The Laughing Lesson

The Laughing Lesson

A Memoir by the Founder of Living Folk Records and Concerts

By Peter Johnson

Peter E. Randall Publisher
Portsmouth, New Hampshire
2019

Published by
Peter E. Randall Publisher
Box 4726
Portsmouth, NH 03802
www.perpublisher.com

Book design: Grace Peirce

Dedication

T he *Laughing Lesson* is dedicated to the following people who
have contributed so much to my life:

Miss Searles, my nurse, who tragically lost her life while
saving mine in the hurricane of 1938 in Newport, Rhode Island

Nora Connors, my parents' Irish cook, whose sad and beautiful
songs, sung in the kitchen of my boyhood, taught me the language
of love

Lorna Porras-Johnson, my wife, who has kept our family focused
while increasing my awareness and appreciation of other cultures
worldwide

"PJ" Johnson, our son, who has inspired me with his *joie de vivre*
and his broad interests from DJing New Age music, and charitable
fundraising endeavors including human rights causes while working
for Independent Diplomat—a unique non-profit advisory group in
the world of diplomacy

Margaret Drew, our friend and attorney, whose advice and
counsel have helped give us a fair shake in life

Howard Glasser, a gifted artist and teacher, who inspired me
and pointed me in a fruitful direction

Genara Banzon, who worked with my wife, Lorna, putting
together the finishing touches on what I had written and bringing
them to life

Freddy Lawrence, my friend and kindred spirit, who gave me a
two-way bridge that connected the present with a usable past

Edward C. Johnson II, my Uncle Ted, who gave me sage advice and, along with Caleb Loring, Jr., helped me create Living Folk Records and Concerts

Elsie Mitchell, my Buddhist cousin and fellow nonconformist, who shared with me her wisdom and common sense

"The greatest use of life is to spend it for something that will outlive it."

—William James

Contents

Foreword

Long before I came to Cambridge, I'd heard about a legendary fellow there who ran informal folk concerts in places like graveyards that today would be called "pop-up" venues. This was during the mid-twentieth-century folk revival, when new communities gathered around singers of traditional songs and players of jigs and reels. I soon learned that the legendary fellow's name was Peter Johnson, and that he had started Living Folk Records and Concerts about a decade before. I also heard that he was a "character," but a character who knew instinctively the power of music and culture. Like a moth to the flame, I gravitated to these gigs.

Folklorists are concerned with context and authenticity. Peter had an ear for the authentic both in story and song and in seeking out performers. In *The Laughing Lesson*, he talks of learning lore from his family's Irish cook and others in 1930s and '40s Newport, in a setting right out of films and television. I find it extraordinary that Peter knew where to find these tradition bearers. This was before the Internet and social media, when recordings on LP vinyl were precious and hard-to-find, when gigs were arranged by a phone call or postcard or even an aerogramme sailing across the waters. He put out the word and audiences and performers turned up at the appointed place and time.

Peter and Living Folk, as well as Peter and his family, are of the same piece. They influenced each other, and, in some ways, Peter's looking to his domestic environment, both upstairs and downstairs, was in keeping with earlier collectors of song and lore by learnéd and avocational antiquarians who looked to their hired help for a glimpse of an imagined—or perceived—vanished world. But, goodness, they were certain they had no lore themselves; they were educated folk.

Peter's glimpses of family life in Newport and Bar Harbor are, in fact, an ethnography of "top drawer" New England society. The notion of the Johnson père teaching his son that then US President Franklin Roosevelt was "a traitor to our class" seems incredible today. Cleveland Amory's *The Proper Bostonians* was filled with similar tales of the same sorts of people, but in a more detached way.

Peter could only have created his Living Folk Records and Concerts in Cambridge—across the Charles from Boston proper—where he went to seek his fortune. He already had an innate sense of history, which is what these towns did best as they served as bellwethers for the rest of North America.

Unlike New York in the late 1950s and '60s, then the center of the entertainment and recording industries where people such as Bob Dylan went to hone their craft and perfect their "act," Cambridge then was all about the music and the people who made the music. Tradition bearers and their audiences intermingled and learned from each other. It was quite democratic. Everyone was literally on the same plane until much later, when, with larger venues, came stages to elevate performers and separate them from audiences. Folk music was giving way to the music business.

Consciously or not, Peter was carrying on the tradition of regional folk-song scholars and collectors. The American Folklore Society was founded in Cambridge in 1888, with Harvard ballad scholar and son of working-class Irish Boston, Francis James Child (1825–1896), elected its first president. The founding statement of the organization talked about documenting and preserving the "fast vanishing remains of folk-lore in America." Each of the cultures mentioned specifically was the Other—American Indians, French Canadians, Mexicans, "Negroes in the Southern States of the Union." In New England, of course, many oral traditions were from the British Isles, Ireland, and France. The lore was very much alive; it doesn't vanish, it just changes.

Peter established ties to Harvard's Celtic Studies Department through its head, Charles Dunn, a Scot; and to Albert Lord, who studied oral literatures and epics; and playwright William Alfred, professor of English; all of whom were stalwart fans of Living Folk.

Many of the performers, especially from England, Scotland, and Ireland, were not professionals in the way we think of them now—or at least didn't have the devoted fans that came later, thanks to Peter introducing their music and traditions to New England and beyond. Performers literally sang for their supper. They didn't necessarily identify a song as "Child No. X"—that would be far too self-conscious—but they might refer, for example, to "Edward" of the traditional murder ballad (Child 13) as if he lived down the block, to create a link between then and now. The vibrant Living Folk community, like others during folk revivals over time, shared a love of the lore, though not necessarily that of their own families or places or times. Tinkers and miners and share-croppers were not part of Cambridge culture, per se, nor were lords and ladies or fairies, but they magically were present here, too.

All roads led to Cambridge. The legendary Club 47 opened in 1958 and was the epicenter of music making on both sides of the Charles River, and home to the "power elite of the folk revival." Cultural revivals crop up during times of societal stress and political tensions, when people look to earlier times for comfort and guidance. In the 1960s and '70s, folk music provided a soundtrack to the times. Ancient ballads were cautionary tales; topical songs echoed old broadsides on everyday injustices; and old-time music and bluegrass got people dancing. A generational cohort literally came of age.

Living Folk introduced locals (and much of North America, through recordings and reviews in folksong publications) to Irish and British Isles performers such as tinker Margaret Barry, Mick Moloney, and fiddler Eugene O'Donnell; ballad singers Ray Fisher, Cilla Fisher, and Norman Kennedy; the Watersons, the Boys of the Lough, the High Level Ranters, De Dannan, Peter Bellamy, the

Battlefield Band, Frankie Armstrong, Louis Killen, Dave Swarbrick, Martin Carthy, and many others.

Likewise, American music was equally unfamiliar. The pre-CNN United States was still a larger, unknown land. Folks who represented that world included Arkansas ballad singer Almeda Riddle, Appalachian singer Hazel Dickens, Cajun fiddler Dewey Balfa and accordion player Marc Savoy, and from the West, Bruce "Utah" Phillips and Rosalie Sorrels. From around New England were Downeast Maine humorist Marshall Dodge (of Bert and I), dulcimer singer Lorraine Lee, Joe Val and the New England Bluegrass Boys, Vermont ballad singer Margaret MacArthur, and the "one man folk festival" Michael Cooney, who sang the many, many verses of "Tam Lin" (Child 39), a traditional ballad performed by an American itinerant in the land of the three-minute Top 40 pop song—kind of the ultimate folk revival.

While fairies may not be holed up in a Cambridge Carterhaugh, as they are in "Tam Lin," Peter brought a different kind of enchantment to these concerts. Gatherings included sets by featured performers, his own or group sings, or recitations from regulars—far different than what usually happened elsewhere. It gave a new spin to the theory of "communal re-creation"—communities embracing the lore and making it their own—what nineteenth-century English antiquarian William Thoms termed "folk-lore," with a hyphen. Living Folk events were much closer in spirit to a kitchen party or a front porch get-together. There was no set list or expectations. This lore was never meant for the stage, anyway; it was a vehicle for self expression or social exchange and entertainment.

I don't recall the first gig I went to—then held at the old nineteenth-century Odd Fellows Hall, later known as the Joy of Movement Center—but it could well have been John Roberts and Tony Barrand, two English transplants. The venue was a proper one— up several flights of stairs to a huge room used as a dance studio, lined with floor-to-ceiling mirrors on the walls and overlooking "Mass Ave" in the heart of Central Square. John and Tony, then teaching in Vermont, sang sea shanties and drinking songs with

John's accompaniment on "squeezebox," a button concertina. They later developed Nowell Sing We Clear, a seasonal program of English ritual drama at Yuletide. All of a sudden, winter solstice Morris dancing and mummers' plays seemed right at home here, just as they had in the early twentieth-century when English folk-song collector Cecil Sharp came to town. His dancers taught English country dance under the patronage of Boston philanthropist Helen Osborne Storrow. Likewise, dramatist Percy McKaye, a student of Child's, produced an Elizabethan pageant at Harvard stadium. Time periods and cultural relics were an imaginative, moveable feast here.

Over the years, Living Folk audiences grew and moved with Peter to ever-larger venues as he brought over soon-to-be-stars like Clannad from Ireland and Silly Wizard from Scotland. After Living Folk ended as an organization, Peter continued to host ceilidhs and hoots at pubs and coffeehouses in Boston and Cambridge.

Peter has always struck me as a better folklorist than many card-carrying folklorists, but he's also a bona fide "folk," as we all are. Peter, though, carries on the patrician lore of Boston, Newport, Salem, and Old England itself. I owe a huge debt to him; he was a mentor. Through him and Living Folk, I learned the professional aspects of the music business and how to produce public folklife events, which I do to this day. And I also learned to step back and just let it happen.

When I met Peter all those years ago, he was already working on these memoirs and would often tell the stories or share the manuscript. I am thrilled that after nearly half a century, *The Laughing Lesson* has made its way to print. The book is a chronicle of his life, revives fond memories, and ideally will bring newer and younger folks into the circle. What a legendary fellow, indeed.

—Millie Rahn
Belmont, Massachusetts
January 2019

Preface

Over the years in which I have been writing *The Laughing Lesson* (named after my father's futile attempt to teach me to laugh "with restraint, propriety, and decorum, in a manner suited to a well-bred gentleman"), I have asked myself whether I am writing an autobiography or a memoir. Some readers would say it is the former; others would say the latter. Giving the question some thought, I realize that my life story offers something of both.

An autobiography narrates the full chronology of the author's life, whereas a memoir is organized around a theme that emerges from that life. What I have written begins with my earliest memory and extends to the present. At the same time, it highlights what I have come to understand as the guiding principle of my life—namely, that to discover and become myself and realize whatever potential I might have had, I had to free myself from the yoke of inherited privilege and prejudice, from a citadel of received meaning and exhausted value that would have held me in a state of quiet desperation amid material comfort.

Born in 1935, I now live in a world very different from the scene of my earliest memories. I hope my idiosyncratic experience of these last eight decades will interest, inform, and amuse you. Feel free to laugh, as long as you're aware that laughter is an inverted tear.

—Peter Johnson
  April 2019

Acknowledgments

I extend my deep gratitude toward those who, over half a century, have supported my writing *The Laughing Lesson* and helped give it life. The story of this memoir begins with those who first encouraged me to write it: Ezra Pound and Robert Lowell. Over the years more than a few editorial hands have given shape to the evolving manuscript, starting with my friend, Don Kalick, with whom I put together the story of my Newport upbringing when he and I were hanging out around Harvard Square. The book also benefited from the skillful editing of Marie Cantlon. Others who contributed thoughtful readings and editorial help included Daphne Abeel, William Alfred, Peter Rand and Genara Banzon, who, working with Lorna, my wife, helped put together the finishing touches on what I had written and brought them to life.

I extend my gratitude to Jane Sloan; Gillian Charters; Audrey Drummond; Elizabeth Calvey; Jennifer Sur, of Revels; and Rosalie Prosser, of Alice Darling Secretarial Services, for helping through different stages of producing the document.

My profound thanks goes to Anne-Marie Sollouière, former president of Edward C. Johnson Charitable Foundation, and to Susan Keats, the archivist and author of *There Will Be Dancing: The History of a Johnson Family*.

I would also like to thank Mary Landergan; Dr. Harvey Mazer, my counselor; Archie and Vicky Brodsky, Simone Payment, Mathilde Duffy, and Tom Stern.

Throughout the years, the following people, each in their own way, have helped me bury the ghosts of the past, navigate the ebb and flow of the present, and traverse the rocky road to the future: Ellen Schmidt; Lori Fassman; Andy Hanley; Al Gutterman; Henry and Sue Bass; Ray and Ann Gomes; Theresa Lavignia-Saunders; Jimmy, Gerri, and Emily Marcantonio; Tonie Marsh and family; Mohamed Adam; and Mary Christie.

My great appreciation to Robin Roberts Howard—singer, music collector, and actress—who inspired my active involvement with folk music. To Margaret Barry, "Queen of the Tinkers," fellow adventurer, "who moved through the fair." Carolyn Kingston, who gave me several voice lessons, taught me a few songs, and introduced me to several musicians who performed at one of my events. Rodger Kingston, who took some photos of family portraits and gave me some lessons in photography.

I'd like to acknowledge Janet Kelley, David Omar White, and Bob Doucette for designing some of my record covers and concert posters.

I'm grateful to David O'Dockerty and Jack Whyte for welcoming me to the Irish musical community and to musical sessions in which I participated; to John Shaw, a member of the Harvard Celtic Department who introduced me to members of the Cape Breton musical community and their music; and to my recording engineers, who over the years since 1970 have recorded long-playing records, concerts, and CDs: Michael Coughlin, Steven Friedman, Scott Kent, Steve Fassett, and Eric Killburn.

Through the good offices of the distinguished writer and singer Scott Alarik, I found Peter E. Randall Publisher. Deidre Randall, the CEO, is herself a folk singer and actress. I am grateful to her editorial staff and to her photographers, Kate Crichton and Kael Randall.

I likewise thank Brian O'Donovan, host of *A Celtic Sojourn* on WGBH-FM in Boston, for his sustained support, and Colin Irwin for portraying me as a character in his show in Glasgow, Scotland, honoring the life and work of Margaret Barry.

Finally, I thank all the boon companions with whom I've made sad and joyful music, the writers and scholars who educated me, the many gifted performers who inspired me and graced my concert stages, the generous souls, including folklorists Millie Rahn and Linda Morley, on the staff of Living Folk Records and Concerts. I am grateful to the good folks who provided venues or funding or helped spread the word, and to the dedicated folklorists and collectors who have kept the music playing.

I hope anyone I have omitted will excuse an old man's fading memory. Every member of this worldwide community, past and present, has a part in the story that follows.

—Peter Johnson
April 2018

≋ Chapter 1 ≋
Stormy Beginning

I came into the world unheralded on May 25, 1935, but my place of entrance was impeccable—Phillips House, that venerable appurtenance of Massachusetts General Hospital in Boston where the well born were wont to arrive. There I was christened Pierrepont Edwards Johnson, Jr., and shortly after was deposited in what was to become my home, Ridgemere, in Newport, Rhode Island.

From Bellevue Avenue, the rear of Ridgemere could be seen at a distance. To approach the house, one turned off Bellevue onto Leroy Avenue and, in order of appearance, there lay the houses and grounds of the Wetmore sisters, Chateau sur Mer; Ridgemere; and Wakehurst, the habitat of the Van Alens. One entered our grounds by crossing under the arch of a fifteen-foot iron gate, whose doors were flanked on both sides by pine trees. Beyond the gate, Ridgemere, sitting solid and secure, became visible a short distance ahead. A *porte-cochère* overhanging the gravel driveway lay between rhododendrons and magnolias.

From the gate, one could see a lawn bounded on the left by an iron fence. On the right, barely visible, partially obscured by a row of elms, were the gardener's cottage, a tool shed, a pump house, a two-story carriage house, and stables containing three carriages—a victoria, a landau, and a phaeton—in good repair but no longer in use. Behind the house was a lawn bounded on the left by trees through which could be seen a well-manicured hedgerow that

1

concealed a garden and greenhouse from view. On the back lawn, within view of the piazza, was a teahouse, covered both inside and out with vines of honeysuckle.

People speak of a house as having a personality or an aura that gives it a distinctive flavor. One hears of spirits that may reflect the personae of its occupants. I once was asked whether Ridgemere was haunted, perhaps by some mistreated or neglected ancestor. If there were spirits in the house, they did not call undue attention to themselves by unseemly behavior such as rattling chains, moaning, or making a spectacle of themselves. In short, they were well behaved, considerate of my family, and remained discreetly in the background. They knew their place, upholding the status quo, a world of order and decorum.

The interior of the house was, for the most part, devoid of smells, sounds, sights, and sensations that are usually associated with households. The aroma of cooking, sounds of human activity, and other signs of life were confined for the most part to the kitchen. In the front part of the house, which excluded the servants' quarters, voices—usually those of my mother and father—were never raised. Only in the kitchen would Nora, our cook, and the maids raise their voices in protest or excitement. Nora's voice had a comforting Irish lilt, and those of the maids—Catherine, Mary, and Margaret— blended agreeably with the clatter of pots and pans, the barking of dogs, and the smell of cooking. The kitchen, which my parents cautioned me to avoid lest I pick up bad habits from the servants, became in fact my refuge where I could feel accepted. There, if I were lucky, I'd hear Nora sing songs that she learned as a child in Connemara. One verse I committed to memory:

We're trampled in the dust, over here, over here,
We're trampled in the dust over here, over here,
But the Lord in whom we trust, will give us crumb or crust,
Over here, over here.

She said, though she wasn't sure, that the song, a famine song, originated in America.

The living rooms and hallways of Ridgemere were lined with portraits of staid-looking ancestors, Audubon prints (in elephant-sized folios), Fitz Hugh Lane (now properly known as Fitz Henry Lane) seascapes, Queen Anne chairs, and other eighteenth-century French family furniture, sparse but elegant, which were restful to the eye.

During my early childhood, I ate all meals with my governess at a small table in the dining room, separate from the large mahogany one where my parents sat. In the morning, my father would have breakfast at the main table, and my mother would be served in bed by one of the maids.

Along with my governess, three maids, and Nora, I lived on the third floor. The hallway leading to the servants' quarters, located next to my room, was put off limits to me by my family for fear that any contact with the servants would instill bad habits.

On the second floor, a small dressing room separated my mother's bedroom—consisting of two large canopied beds, chairs, and sofas—from my father's room. There were two guest rooms and a large linen closet, which contained sheets and large white towels bearing the initials of Fanny Foster, a deceased relative of my mother and one of the former owners of the house.

On a staircase landing between the first and second floor was a grandfather clock. In order to wind it, my father, who stood around six feet five, would climb up on a stool.

Descending the stairs to the first floor, one came upon the main hallway, which, like the aisle of a church, divided the house into two equal parts. To the left of the stairs was a large dining room with a fireplace, which one entered through two sliding panel doors. To the rear of the dining room was a pantry that led to the kitchen, with its view of part of the back lawn and garden. On the other side of the dining room was the den or library, which contained old leather-bound books encased behind locked doors. Across the hall was a living room, where my parents would entertain their friends at cocktails or a dinner party. At the right of the stairs were a coatroom, a guest bathroom, and a vestibule opening up to the *porte-cochère*.

At the end of the hall, facing away from the stairs, was a grand Steinway piano, which my mother played occasionally. Behind the piano was a large door that led to the veranda overlooking an Italian-style terrace and a restful expanse of lawn.

* * *

My earliest memory is of a fateful day in the late summer of 1938 when a hurricane raged over most of New England. I recall being a child of three, sitting in a Coast Guard station, hearing the steady patter of rain beating against the wagon and the wailing and keening of the wind, a howling wildness, bending and breaking the trees, shaking the leaves. Looking out the window, I saw the stars, flecks of gold, glittering in the dark sky, and the moon, her yellow streaks of light illuminating the windswept trees below. I recall getting a glimpse of a ghostly galleon of gray clouds. Not knowing where I was or what happened, nor feeling afraid, I was at peace with my companions in the sky.

Years after that, when I was maybe fourteen or fifteen, my parents explained to me what had happened on that day. In the late afternoon, when the wind was at its peak, Miss Searles, my nurse, holding me in her arms as she stood on some rocks that overlooked the turbulent sea, gently handed me to Andy, the gardener, telling him, "Don't let any water get in the baby's mouth." Just then a giant wave cascading over the slippery rocks caused her to slip into the raging waters below and drown. Shortly after that, I was rescued by the Coast Guard wagon and taken to the station. A brief account of this rescue and tragedy can be found in a well-documented book, Everett S. Allen's *A Wind to Shake the World*.

Hearing about Miss Searles, I felt sad and helpless, knowing there was nothing I could do. She gave her life for me. It seems more than coincidence that so many of the songs that have left their mark on me over the years are tragic ballads of death and unrequited love, such as "Who Killed Cock Robin?", "Geordie," and "The Unquiet Grave." When I shared that thought in later years with my psychiatrist, Dr. Harvey Mazer, he said, "Perhaps the reason you keep recalling Miss Searles is that you feel deep down that her warmth and love for you represent your real mother and that in saving your life and losing hers she left you to your cold and aristocratic parents, who brought you up in a cloistered world of good form without love, and it was only by discovering folk music and the people who made it that you discovered your real home, your real community."

* * *

Until I was nine or ten, I never saw much of my family except perhaps in the late afternoon when, at the request of my parents, my governess would usher me into the living room. My mother and father would then introduce me.

"Peter, come in and say 'how do you do' and shake hands with Mr. and Mrs. Drexel, Admiral Ingersoll, Mr. Van Alen, Mrs. Schuyler," and so on. After I had politely shaken hands and paid my respects to all the guests, I would dutifully kiss my mother on the cheek and say goodnight to the company. Then my governess would escort me upstairs. She would give me a bath and supervise me as I brushed my teeth. We would go up to my room on the third floor and prepare for bed.

I remember coming down for breakfast when I was twelve or thirteen, at home on Christmas vacation from the Fessenden School. There was my father seated at the head of the table.

"Good morning, young man. Come on over here where I can see you."

I walked over to where my father was seated and obediently stood about a foot away from him, waiting to be inspected. As I no longer had a governess to oversee my appearance, he personally would make sure that my clothes were neat and clean. On this particular morning my father, acting as the commanding officer he had been in the Navy, looked me up and down and said, "Go upstairs, wash your hands, clean your nails, and do something about that perfectly dreadful cowlick. Remember, you're my son, not the Wild Man of Borneo or something out of *Tobacco Road*. After you've made yourself presentable, I'd like you to say 'good morning' to your mother and then come down and report to me."

Looking contrite, I murmured, "Yes, Daddy," and promptly did as I was told. Having performed my ablutions, I knocked at Mummy's door as instructed. Hearing her say, "Good morning. Do come in," I entered. She was sitting in bed having her breakfast from a tray while one of the maids was in the corner of the room diligently dusting the furniture. Margaret was always there punctually at nine o'clock, when she would commence her round of chores: drawing the blinds, running the bath water, and serving my mother breakfast from a lazy Susan. If it were winter, she would start a fire in the fireplace. I tiptoed to my mother and politely kissed her on the cheek.

"Hello, darling. How are you?" she said, barely turning her head. Attempting to summon cheer in my voice, I replied in a barely audible tone, "I'm fine, thank you. It's nice to see you. How are you?"

"Fine, darling. Oh, look at you. Don't you look cunning in your blue shirt."

Finding time between sips of tea and dainty bites of toast, my mother made pleasant chit chat with me. After a few minutes of this, I politely dismissed myself and went back downstairs to report to my father, who was, by this time, in the middle of his breakfast.

"Now, Peter, let's have a look at you!"

He examined my hands, closely inspecting my fingernails, and was pleased to note that every hair on my head was in its properly appointed place. To his satisfaction, everything about me was in order.

After breakfast, he continued his interrogation: "Well, young man, what are your plans for the day?" There was no satisfactory answer to this question. If I hadn't any plans, my father would scold me for lacking initiative, and if I had plans he would admonish me for not checking with him first.

I coped with this question as best I could. "I was just waiting to consult with you first, Daddy."

My father pronounced his advice. "Why don't you go outside? Make yourself useful and give Andy a hand on the place. It will do you good." As an afterthought, he added, "And pay attention. Who knows, you might learn a thing or two. Now, off you go, make it snappy!"

Andy lived in the small cottage adjacent to the stables. Among his tasks was the care of the three carriages that generations earlier had served my mother's ancestors. By my time they were relics, ornamental but useless. The phaeton, a two-passenger carriage with a box in front for the driver, was the apple of my eye.

Working with Andy was not without its rewards. He would capture my imagination with stories of his youth in old Newport; a world of livery, pomp, and splendor seen from afar by a boy who was to serve that world throughout its graceful decline.

Despite my family's firm belief in class distinctions, the separation of master and servant, I was encouraged to be present as Andy and the other workmen attended to their various duties, feeding our chickens, pulling weeds, raking the leaves. This experience was expected to give me a feel for the place. After all, whether I liked it or not, I was being groomed as the future master of Ridgemere.

In retrospect, the idea of being the master of Ridgemere and having to behave like my father terrified me. Strutting, stammering, pigeon-toed, and lacking in self-confidence, I found myself mistakenly addressed by the maids as Master Peter. I wasn't allowed to go to the bathroom by myself until I was six years old—I was always accompanied by my governess to make sure that I, in the words of my father, performed my "salutary ablutions with meticulous solicitude." Not knowing how to "shed a tear" or "test the facilities," again my father's words, was a source of embarrassment when I had to go to the bathroom at school in the first grade.

Groomed to be the master of Ridgemere, I was its slave, or so it seemed to me. I vowed that sometime in the future, when the time was right, I would re-create myself and feel free to live and laugh in my own way. Laughter is an inverted tear, is it not?

⧽ Chapter 2 ⧼

Nature

As early as I can remember, my conversational ability was severely limited by one of my father's favorite maxims, "Little boys should be seen and not heard." There was always something on my mind, but not being encouraged to enter into conversation with my family, I would keep all of those thoughts and feelings inside and save them for those special occasions when I would go walking in the garden, secure in my solitude. There, I would address my questions and deeply felt grievances to the flowers, trees—anything that had a soul and was a good listener. They were a sympathetic audience. Sometimes I would walk down to the chicken coop and enter into conversations with my feathered companions.

In front of Ridgemere stood a wonderful and mysterious weeping willow tree that appeared to me to be kind and very wise. I would sit under the branches and console myself with the thought that somehow I was different from other people. I first stood under the tree when I was a boy of six, and over the years I continued my visits.

The kitchen was another very special place, as I felt free to talk to Nora, our cook, and the maids. They encouraged me to say whatever was on my mind. In a way, they seemed more like my real family than my own mother and father. Nora had such a kind, loving nature. Despite all my flaws—being pigeon-toed, stammering, and sucking my thumb—I felt that she loved me as much as if I had been one of her own.

Although forbidden by my family to go to the servants' quarters for fear I would pick up vulgar habits, I would go and pay Nora a visit in her room. Sometimes I'd lie on her bed and she would run her hand through my hair and soothingly tell me that everything would be all right. My two friends were Nora and my tree. And I felt that, just as there was a bond between them and me, so was there some unspoken but sympathetic connection between them. They reminded me of the mysterious helpers in fairy stories read to me by my governess, who would come to the rescue of the hero as he ran away from the wicked stepmother or the giant. Nora and the weeping willow seemed to be cut from the same magical and spiritual cloth as these fairy-tale figures, and I longed to be a part of their world.

One time, I had a wonderful dream in which some of the animals remembered from bedtime stories, together with Nora and my weeping willow, were flying through the sky. We all sang songs and said hello to the passing stars, birds, flying dogs, and other friends. From Nora, the weeping willow, and my friends in nature, I felt comfort, and to them I was—and still am—grateful. Largely through them I learned that it was all right to laugh and cry. They gave me something intangible yet very real and good that enabled me to keep on going.

When I visited Bailey's Beach, if I wasn't swimming or playing in the sand, I would just walk by myself, enjoying the feel of wet sand under my feet and marveling at the sea and all it had to offer— sandpipers, starfish, crabs, and seaweed. My solitary sojourns gave me a feeling of independence, as I was temporarily freed from the mundane boundaries of my other world, the cloistered one of my family and people in general. In nature, nothing could be taken for granted. She revealed herself constantly in new and wonderful ways. Even the dirty seaweed was mysterious and oddly beautiful. All of these things—alive, fresh, and welcoming—were my friends. We demanded nothing from each other. All was freely given in an exchange of mutual appreciation, or so it seemed. In my sunlit, windswept, and water-soaked imagination, the crabs and even the starfish took a benign, comradely interest in me.

I remember late one morning in 1944 when I was in Bar Harbor, Maine, going for a walk in the woods around Eastcote, our "summer place." With bare feet I stole downstairs, walked out the front door, and made my way to the back. It was seven o'clock, the dawning of the day, and the dew was still fresh. The sun (observer of all living things) was renewing herself, emerging from the ocean and starting her majestic climb through the sky, caressing the Earth and suffusing everything with a touching tenderness.

Instead of following the usual path that led down to our pier, I took a less familiar one. I was alone save for my stalwart companions, those tall green pointed firs that reached up and supported a vast vault of blue sky that seemed inconceivably immense. A family of white clouds trailed each other at a leisurely pace. The largest ones seemed to be swimming with a sense of purpose as they all headed in the same direction in their great expanse of dense indigo blue. Some of the clouds, the ones farthest away, appeared to stand motionless or barely moving, as if anchored safely at rest. In the distance I could see seagulls, travelers of the sky, and swallows, companions to the high cliffs, clad in their cloaks of white and black, sporting with a fickle wind as it unpredictably changed its course. The folk of the air knew how to have fun. I looked across Frenchman Bay and could see the shoreline of Sorrento, stretched out like a lilac streak. The cliffs in the distance were overhanging the shore, descending precipitously to the sea. Like smoke, the last of the morning mist rolled up, and a rainbow connected the land with the sky like a bridge between dreams. The tall blades of grass and scattered layers of pine needles tickled my ankles. A faint sea breeze, breathing its cool-smelling freshness, sent little chills rippling up my arms.

After walking for some time through the wooded path where patches of receding shadows mingled with advancing golden threads of light, I came upon a clearing that momentarily dazzled my eyes

as the genial radiance of the sun illuminated the softly shining
green leaves, white daisies, and goldenrod. Farther ahead, to the
left of where I stood, a gray-brown squirrel scolded from an overhanging branch, darted down the limb, paused, and ran part way
across the clearing. He stopped for a brief second and looked up,
as if to address me: "For Pete's sake, what are you doing here?" He
then darted to the other side of the clearing and disappeared into the
woods. Stunned, I quickly recovered my wits and realized that my
imagination, tinged with quiet, had played a trick on me. I had tres-
passed on the squirrel's sacred ground.

Leaving the clearing behind, I followed a path where a thick
wood rose up like a wall and darkness floated down. My meander-
ings continued for several hundred yards until, suddenly, another
clearing burst brightly into full view. This one, larger and brighter
than the first, seemed to be encased in a mantle of many colors. The
leaves and the grass were burning brightly, a dark and light green.
Flowers of all kinds were everywhere, and they swayed gently with
each little puff of wind. Tiny droplets of dew, shining like pearls of
frozen tears, were melting beneath the genial smile of the sun. On
the canvas of that still water, the sunshine painted the picture of
the day.

Just a few feet away was a raspberry bush whose berries dotted
a sea of green wheat with fields of brilliant red. I picked several
handfuls, and their tender, tart sweetness lingered almost as an afterthought. They tasted better than any berries served at the dinner
table. After getting my fill of them, I lay down on a patch of grass
near a bush of wildflowers and looked up as the fleeting aroma of a
passing sea breeze mingled with the smell of fresh sap. The chirping
of a nearby cricket kept a steady beat, counter-pointing the stately
lapping of waves on rocks. A loon cried sadly in the distance. The
whisper of my breathing mingled with all those sounds and I knew I
was in good hands. My heart was in this place with the clear air and
the morning dew. I felt I was one with everything surrounding me.

Lost in my peaceful reverie, I thought of my storybook friends
who years earlier had visited me at bedtime. I shut my eyes and

could see old Mother West Wind and her children, the merry little breezes, scampering across the green meadows to the smiling brook where they would politely pay their respects to old Grandfather Frog in the hope that he would tell them a story. They were all my friends: Johnny Chuck, Jimmy Skunk, Little Joe Otter, Freddy Fox, Hooty the Owl, Sammy Jay, and others as well. They were good-natured, had a sense of fair play, and could be helpful. In their world, wrongs were usually righted and the victim was usually compensated.

On that grassy green, it seemed that everything—the sky, the sea, the trees, and my beloved friends from storybooks—was all on the same footing with me in a common flow of feeling. It seemed as if all things were alive and aware of me as I was of them and that we were enchanted by one another's presence. The pastoral splendor of the rising slopes of green mountain and the mysterious majesty of those tall trees wiped away all worries, desires, and feelings of guilt. I imagined this was what the world looked like on the first day of creation. In the back of my mind, I could hear Nora singing her folk-songs, the ones that she sang while preparing dinner, old songs that could make one laugh, cry, or sleep.

All of a sudden: putt, putt, putt—the spluttering of an old Model T broke the enchantment. It was a friendly enough sound but had a slightly alien ring to it, and I remembered sadly that a part of me belonged to my everyday world. Everything that had been so beautiful, fresh, and pleasing now appeared ordinary. I felt abandoned like a broken wheel and alone like a crumbling wall. There were no breezes to take away my sadness and loneliness. No longer were the large oak trees and the green mountain my mother and father. Gone were the smaller trees and bushes, my brothers and sisters. Their leaves no longer sang loving words. Those tall trees with their long, sad, bony faces were no longer weeping their long sorrow. Light was no longer dripping from their leaves.

Poised on the threshold of two worlds, the one mysterious, intuitive, and everlasting, the other logical, calculating, and perishable, I felt cut off from the promise of eternal love and acceptance. This place was full of death!

Putt, putt, putt. The sound of the Model T sputtered in the distance. This time it had a more reassuring ring, like a beacon. Then I fully realized that those fresh green leaves, leaves that were greener and fresher than I had ever seen, were no longer immortal. They would in time turn yellow, fall to Earth, and perish. Yet, nonetheless, how beautiful they were now.

I yearned for my familiar surroundings and looked forward to breakfast at the dining room table. On some deep level of under-standing I realized it was time to leave, for to stay in such a place would eventually be suffocating. As I pensively trudged homeward, I understood that there were two worlds that existed for me. I knew that I'd always carry the memory of that morning when I experi-enced what seemed like the creation of the first day of the world, with the dew still fresh like a seabird's egg—lovely, perfect, and laid this very morning.

≋ Chapter 3 ≋

The Dinner Party

I was eight years old and World War II was ravaging Europe. In the kitchen, the old RCA Victor radio was playing. The ponderous, gloomy voice of a newscaster named Gabriel Heatter would hold forth on recent military developments. All within earshot would listen intently to his words and his portentous tones that seemed to augur doom.

One winter afternoon I remember plotting, if not doom, at least mischief. I had managed successfully to stay out of my family's way, and I was to have dinner alone because my parents had invited guests for the evening. Eating at a small table in the dining room, I hatched my plans.

Shortly after I had finished my dinner, some of my parents' friends arrived at the house. A few of them were elderly, too old to drive, especially with the bad weather conditions. Miss Wetmore, a neighbor of ours, arrived in an old touring car and was carefully deposited on our doorstep. The chauffeur drove away.

Mr. and Mrs. Coolidge also were driven by their chauffeur. However, the chauffeur did not leave. He dutifully parked the car and braced himself for the hours-long wait. I remember the Grosvenors ringing the doorbell and one of our maids answering it. "Good evening. The Johnson residence." She showed them in and helped them remove their coats, which were then deposited in the coatroom.

Fraülein, my governess, returned from her day off and responded to my parents' request to bring me downstairs to make a brief appearance, say how do you do, and shake hands with the guests. After being made presentable in my new Brooks Brothers sailor suit, I politely greeted the guests.

It was cocktail time and drinks were being served in the living room. Before long, some of the guests were standing in front of the fireplace with glasses in hand. With the aid of Scotch on the rocks, bourbon, dry martinis, and gin and tonics, a cozy conviviality descended on them. In the course of the next few hours, people were getting somewhat "tiddly," to use my mother's expression.

Mr. Lighter, who couldn't hold his Scotch very well, was slurring his speech. Even so, some inner principle kept people on the right side of good form. A short while later one of the maids came in and announced that dinner was being served, and soon all the guests were ushered into the dining room. And yet, within this elegant tableau with its stately décor, the mischief was afoot.

Taking the seat next to my father, Mr. Auchincloss remarked to him, "I see your boy has grown. He has such good manners." Indeed, my parents had instilled in me those habits of carriage and comportment that their friends would instantly recognize as flawlessly correct. However, before the guests seated themselves, I had secreted myself beneath the dining room table.

On previous occasions, I had noticed a peculiar custom among the men who attended dinner parties. Toward the end of the meal, and after having consumed liberal amounts of liquor, they would carelessly kick off their black patent leather pumps under the table. With this recollection the seeds of a prank were sown. From my hiding place, I could wait for the pumps to come off and proceed to take action.

First the soup was served and then, after an interminable interval, several of the maids came in, took away the soup bowls, and brought in the main course.

One gentleman, sitting right across from my mother, said to her, "Lilias, you remember my boy Chauncy? He's in the army and is stationed in London. Loves it. He keeps himself very busy; he's always getting invited to dinner parties and dances. On weekends, he takes a suite at Claridges and entertains his friends. Jolly good fun. I think London will do the boy good. His tailor is not far away."

"Who is his tailor?" asked Pip Cutler.

"He goes to Poole's."

Poole was a familiar name. I remember seeing Poole's boxes in the attic. For generations my father's family had had their clothes made there.

"Marvelous place, Poole's," said Mr. de Peyster. "Years ago, when I was a young man and getting outfitted there, they used to serve their customers brandy and cigars. It was like a club. All very civilized. Unfortunately, with every Tom, Dick, and Harry going there, it's changed."

I was getting cramps in my legs and could hardly move for fear of accidentally disturbing any one of those important limbs that surrounded me on all sides. They were all sizes and shapes. The conversation was getting on my nerves and I was getting impatient.

Mother and Father and several of their friends were discussing the servant problem right in front of the maids, as if they didn't exist.

"Well," said my mother, "it's always a problem. Nora, our cook, is Catholic and she's got to have fish on Fridays, but Margaret, one of the maids, absolutely detests fish. It's very difficult to keep everyone happy."

"Oh, Lilias, you poor dear, I couldn't sympathize with you more. It's so tiresome," said Mr. Drexel.

From the other end of the table, Hank Phelps added, "We had to let one of our maids go. I caught her nipping in the liquor closet. Servants don't behave the way they used to."

"Well, what do you expect," said Mr. Hallowell. "If it weren't for Roosevelt, we wouldn't be having any of these problems."

"You're right on the mark there," my father interjected. "This is the day of the common man. People don't know their place or their betters any more. Today anything goes."

I gritted my teeth and just hung on, knowing that soon I'd be able to make my move. My expectations were gradually rewarded as the maids removed the dessert plates, with only the finger bowls and wine glasses remaining. The men were relaxed and most of the patent leather shoes were either on the floor or casually dangling from their well-hosed, important-looking feet. Remaining quiet, I deftly managed to navigate the tortuous passage from one end of the table to the other and carefully interchanged several of the pumps.

Closely inspecting the venerable footwear, I noticed that there were two kinds: black patent leather shoes and pumps with a small bow. Some of the shoes were made in England, bearing labels such as Poole's or Maxwell's, while others were homegrown vintages à la Brooks Brothers. The only difficulty I encountered was removing a pump that was still half on the owner's unsuspecting foot. Throwing caution to the wind, I gave a yank and was rewarded as the pump and silk-stockinged foot parted company. The man whose foot I had robbed became dimly cognizant that something was "afoot." By an odd misdirection, he managed to put his hand on the lower part of the leg that belonged to the lady sitting next to him. In quiet tones, icy and measured, she addressed him, "John Archbold, please remove your hand. It doesn't belong there. You are the rudest man I've ever known."

There was total silence followed by a few subdued titters and coughs. Poor John Archbold was totally bewildered. He was obliged to make an apology, although he had no idea how or why he found himself in that ignominious position. Luckily for me, he didn't initiate an investigation or my presence would have been discovered.

To my relief, a maid came in and quietly told my mother that there was a long-distance telephone call from Mount Kisco, New York. It was from Aunt Helen. My mother got up to answer the phone and as soon as she left the dining room I decided to take my chances. I crawled next to her vacant chair and waited until the guests started laughing at some joke in progress. I then disappeared into the pantry, crossed the kitchen, and went up the back stairs, finally gaining sanctuary in my room.

There was no mention of the effects of what had transpired

under the dining room table until several days later when my mother casually mentioned that one of their friends, on returning home from the dinner party, had discovered that one of the shoes on his feet was not his own. Feigning shock, I exclaimed, "Oh, Mummy, that's terrible. Do you suppose he had too much to drink?" She readily concurred and I was left in the clear.

Reflecting on my successful adventure, I remembered one of my father's many prior admonitions: "You are to keep out of the dining room unless you're having your meal. I'm laying down the law, no more playing under the dining room table; you don't belong there." I further recalled one of his oft-repeated maxims: "When you know the rules of law, you may break them." However, that was not to say that I was actually encouraged to do so. Under the tutelage of my parents and governess, I was still at that awkward stage of learning the rules; hence, breaking one of them was simply out of the question.

Further consideration of this matter led me to believe that my breach of etiquette was permissible only because I had not been caught under the table. I imagined that if I had indeed been caught flat-footed, the guests would have thought, "How clumsy of him. He can't do anything right."

Chapter 4

The Laughing Lesson

I was a good student, but not an excellent one. There were several areas in which I was found wanting, but I was willing to wink at them. A different kind of educational challenge—this one imposed not in school, but at home—was more difficult to disregard.

During the years spanning childhood and adolescence, I developed a secret crush on one of my mother's friends—a Mrs. Strawbridge—and my admiration prompted me to imitate her odd-sounding laugh. My father, horrified at my high-pitched cackling, informed me that my laugh was "not the laugh of a gentleman."

To rectify this very serious situation, he announced one evening after dinner, "Peter, it's now 7:30. At eight o'clock, I want you to report to me in the den, and don't be late. I want you on deck on time." Whenever stressed, my father reverted to his naval background.

Playing Burl Ives records in my room, I spent half an hour puzzling over the nature of my infraction. "What have I done now?" I wondered.

At eight o'clock in the den, my father commenced his lecture without hesitation. "Peter, this way of laughing of yours can't go on. How can you possibly laugh the way you do? What will people think? Do you know how unattractive it sounds? That is not the way I laugh nor the way my father laughed. My friends don't go around laughing that way, and I dare say their children don't either.

Very unbecoming. I won't have it in my house. You simply can't go around laughing any old way you please. I'm going to have to give you laughing lessons and see to it that you can once and for all learn how to laugh properly in a way that is suited to a gentleman, especially when you're in the company of your mother and me and your elders. What's got into you? You are my one and only son, my flesh and blood, my legal issue, and I expect better things of you. Remember, this is serious business. If you've got to laugh, you've simply got to do it correctly. This is no laughing matter."

Thus was I consigned to learning the correct, well-bred forms of laughter. My father could not abide the chance that I might be heard to titter in an unseemly way that could betoken bad blood in my family.

"Gentlemen should not laugh too much," he cautioned. "A laugh should be short, not effusive or prolonged, and it should be about the right things, not coarse jibes. It goes without saying that a gentleman laughs only at appropriate times, never at the dinner table with one's elders." My father stressed the manly aspects of the laugh, but with the admonition, "You mustn't laugh too loudly or too long or you'll sound like a truck driver." He emphasized those sounds that resonated with a baritone voice as ringing true to a gentleman's ears.

I practiced in front of the bathroom mirror, but with disappointing results. I even went so far as to place several fingers in my mouth in an effort to create the right shape. Nothing seemed to produce the right sound, and in due course I was summoned back to the second-floor den, where the maid was drawing the blinds.

"That will be all, Adelaide," my father said, dismissing her. Turning to me he said, "Well, my boy, get comfy but not too comfy. This is serious, and we've got to get down to brass tacks."

Trying to remember what I'd practiced, I let out a pathetic bleat that continued for about two minutes. My father grew red in the face and left the room in disgust, saying to my mother, "Lilias, it's no use, it's quite impossible. God knows I tried. We've reared a jackass for a son."

My mother blithely replied, "Oh, darling, don't be hard on him. It's all our fault. We've made such poor choices of governesses."

Henceforth, I became very self-conscious about laughing in front of my parents or their friends. I refrained from doing so unless it was absolutely necessary. Thus was I spared the ignominy of future lessons. What remained most troublesome was not knowing how to laugh when laughter was called for. I didn't even know what my family considered funny. My parents rarely laughed in front of me, but occasionally did so with their friends at cocktail parties. Disdaining anything that reeked of emotion, my parents wished to be no more than lightly amused.

I vowed to continue my laughing lessons unofficially on my own. I was duty bound to heed my father's directive, "You've simply got to knuckle down, get down to brass tacks, and laugh properly."

On those rare occasions when I heard my father utter a restrained "ha-ha-ha," I would listen intently, hoping to learn something. I noted his laugh never lasted longer than a second and a half. I wished it would last longer, to give me more to go on. After watching and listening carefully, I quietly practiced the well-bred laugh in my bedroom or bathroom, trying to capture the right pitch, nuance, intonation, accent, timbre, intensity, and duration. After many tedious hours of practice, I felt that I was making headway.

One day, perhaps vaguely aware that I was pushing my role of backward but earnest son to the limit, I asked my father, "Daddy, this may sound just a little peculiar, but please tell me, do I need crying lessons or do I already do it correctly?"

"Lessons in crying? Indeed not!" he replied in a brusque tone. "Don't be silly. I've never heard of such a thing. Since when do gentlemen cry? Really, Peter, you should know better. Frankly, I'm surprised at you. Crying, indeed. That's very bad form! It's not done! If you're feeling grief, you keep it to yourself, and you don't go around with a long face where others can lay eyes on you. Little girls may give in to their feelings, but whatever you do don't make a dreary spectacle of yourself. Remember, crying is a show of weakness. If you knew how unattractive it sounds, you wouldn't do it.

You've got to learn to bite the bullet and not give in to your feelings. Tell me, why would you ever want to cry in the first place? After all, your mother and I have seen to it that you've been given every advantage in life, so you should be thankful. Let's hear no more talk about crying. Really!"

I hoped to find further guidance by looking up the meaning of laughter in the dictionary. Unfortunately, the family dictionary was inaccessible to me, locked behind glass doors in the library, so I paid a visit to the Redwood Library in town. Slightly bemused, I confided to the librarian that I wished to learn how to laugh correctly to please my father. She looked at me oddly but kindly, perhaps wondering whether she had heard me correctly, and replied in a gentle tone, "Laughing correctly? I've never heard of such a thing. Isn't that something you do naturally?" Disappearing into another room, she returned shortly with several dictionaries and encyclopedias.

According to one of the dictionaries, the word "laughter" referred to a variety of sounds, all of which had different connotations. First there was the guffaw, described as loud and coarse laughter. Out of the question, I mused. That's fine for truck drivers, but not for my family. Then there was the giggle, which consisted of a series of high-pitched sounds suggesting silliness. That won't do; that's what I do now, I thought. Next was the snicker, a snide reaction to an off-color joke, not that I knew any. It manifested itself in a derisive manner. "Most unattractive," I murmured. Studying the matter further, I chanced upon the chortle, described as a snorting sound. No dignity, I reflected. Growing impatient, I silently demanded, "Where, for Pete's sake, is the well-bred, upper-class laugh that my father talks about?" Next was the chuckle, which was mentioned as laughing in amusement in low tones in a self-satisfied way. "An improvement," I whispered, "but it's not quite right—or is it? No, I don't think so."

What's next? I wondered. I knew the cackle was beyond the proverbial pale, so I didn't even bother to look it up. Finally, I came upon a form of laughter that appeared not only *comme il faut*, but also funny. I am, of course, referring to the titter, characterized as a laugh of mild and restrained amusement and affected politeness. Strikes close to home, I thought. I then remembered a cartoon that I had seen at school. It depicted a well-endowed woman running naked through a crowded room at a party. The caption read, ". . . and a huge titter filled the room." Perfect, I thought. On second thought, however, I realized this was not quite what my father had in mind.

To be on the safe side, in my parents' presence I refrained from showing emotion and instead affected an enigmatic, noncommittal smile. This smile, with the corners of my mouth turned ever so slightly upward, had respectable antecedents in the statues of youths and maidens of pre-classical Greece that I had seen on a school field trip to a museum. By re-creating their antique facial demeanor, I fulfilled my parents' highest expectations of me, namely that "little boys should be seen and not heard."

Chapter 5

Pets

It was during World War II, when I was seven or eight, that a friend of my parents gave me a pet chicken that was cross-billed and needed to be fed by hand. We had a chicken coop behind our stables that contained at any one time between forty and fifty chickens. Every morning, Andy (the gardener) and I would feed them, collect the freshly laid eggs, go back to the big house, and give the eggs to Nora.

"When I was a girl," my mother noted, "I was presented on my birthday with a bantam rooster and his three wives. My rooster strutted around the coop, all puffed up, very pleased with himself. So I decided to call him Theodore, after Roosevelt."

"Oh Lilias," said my father in a tone of dismay, "how could you bear having a Roosevelt in the family? That is too much for words. How naughty of you."

"Well, if I remember correctly, young Elsie, your niece, had a Roosevelt in the family."

"Yes, she did, but look what happened to him." Turning to me, my father explained. "Last year, your cousin Elsie was given a rooster. Aunt Elsie and Uncle Ted were not terribly pleased with him as he made a perfectly dreadful racket in the backyard. He crowed so loudly that Uncle Ted decided to call him Franklin, after Franklin Roosevelt who, as you may or may not know, has a loud voice. You need a loud voice when you talk to the masses. It was all too terribly sad. When young Elsie was away at boarding school in Farmington, her mother decided that she simply had had enough of Franklin's cackle, so she had him incorporated into a stew. Little Elsie was anything but pleased when she found out about it."

At the time, my parents owned a donkey called Neddy who was domiciled in the stables. On a summer day, if the weather was good, Andy or one of the workmen would hitch Neddy to his cart and with Mademoiselle (my French governess) at the helm, we would trot to Bailey's Beach. I was fond of Neddy and, contrary to the prevailing wisdom on donkeys, I never considered him to be stupid. Whenever I paid him a visit, he would look up at me, blink his eyes, cock his head knowingly, twitch his ears, and look at me in anticipation of sugar, which was usually forthcoming.

One summer afternoon my parents were having a cocktail party on the piazza that overlooked the veranda. Along with my friends Brad Norman, Allan Moulton, Peter Altemus, and Freddy Prince, I gave our governesses the slip. Stealthily we made our way to the stables and there let Neddy out of his stall and guided him in the direction of the front lawn. To our glee, we saw Neddy deposit his calling card near the weeping willow tree where he was grazing. In a matter of minutes, we noticed some of the male guests waving their arms, shouting, and heading for Neddy.

My father in the lead, dressed in a blue polo shirt and long yellow trousers, with similarly dressed friends in tow, called, "Whoa, Neddy. Easy boy. Steady, steady. Whoa boy. Steady now. Easy as you go." This picturesque and comical sight of Neddy leading his pursuers a merry chase didn't last long, as he was captured in a matter of minutes and brought back to his stall in the stables. My friends and I were duly scolded. My father said to me sternly, "Haven't you got anything better to do with yourself than play silly pranks and inconvenience your elders?"

No, I thought, but answered contritely, "Yes, Daddy, I'm very sorry. I promise you that I won't do it again."

"Well, see to it that you don't," he said.

The next morning I paid Neddy a visit and addressed him.

"Good morning, Neddy. Didn't we have fun yesterday?" Dignifying this rhetorical question with a toss of his head and a switch of his tail, he broke wind and remained noncommittal.

* * *

Other pets included our parakeets, Cyrano and Roxanne, for whom Mademoiselle had expressed a strong affinity. She would talk to them in English and in French, but mostly in the latter as it was her native tongue. A devout Catholic, her favorite topic of conversation was religion. She lectured, prayed, preached, and even sang a few hymns to those poor innocent parakeets. Mademoiselle's most cherished and oft-repeated idea was that once the birds learned the Bible, their prayers, and their catechism, she would let them loose and they would fly to the four corners of the Earth and spread the gospel to their brethren for the greater glory of God.

On several occasions, while talking to the birds, she would digress from her religious themes and make mention of the old French monarchy with such phrases as *"le roi qui veux"* (the king wills it). My parents attributed much of Mademoiselle's behavior to senility as well as genuine religious feeling. "Let's hope," said my father, "that Mademoiselle succeeds in converting the birds and sends them on their way. Then we'll have some peace and quiet."

"Don't count on it, dear," said my mother, "Cyrano and Roxanne have never struck me as being particularly religious. Not everyone gets the calling. Just remember if the birds ever left, Mademoiselle would miss them and we'd have to get some more birds or we'd never hear the end of it."

"Perish the thought," sighed my father in a disconsolate tone.

"She has a messianic complex. Poor Mademoiselle, she's going around the bend. She's just a little batty. When I was a child and she was my governess, she didn't have this unfortunate thing about religion."

"What are we going to do with her?" asked my father.

Though my mother was fluent in five or six languages, my father was limited to English. Nevertheless, he did possess a small repertoire of expressions such as "comme il faut" and "de rigueur" that he considered good form to use from time to time. Apropos of all this, one late afternoon when Mademoiselle was conversing with the birds, my father exclaimed in a tone of annoyance to my mother, "Really, dear, this can't go on. I won't have it in my house. We're all very fond of Mademoiselle, but we've got to call a halt. If this continues, those damn fowl and our one and only son will be oblivious to the King's English and turn into a frog." Shortly thereafter, Mademoiselle retired and a German governess, Fraülein, took her place.

* * *

As far back as I can remember, my family always had dogs in their company. First there was Flipper, our wirehaired terrier, who eventually became blind and died of old age. Then there was a succession of Pekinese: Mr. Percy, Mr. Pims, Miss Primrose, Poppy, Miss Phipps, Peppy, Portia, Mr. Peabody, Parnsip, and Solly. The last, being Nora's favorite, spent most of her time in the kitchen. When discussing the names of the dogs, my father explained to me, "Mr. Percy was named after Percy Dove, an ancestor of mine who summered in Bar Harbor. The Doves lived in Andover."

During our conversation, Mr. Percy padded into the room, put his paws on the chintz sofa, jumped up, landed next to my father, and then lay down. My father had no recourse but to scold him for this breach of etiquette. "Mr. Percy, how many times have I told you that little dogs don't belong on the sofa? Really, you are being very naughty! Bad dog! You should know better. What are we going to do with you? You don't see other dogs jumping on the sofa and misbehaving, do you? We've been through this so many times I don't want to have to mention it again. Have I made myself perfectly clear? Now be a good dog and off with you."

Obeying my father's instruction, Mr. Percy jumped down, waddled under a Queen Anne chair, curled up, and went to sleep. Coming to Mr. Percy's defense, my mother said, "We mustn't be too hard on him. He's been a good dog all day and, as you know, he has a mind of his own. He's very *contra-corrente*."

Surprised and thinking it unusual but funny that my father named one of our dogs after an ancestor, some bit of mischief possessed me to ask a question in the most ingenuous tone I could muster. "If I'm married and have a son to carry on the family name and decide to name him Percy Dove, would I tell him that he's named after Percy Dove your ancestor or Percy Dove our dog?"

"Oh, Peter," sighed my father wearily. "I don't know whether you say these odd things for effect, to get attention, or whether it's because you don't know any better. You should know by now that people in their wildest dreams wouldn't name their descendants after their dogs, but after their ancestors."

"Oh, dear," cajoled my mother, adopting the same tone that she had earlier used for Mr. Percy. "Don't be hard on the boy. He doesn't know any better."

"Yes, dear, I suppose you're right," sighed my father. "It's just that I wish he'd make some sense. All it takes is more effort on his part and that's not too much to ask of him. He's a great talker, but he's got to learn to think before he says any old thing that pops into his mind."

Later that summer, sitting in the living room in Eastcote, Mr. Pims played one of his usual pranks. He made off with one of my father's monogrammed felt Brooks Brothers slippers. "Oh drat," said my father, "I'll wager that Mr. Pims has been up to his tricks." Raising his voice ever so slightly, but not enough to breach etiquette, he called out, "Oh, Mr. Pims, where are you? Come here this very minute. I want you to return my slipper *tout de suite*. I'm not amused."

I broke into a giggle, whereupon my father with a look of profound chagrin remonstrated, "Peter, how can you laugh that way? You're not developing a proper laugh. You may think that you're being clever, but take it from me, you're not."

"I'm sorry, Daddy," I mumbled with an air of repentance. "I thought it was funny. I mean Mr. Pims and your slipper."

"Well, you thought wrong. It's not funny, not in the least. Don't you know what's amusing and what's not? Mr. Pims has been a naughty boy and I don't find his behavior the least bit cunning. I don't want him to get the idea that we think he's being amusing. When I see him, I'm going to give him a piece of my mind." *Sotto voce*, he added, "Now we all know that we're terribly fond of Mr. Pims, but he's got to realize that little dogs cannot do as they please and willy-nilly play pranks on their masters." Sternly he said, "Peter, get that silly smile off your face. It's most unbecoming."

"Oh, poor Mr. Pims," said my mother. "He's probably picked up bad habits from cavorting with stray dogs. Perhaps he's been hobnobbing with the Wetmore dogs."

"It's so annoying," replied my father. "When the dogs are taken out for a walk, it's hard to keep an eagle eye on them all the time."

"The last time Mr. Pims absconded with your slippers, he went up the back stairs and left them in the servants' quarters," said my mother.

"Ah, Mr. Pims, there you are," exclaimed my father with a mixture of relief and exasperation. Sternly, he addressed our late arrival. "Mr. Pims, you're a naughty, naughty boy. What do you have to say for yourself?" Having deposited the slipper at my father's foot, Mr. Pims stood there as if nothing had happened, with that "sugar wouldn't melt in my mouth" look, full of guile, a real charmer. My father put on his slipper, stood up straight, bent his six-foot, five-inch frame forward at the waist until his head was within two feet of the floor, and wagged his finger within inches of Mr. Pims' pug nose. He chastised, "Mr. Pims, that's not the way for little dogs to behave. Now I know you know better than that, and don't look so pleased with yourself. Shame on you!"

Wishing to please my father but also feeling sorry for Mr. Pims and attempting to placate both parties, I cooed, "Oh, you naughty little dog. You must never hide Daddy's slippers ever again." Mr. Pims, perking up at my soothing tone, wagged his tail and smiled.

"Peter, what is wrong with you? Can't you do anything right? You don't sound very convincing. You're saying the right things, but it comes out all wrong. The sound of your voice is way off the mark. When you scold a dog, make him realize you're scolding him.

Otherwise he'll get the wrong idea and think that you're molly-coddling him.

"Why is it that you always seem to do things backward? Don't you ever do things in a normal way? Tell me, if you can't discipline our dog and sound as if you mean it, how, when the time comes, will you ever discipline your child? Remember, if one is too lenient with one's offspring, in the long run it will be hard on both of you. Peter, your mother and I would appreciate it if in the future you try to do things in the right way. We are asking this for your own good, because we care about you. Once you get the hang of it, it's not too difficult. I don't feel that I'm asking too much of you. Just keep a weather eye on your mother and me, see how things are done, and you'll be better off, I promise you."

Another time, coming into the living room, I heard my father say, "You've been a naughty boy. You can't go on like this. Look at you! How do you account for yourself?" Fearing the worst, I wondered what I had done now. Unsure of the nature of my alleged transgression, I capitulated, "I'm sorry, Daddy. I didn't mean to do it."

"Oh, hello, Peter. It's you, is it? What on Earth are you talking about? What's wrong with you? You're a silly Billy. If you had been paying attention and listening carefully, you would realize that I wasn't talking to you but to Mr. Percy."

Out of the corner of my eye I caught a glimpse of Mr. Percy, who was wagging his tail in appreciation of my unintended diversion.

"As you can see, he's been lollygagging in the mud where he doesn't belong," said my father. "Peter, can't you screw your head on straight? Can't you even tell when I'm talking to you or when I'm addressing one of the dogs?"

Sad to say I could not, but not daring to admit it, I replied, "Yes, Daddy. I'm afraid I was just daydreaming."

"Peter, I can't tell for the life of me whether you're just trying to get my goat or whether you really are in a fog. Snap out of it. I'm glad you realize that you are not a dog. Thank God for small favors.

At least you know something." Standing up straight in his Savile Row jacket, staring ahead, my father staunchly avowed, "Peter, would I be talking to you as if you were a dog?"

Yes, you would, I thought. In all honesty, I had almost felt that the lectures to the dogs when I was present were partly directed at me. I replied, "I'm so terribly sorry. It was all my fault. I just wasn't paying enough attention."

"By the way," my father quizzed in a suspicious tone. "At the beginning of our conversation you said that you didn't mean to do it. What didn't you mean to do?"

Momentarily stuck for an acceptable answer, I cogitated, I'd better get out of here. This conversation is getting the better of me. I replied, "Silly me, I left the faucet dripping in the bathtub. Please excuse me so that I can go and turn it off."

"Faucet dripping?" exclaimed my father. "How many times have I told you not to waste water? Go turn it off. What were you doing, taking a bath?"

"No, not really. I was just playing with my toy boats in the bathtub."

"Toy boats? Aren't you a little old for that?"

* * *

My education regarding pets was furthered at school, where I came to understand how some people regard their dogs as their best friends. My old headmaster, Mr. Hart Fessenden, once mentioned over high tea, "Miss Suckley was very fond of her dogs. Nothing was too good for them. She flew her poodles by her own private plane to Palm Beach. The dogs lived very well. She had food specially prepared for them at the Ritz. Miss Suckley had her own veterinarian, who cautioned her not to feed them such rich food. Despite the dogs getting sick, she disregarded his advice. She said she knew what was good for them and what was not."

Mr. Caswell, my old headmaster at Dexter, once described a certain Boston Brahmin dowager. "She absolutely doted on her dogs. She and her dogs were inseparable. They were always driven by her chauffeur. In her will, she left them all her money, which was considerable. The family inherited the dogs, but the fortune belonged to the pets."

Hearing that, my friend George Rhinelander quipped, "If my family left all their money to the dogs, I'd try to persuade the dogs to share some of it with me and then we'd all be happy. There'd be no family squabbling."

"Well, that's pretty much what happened," said Mr. Caswell. "I'm not sure of all the legal ins and outs, but apparently the family, not wishing to be left out in the cold, convinced the dogs, or their lawyer, that when the dogs passed away and went to dog heaven, the money would revert to the family. I am led to understand the dogs didn't live that long."

* * *

At Camp Kieve in Nobleboro, Maine, I heard more dog stories from one of my friends, David Cadwallader, who confided, "My great-grandfather was a classics scholar. He loved Latin and Greek literature, philosophy, all that stuff. He also loved his dogs. Whenever one of them died, he built a giant tomb for the mutt in Renaissance style, whatever that is. The marble was hand carved and came all the way from Italy. And on the tomb he inscribed something in Latin. He composed it himself. These tombs were in the family cemetery and were a lot bigger and grander than the ones for people." David screwed up his face in a pensive expression and said, "It's strange, but kind of sad, even funny, how rich people seem to care more for their animals than for their own family."

"Yes, I know," interjected "Uncle" Don Kennedy, the head of our camp. "Sometimes families just don't know how to show love to one another, so instead they give it to their pets. It's the only thing they can do."

* * *

When I was ten or so, I'd visit the dogs in their yard behind the greenhouse and bark at them conversationally. All of them, without exception, would reply collectively and individually, and why shouldn't they? We were all friends and on excellent speaking terms.

On one occasion, I committed a faux pas by emitting a bark. No sooner had Mr. Pims replied with a definite woof of his own than Mr. Peabody, Mr. Putnam, and the dogs in the kitchen joined in the canine chorus.

"Oh, doggies, do hush," scolded Daddy. "It's way past your nap time. Little dogs should be seen and not heard." Addressing me, he said, "You may think you're being cunning and clever, but take it from me, you're not. It's very well for you to amuse yourself at the expense of the dogs, but you're hardly setting a good example for them. I suppose one might say it's a sign of the times. Young Freddy Lawrence warbles like a bird in church while his father gives a sermon. Our one and only son howls like a hound in the middle of a conversation. The next thing you know you'll be baying like a banshee. Reveling in the lower orders of nature appears to be the going thing among the young. I'll wager the Van Alen or Cushing boys know better than to carry on in that fashion."

In deference to my father's remonstrance, the dogs finally fell silent. Wouldn't it be funny, I thought, if Daddy decided to give the dogs barking lessons. I envisioned my father stiffly bending over, wagging his finger, and saying something like, "Dogs! It's now 6:30. At 7:30 report to the den for your barking lessons and I'll teach you how, when, and where to bark correctly."

Chapter 6

Summer Vacations

My early childhood summer vacations consisted of playing with the children of my parents' friends. Under the supervision of our governesses we would have a turn at croquet, play hide and seek, make castles in a sandbox, or push a large Victorian hoop with a stick. During these festivities a maid would invariably produce refreshments in the form of ginger ale, cookies, and watercress sandwiches.

Age ten was a turning point for me. Fräulein, my governess, had left and my parents decided to send me off to summer camp so that I could learn to strike out on my own. During the late forties and early fifties the people in my family's social circle commonly did this. It was a satisfactory arrangement for all concerned. The brief parting of the ways between family and the "young" meant a growing sense of mutual independence: mothers and fathers (and governesses, if they were still around) would have more leisure time, and their offspring could derive some benefit from coming into contact with nature.

My parents selected Camp Wyanoke, which was recommended to them by friends. Camp Wyanoke, located in Wolfeboro, New Hampshire, was run by Brad Bentley and overlooked the largest body of fresh water I'd ever seen, Lake Winnipesaukee. All that I remember of the camp is that I caught a bad case of poison ivy, slept in a cabin while the older boys slept in tents raised on platforms, and cried upon leaving for home. It had been my most enjoyable summer yet.

Several summers later I once again was packed off to camp. This time it was Camp Kieve, located in Nobleboro, Maine. Activities consisted of tennis, archery, riflery, canoeing, sailing, fishing, swimming, volleyball, and arts and crafts. At night, after taps was sounded and the lights were turned out, I'd pull the blanket over my head and read such forbidden literary material as funny books.

On Sundays after breakfast, we'd clean our cabins inside and out, fold our clothes in the prescribed manner, and sweep and swab the floors until the last speck of dust was removed. Wearing our freshly cleaned and pressed uniforms and standing at attention by the foot of our beds, we stood inspection, the results of which would be announced at the noonday meal after a compulsory church service held outside in a clearing in the woods.

As smoking cigarettes was forbidden and in any case cigarettes were not available, we resorted to other means. I, along with a few of my friends, took toilet paper from the outhouse, wrapped it around dry pine needles, and smoked what we called "bumwados," which tasted awful, burnt our lips, but made us feel very grown up.

Of the many pleasant things to do at camp, canoeing became my favorite. I enjoyed the feeling of being able to steer the canoe, controlling it and making it go where I wanted to go. It was a great feeling to meet the challenge of rough water, where I'd have to paddle as hard as I could to make the boat go at all.

One day, a few friends and I decided that we would demonstrate our canoeing prowess and go on a short trip across the lake and back. On the same day as our canoeing trip, the entire camp and staff had planned to go skinny-dipping.

At the far west end of the lake there was a girls' camp. We campers never came in contact with its inhabitants, though, so we decided that we would break the ice. We took a large war canoe and straightaway commenced paddling as hard and as fast as we could until we plowed right up onto shore at the girls' camp.

Upon our arrival we were cordially received; hospitality came in the form of food and hot cocoa. Feeling that we owed them some explanation for our sudden intrusion upon their shores, we fabricated some silly story, saying that we wanted to borrow girls' clothing—dresses and bonnets—for a play we were putting on back at the camp. We assured them that we would take very good care of the borrowed attire and return it as soon as possible.

After we got the clothes we departed, leaving the girls' camp in a state of semi-bewilderment. As we paddled back to camp, we precariously managed to change into our borrowed clothes, taking off our shorts and putting on the dresses and bonnets. We even had a few cameras with us to heighten the effect of our forthcoming caper.

When we were within sight of the skinny-dippers, we found that our disguises had a profoundly gratifying effect. We must have borne some resemblance to the female sex because almost immediately there were cries of dismay. "Help!! It's some girls! Everybody out!"

Counselors and campers alike made a beeline to the relative safety of the boathouse. Their swift departure reminded me of a school of fish or a herd of antelope who, their tranquility disturbed, quickly disappear into the protective coloration of the environment. Even those campers who were a little too pleasantly plump for their own good and, by their nature were a bit lazy, moved with stunning alacrity that amazed us all.

We laughed and laughed until we managed to tip over our canoe, and there we were, flailing in the water, still laughing. A few counselors witnessed our tragedy and, still thinking we were damsels in distress, rowed out quickly to rescue us.

I have never seen a more pronounced shock of recognition, a more perplexed and surprised bunch of people, than the counselors as they righted us bedraggled campers, clutching at the gunnels of our canoe. Their reaction also was one of relief, as we had been gone a couple of hours. I guess our little caper put them in a good mood, seeing as they did not punish us. One of the counselors even admitted, "That was pretty funny. You had us in stitches." It occurred to me that our camp counselors were more flexible than my masters at school and that being away from my family was a pleasant respite from the confining nature of home. The counselors told us to wash our borrowed clothing and return it the next day.

The day's amusement had been so much fun that we daring campers couldn't just let our joke expire on the spot. So, the next day, renewing our poetic license (so to speak of the joke that lay dormant within us), we did as we were told; we washed all the bonnets and dresses and headed across the lake once more.

This time the joke lost some of its impact because the girls, seeing us even at a distance, knew who we really were. Besides, they all had on bathing suits and so had nothing to hide.

The day ended happily as the female campers were highly amused that their clothes were so instrumental in pulling off a good practical joke.

⁌ Chapter 7 ⁍

Religion

After the dramatic and terribly sad loss of Miss Searles, my next governess was French. I called her Mademoiselle. Interestingly enough, she had been my mother's governess some twenty-five years before.

After she had given me my bath, I would put away my toys, kneel next to my bed, and mechanically recite a little prayer that she taught me:

> *Now I lay me down to sleep*
> *I pray the Lord my soul to keep.*
> *If I should die before I wake*
> *I pray the Lord my soul to take.*
> *God bless Mr. Percy, Mr. Pims, Miss Primrose, Peppy, and*
>   *Solly. Amen*

When I remembered, I would include in the litany of names Neddy, our donkey, and Cyrano and Roxanne, our parakeets. Mademoiselle would tell me a bedtime story and then leave me alone with the night. The stories tended to be fanciful and not very cheery—cautionary tales in which rash young heroes or heroines ran the gauntlet of threatened injury or mutilation as a price of those venturesome impulses. My father was a firm believer in these stories as a way of "disciplining the young." Left to my own devices, I tucked myself safely under the blankets and pillows and gathered all my stuffed animals about me before going to sleep.

Religion was not an issue of ultimate concern for our family. My parents never discussed such tiresome subjects as salvation, nor was I threatened with the dreary promise of eternal damnation if I didn't toe the line. That sort of unpleasantness was too gauche for polite conversation. Although passionate religious beliefs and behavior were the province of the lower classes, there were nonetheless forms to be given their due. My family periodically took me to Trinity Church in Newport. We sat in the family pew that looked down on the congregation below. The minister, it goes without saying, conducted himself properly and refrained from displaying excess emotion or waxing overly cerebral. My mother explained to me that she went to church only to see who among her friends were in town so that she could have them over for drinks.

Despite my family's lack of interest in matters religious, they occasionally made casual reference to religion as an inadvertent way of communicating some social truth. A case in point was one spring when I was eleven years old. I had made the mistake of bringing back to the house a boy of my own age. To begin with, I was never allowed to bring anyone home without permission from my family. Worse, Kevin was a townsperson. Nevertheless, not knowing any better, I liked him. We had struck up a conversation one day at the drugstore in town. Soon we discovered that our mutual interests included funny comic books, so I invited him home with the hope of trading some of them. Upon our arrival, my mother and father met me at the door. Judging by the look on their faces, they were not terribly pleased. My parents were civil but not warm to Kevin. I sensed that he felt ill at ease in these cold, imposing surroundings. Soon he excused himself, gathered up his books, thanked me quietly, and left. After his departure my mother took me aside and explained to me one of the basic facts of life.

"Darling, you know Kevin is terribly nice and he may get to Heaven before we do, but that is absolutely no reason on Earth why he should be allowed inside this house."

Stunned, I realized that according to my mother's theology

everything was Earth-centered and that Heaven had very little to do with anything.

My father, realizing the gravity of the situation, followed suit with, "Your mother is absolutely correct. The next time that boy comes to the house he should enter the servants' entrance at the back door, where he belongs, and should not be seen in the front part of the house." My father and mother didn't reprimand me further for my faux pas, as they assumed that I simply didn't know any better.

My mother, noticing my hurt and confusion, explained, "We are doing this for your own good. Some day, when you're grown up, you'll see the wisdom of it all and thank us. After all, you don't see us cavorting with the servants."

My father concluded with, "Peter, stick to your own kind and you'll be better for it, I promise you. I know you mean well, but you've got to think of the consequences."

After that I never invited anyone to the house unless my father gave me explicit permission to do so, permission that was not forthcoming unless the children in question were of a socially acceptable background. For the first time I gave religion some serious thought, as I failed to understand why, if Kevin was good enough to reach Heaven, he was considered an outcast in our house. After that, having lost a friend, I came to understand that religion was quite irrelevant to my family life. My parents, adding a note of ecumenism, explained that there were upper-class Catholics as well as Protestants. My father further explained, "Upper-class Catholics control their lower classes more effectively than the Protestants who, sad to say, are more permissive."

My religious education was enhanced by one episode in particular. While I was on Christmas vacation from Fessenden, a boarding school in West Newton, Massachusetts, that went up to the eighth grade, my family decided to go to church. Prior to our departure, my father inspected me from top to bottom, noticed that I was wearing short socks, and addressed me sharply, "You really must do something about those perfectly dreadful socks. This is not the summer and you are not playing tennis at the Casino. Really, Peter, I don't know what's got into you, but you should know better. You can't pray to your God looking that way. What would people think? There's no reason on Earth why your mother and I should have to look at you cavorting about the house, half naked, making a dreary spectacle of yourself. It's not cunning. Your mother and I didn't bring you up to look like a guttersnipe. Now go upstairs, get yourself squared away, and come down *tout de suite* and I'll inspect you. And for God's sake, comb that cowlick of yours. You're not Lord Byron or some dreamy-eyed poet. You're a perfectly nice-looking boy and you don't have to hide behind a mane of hair. Besides, your mother and I would like to see what you look like. Tomorrow I'm taking you to my barber and I'm going to supervise your haircut. Now get going and make it snappy. Don't dawdle."

I then realized that a proper dress code was a means of gaining social acceptance to Heaven.

* * *

Although I had attended chapel every day and twice on Sunday for years at boarding school, I felt a trifle blasé and even skeptical about God and religion. Attendance at chapel was compulsory and most of the sermons were designed to show how to succeed and prosper here on Earth. Perhaps if I had aspired to become a captain of industry I would have listened more attentively. However, my prospects for going into business were nil, as my father insisted that gentlemen don't work but merely inherit their money gracefully.

One of my father's pet passions was sailing. Starting as a young boy spending summers in Bar Harbor, he had sailed the coast of Maine. He regularly made known his dislike for motorboats and the people who owned them. As he explained, only nouveau riche types owned motorboats because they simply did not know any better. "A gent doesn't go nipping and cavorting about on a motorboat," he noted. "I'm appalled that John Archbold bought a motorboat. After all, he does know better. God is on the side of the gentlemen who sail their boats."

I was at a loss as to why God should be on the side of those who owned sailboats and not motorboats. My father owned the *Flying Cloud*, a fifty-eight-foot yawl. Perhaps that was a visible sign that he was one of the elect, predestined for Heaven. In my silly, childish way, I wondered about the theological status of people who owned rowboats or canoes. I didn't own a sailboat but did enjoy sailing, as well as rowing and canoeing. For a few seconds, I actually contemplated my standing in the next life. Would I be among the saved or the damned? It occurred to me that because some sailboats had auxiliary engines, their owners might go to Purgatory. It struck me that St. Peter, if alive today, would probably conduct his fishing business out of a motorboat and not a sailboat.

To my knowledge, the only time religion was a practical issue in our household was when Nora, our cook and a Catholic, had an argument with one of the Protestant maids as to whether fish or liver should be served for Friday lunch. My mother, being very fond of Nora and dependent on her, went into the kitchen to settle the argument. We had fish for lunch and didn't give religion a second thought.

* * *

During my childhood years, we would spend one summer month at Eastcote, my paternal grandmother's summer house in Bar Harbor, Maine. Although I was fond of my grandmother and was glad to see her, the month was a lonely time for me. I was no closer to my parents at Bar Harbor than in Newport, and I missed the warmth of contact with my friends, the servants at Ridgemere. Strangely enough, my loneliness was not diminished at dinnertime when, in an exception to the usual rule of dining alone, I got to eat at the table with my grandmother and my parents. I wasn't truly with them, however. I felt straightjacketed by the role I was required to play—the well-mannered young man who was to be seen and not heard. Once at dinner my father remarked to me, "Your grandmother is very fond of Bishop Lawrence. If you remember, she has a photograph of him on her desk. The bishop makes perfect sense. He speaks plain English. No beating around the bush."

While Adelaide, one of my grandmother's maids, served Grandma and my mother and father from a silver tea service, my father continued in affectionate tones, "The bishop was fond of saying 'Godliness is in league with riches. National prosperity is helping to make the national character more joyous, more unselfish, and more Christian. There is nothing wrong with money. It is our godly duty to have it.'"

Slightly confused by this pronouncement by the Bishop of Business, as I thought of him, I gingerly enquired, "But Daddy, if the bishop is right, how do you explain the saying that money is the root of all evil?"

"Oh, fiddlesticks and balderdash," snapped my father crossly. "It sounds as if you've been listening to your Commie masters at school. Is that what they teach, may I ask? That money is not important?"

"Oh, heavens no, Daddy," I replied defensively, "but do you mean to say money is the root of all goodness and not badness?"

"Well, yes, but not all money," my father replied. "Old money that's been around, that's been in the family for generations, that's tried and true. It is more trustworthy. It's got some value. But new money is always a bit suspect."

"Thank you, Daddy," I replied in a grateful tone. "I think I understand. Old money is the source of goodness but new money is the root of evil." I wondered whether a rich man and a poor man shared the same God.

* * *

There was no further mention of religion until one evening when my parents were getting ready to go to a dinner party given by the Strawbridges. With my parents were Caleb and Rosemary Loring, recently arrived from Prides Crossing in Massachusetts. My mother looked lovely in her evening gown and jewelry. While one of the maids was helping with her coat, she remarked with an offhand air, "Some of the Eastern religions make a lot of sense. They're not concerned with the dreary business of making money." With a simple gesture of her left hand that revealed a diamond ring with glittering stones and a gold bracelet that dangled carelessly from her wrist, she proclaimed, "Material things are a dreadful bore."

"Lilias," said my father, "I couldn't agree with you more. These days the common man wants more money, more handouts, something for nothing. My answer to him is let him do an honest day's work and he'll feel better about himself. Too much money can spoil and corrupt him. I'm only speaking for his own good."

Hearing that, I wondered whether my parents' life would become more enjoyable and interesting—not to mention virtuous—if their jewels, furs, silver, servants, and houses were all suddenly to vanish.

Wondering whether my father would expect to be admitted to Heaven ahead of the common people who happened to arrive at the same time, I even wondered whether he would expect them to gain admittance only through the rear entrance.

≋ Chapter 8 ≋
Fighting a Duel

When I was twelve or thirteen, at breakfast one day my father asked, "If it should come to pass that one of your contemporaries, a social equal, should ever cast aspersions on our family name, would you be willing to avenge the slight?"

I was not really sure what he meant and was surprised by the unexpected nature of the question, but, wanting above all to please him, I blurted, "Yes, Daddy, of course I'd be willing to fight a duel." I thought it was a strange request, as dueling had gone out of fashion hundreds of years earlier, but I realized that my father's cast of mind was somewhere in the eighteenth century, when people dueled at the drop of a hat.

It just so happened that at the time of my father's unusual request, I was taking fencing lessons with some friends—Bobby Grosvenor, George Strawbridge, Lance Reventlow, and Freddy Cushing. At one of our fencing lessons Bobby called my father a "stuffy windbag," which of course was true.

Hearing that, almost jumping for joy, I clapped him on the back and exclaimed, "Bobby, you've saved the day. We're going to have to fight a duel because you insulted the family name. But don't worry; just nick my left cheek with your pocketknife to make it look like we fought a real duel. In return, I'll give you several of my most prized funny books." I was loathe to part with them, but then I was willing to bend over backward and do anything to please my father and gain his approval. "Please agree," I begged. Bobby was reluctant at first, but finally he agreed, especially as I had promised him those funny books.

After the "duel," having received my badge of courage, my scar, I proudly showed it to my father later that evening. To my disappointment, he looked at me askance and remarked, "What hath God wrought? I ask you. Where on Earth do you think you are, in Heidelberg, making a dreary public spectacle of yourself?" He then put an end to my fencing lessons and admonished me to stay out of trouble and not be the goat holding the bag.

Chapter 9

Lessons in Economics

My family taught me the principle of private property and the virtue of thrift needed to maintain ownership of that property. If I perhaps failed to grasp some of their advanced theories, I can only blame myself. My father, who maintained that gentlemen don't work but simply inherit their money gracefully, lived off a traditional Boston trust fund.

One morning, while on vacation from the Fessenden School, a small private school in Massachusetts where I was a fourth-form student, I asked my mother's permission to play one of my records on the phonograph in the living room, having left my own at school. My mother seemed quite shocked at the request. She curtly replied, "Your father gives you a generous allowance of twenty-five cents a week. If you save your pennies and don't spend them frivolously, you can afford to buy yourself a phonograph to keep at home."

I politely mumbled, "Yes, Mummy," went upstairs to my room, sat down at my desk, set pen to paper, and tried to figure out how long it would take before I could purchase a record player. Twenty-five cents a week yielded one dollar a month. In a year I'd have twelve dollars. That seemed like a lot of money. I hadn't the vaguest notion of how much a record player would cost. If I could save all my allowance, perhaps I could purchase one in two or three years.

Generally, I was very careful and considerate of anything that didn't belong to me. To my knowledge, I never damaged or broke anything at Ridgemere or Eastcote, our family homes in Newport, Rhode Island, and Bar Harbor, Maine. I was mystified as to why mother wouldn't let me use one of her phonographs. Perhaps she suspected my mechanical and motor skills were not up to the task of running the machine. Several days later I summoned my courage and asked her why I was not allowed to play a record on her machine. Without looking up she answered crossly, "Let me put it to you this way, darling. What's yours is yours and what's mine is mine. Frankly, we haven't gone communist yet!"

Not wishing to display my ignorance by asking her the meaning of the word "communist," nor to appear tiresome by continuing the discussion, I mumbled, "Yes, Mummy. Thank you." Being twelve at the time and ignorant of much of the outside world, I had no idea what a Communist was except that my mother didn't approve of them.

The next day I went to the library to look up the meaning of the word and found that "communist" referred to a society devoid of social classes. I remember wondering why, if Communists were people who on occasion shared a few of their possessions with their children, they were so bad.

Years earlier, my parents had told me to be generous and share my toys with my friends who, along with their governesses, came to visit. Apparently, there were two standards of behavior, one for parents and another for children. I later learned that after World War II, Marshal Tito's Communist government had confiscated an ancient Croatian castle that had been in my mother's family for hundreds of years. It had last belonged to Baron Joseph Von Gill-ming, my mother's grandfather. Why she equated me with Marshal Tito and the phonograph with the family castle gave me pause.

When I reached the age of thirteen, my father decided that it was time to instill in me a sense of responsibility about money. While continuing to grant me the handsome sum of twenty-five cents a week, he attached the stipulation that I should have to account for every cent I spent. Twenty-five cents in 1948 went a long way. One nickel could purchase a second-hand funny book, an ice cream cone, or a bottle of ginger ale. It also could have purchased a bottle of Coca-Cola had I not been enjoined from drinking that plebian beverage.

At the end of each week, I would go to my father and submit an official-looking sheet of paper containing all pertinent information regarding the previous week's expenditures. This fiscal review would take place in the library, sometimes referred to as the den. I remember one such occasion when I was fourteen. I stood outside the room and asked permission to enter.

"Yes, Peter, what is it? What can I do for you? Do come in and sit down."

"Thank you, Daddy," I diffidently replied. "Here is my accounting for last week's expenses. I hope I added it all up correctly."

"Thank you," he replied. "Let's see what you've got."

He perused the piece of paper. Looking up, he asked, "Peter, how much money do you have left?"

I fished in my pocket and pulled out six cents.

"Peter, according to these figures you should have nine cents left, but you seem to be short. Look here, you have spent five cents for one ice cream cone, five cents for a funny book—I wish you'd stop reading those things—and one penny for a piece of gum." At the mention of the word "gum," he looked at me sternly, with a hint of distress. "Gum! Since when do you chew gum? Most unattractive! You don't see me or your mother or any of our friends chewing gum. What's gotten into you? Really, Peter, you should know better. We didn't bring you up to be a gum chewer. In the future you will curb this practice. Very unbecoming!" He paused and concluded, "Only servants and common people chew gum, but you can't blame them for they simply don't know any better. But you do. If you have to chew gum, please have the decency to chew in private where we won't have to lay eyes on you. Let me put it to you this way. How would you like it if your mother and I went around chewing gum? It would be a pretty sight, wouldn't it?"

Wishing to get back into my father's good graces, I stood ramrod straight, chest puffed out, chin up, and in a pompous tone replied, "Why, Daddy, I'd be appalled. I just can't imagine it."

"Appalled, you say. Good for you. Indeed, you should be appalled. Now you're showing some sense. I trust I've made myself perfectly clear." He looked at me with gravity, making sure his words registered with their full weight. "Now let's see," he added, looking at the paper. "Peter, according to the figures you've given me, three cents are not accounted for. You have only six cents left but you should have nine. Look, let me show you. You spent five cents last Tuesday, and on Thursday you purchased three items, which I'm glad to say you list correctly, the sum of which is eleven cents. Do you follow me? You spent five cents one day and eleven cents two days later." He paused and looked at me intently. "It's a matter of simple arithmetic. What's five and eleven?"

Vexed and embarrassed, my mind went blank. I screwed up my face apprehensively. My father's face registered annoyance. "Oh, Peter, don't be difficult. You know very well what five and eleven are!"

"Let me see," I blurted out. "It's sixteen cents, Daddy."

"Peter, you know very well that it's sixteen cents," he scolded. "Close your mouth, you'll catch flies. Now you have spent sixteen cents and I gave you twenty-five. How much should you have left?"

"Well, as you said, Daddy, I think I'd have nine cents left," I replied hopefully.

"You think! Why of course you'd have nine cents left, but you tell me that you only have six cents left."

"Gosh, Daddy, I just don't know. I think something is wrong."

"Don't say 'gosh'; it's not becoming," he snapped.

I went through the motions of searching my pockets. "I'm sorry, I don't know where those three pennies went. I thought I had them."

"You thought. Well, you thought wrong. It's carelessness on your part. You've simply got to learn to assume responsibility for your financial affairs."

Perhaps taking pity on me and probably finding the situation hopeless, he added, with more accommodation in his voice, "Maybe you lost those three pennies when you were playing outside. Peter, check your pockets and make sure they don't have any holes in them." At the time I was wearing tropical worsted gray flannel shorts. "If you have any holes, give your shorts to Margaret or Adelaide and they will be glad to sew them up for you." Still not letting me off the hook, he asked, "Is it possible that you spent those three pennies and just forgot about it?"

"Well, maybe, Daddy, but I don't remember doing that." I attempted to convey the appropriate look of one recalling an important fact.

"Don't remember? You've got to remember," he said sternly. "Otherwise how will you ever keep your finances straight? Next time be more careful. You can't go around losing money." Mercifully, my father reached into his pocket and pulled out a quarter and gave it to me. "Now here's your allowance. This will last you for one week until next Friday. Make sure you keep track of your expenses and make no mistakes, please."

"Yes, Daddy, thank you. I'll be more careful in the future." Just for safety's sake I checked all of my pockets to make sure they hadn't any holes.

After my father gave me permission to leave, he issued these final words of admonition: "Peter, don't spend all your money in one place. Remember, twenty-five cents should go a long way. Think carefully before you spend it. It's always better to save money than to spend it; then you'll have some left over for a rainy day. That's what I call smart thinking."

After that talk with my father, I always felt a little guilty if at the end of a week I had less than a nickel in my possession. As for the errant pennies, they never did turn up.

* * *

Even though my father despised "business," he never allowed anyone to take advantage of him financially. One day in 1947, Charlotte, one of the kitchen maids, interrupted my parents' lunch to inform them that a piano had arrived at the front door. My mother explained to me that she had lent a piano to some friends, Lawrence (Lolly) and Kitty Reeve, who lived in Manchester, Massachusetts. The understanding was that eventually it would be returned. The Reeves, laboring under the misapprehension that the loan was a gift, were loath to return it. After some curt exchanges, the Reeves returned the piano. Accompanying it was a bill addressed to my father for the sum of five dollars for storage. With the Steinway piano safely tucked away in the front hall, my father retired to the den, wrote Lawrence Reeve a five-dollar check, and along with it sent a bill in the amount of $5.25 for rental. He matter-of-factly announced to us that a gentleman should not feel above coming out ahead in matters such as these. A week later the Reeves's check for $5.25 arrived.

Years later, it occurred to me that my father had earned back my weekly allowance on the deal. If he had ever deigned to work, he would have made an excellent businessman.

Chapter 10

History

Although I grew up surrounded by old family portraits, it wasn't until I had reached the age of fourteen or fifteen that I became consciously curious about all of those ancestors. As with my bedtime friends in early years, these personages seemed to come alive for me. August in countenance, peering out through gilt-edged frames and looking resplendent in their old-fashioned garb, each visage had an air of remote superiority, regarding the world of which they were the overseers. Caught up in their impervious gaze and feeling disconcerted at the prospect of their passing judgment on me, I made a determined effort to think and feel only respectful thoughts whenever I encountered them.

One evening while sitting in the den I asked my father about the portraits.

"I'm glad you're finally coming around and taking an interest in your family," he pronounced. "Remember that they are your flesh and blood as well as mine and your mother's. You should know that my father, Reginald Mansfield Johnson, is your grandfather who married my mother, Julie Pierrepont Edwards, who couldn't be fonder of you. She always asks for you. My father was a senior partner at Ropes & Gray in Boston. My mother's father, your grandfather, who I needn't tell you was Pierrepont Edwards, was a vice consul from the Court of St. James in England. His portrait, in case you hadn't noticed, hangs over the sideboard in the dining room.

In turn, his father, Charles Pierrepont Edwards, my great-grand-father, is your great-great-grandfather. He wrote a book about the law entitled *Pleasantries About Courts and Law* and dedicated it to his son, Pierrepont Edwards. If you bear with me, I'll read his inscription." Returning from the library with a leather-bound book he commenced: "It reads as follows: 'Dedicated to Pierrepont Edwards, Esquire, his Britannic Majesty's Vice Consul at the Port of New York, to my son and from my pride in him as a man.'

"My grandfather built Eastcote in Bar Harbor," my father reminisced. "He married Antoinette Waterbury, and if you're paying attention, you will know she is your great-grandmother. The Waterburys made their money in cordage during the very latter part of the seventeenth century and the early part of the eighteenth century. They had a daughter, Dorothy, my grandmother's sister, who married Robert Turnbull. You haven't met Uncle Bob and Aunt Dorothy; your mother and I visited them at Twickenham in Yemassee, South Carolina. It might interest you to know that the first Turnbull was given Twickenham Plantation as a land grant by King Charles II sometime during the latter part of the seventeenth century. If you recall, George de Peyster and I went to Twickenham last winter to go shooting—very festive. It was all very gay."

When my father mentioned the Waterbury ancestors, my mother entered the room and assumed her rightful chair by the fireplace. "I'll have you know the Waterburys are all quite mad. Mad as March hares!"

"Do you mean to say there's madness in the family?" I asked, disguising a tiny note of hopefulness.

Disregarding my question, she explained, "Antoinette Waterbury was mad as the Mad Hatter. Completely around the bend. Her husband, Pierrepont Edwards, already living in this country but still a British subject, was offered a knighthood for his services to the British crown. Antoinette made him refuse it. She informed him that it was un-American. He was also offered an ambassadorship and she made him refuse that, for what reason we'll never know. Furthermore, when Pierrepont Edwards died, what was the first thing Antoinette did? I'll tell you. She promptly married his valet, whose name was Burden. I've been told he read poetry to her. All quite mad!"

"Ah yes," sighed my father with a weary note of resignation. "Had Antoinette lived in the eighteenth century she would have made more sense. Unfortunately, she became infected by this thing called democracy that was in vogue in the nineteenth century. Poor Antoinette had a strong will but was very impressionable. She got taken in by liberalism and intellectuals who had all the wrong ideas."

Turning to me, he added, "You are descended from His Grace, Evelyn Pierrepont, Duke of Kingston, whose portrait hangs in the vestibule. The Pierreponts were Norman knights who rode with Duke William in 1066. Tell me, Peter, what have you learned in history this past year at Brooks?"

"History? Well, Daddy, let me see. Last semester I was studying American history with Mr. Bartlett. I enjoyed reading about Theodore Roosevelt." At the mention of Roosevelt my father flushed crimson and explained, "I'll tell it to you straight. Roosevelt was a traitor and a disgrace to our class. He sold us down the river."

My father issued such pronouncements whether the Roosevelt in question was Theodore or Franklin. He made the subject of history come alive for me on several occasions when he made me empty out my pockets and if FDR dimes (first issued when I was eleven years old) were found he would confiscate them, saying that they had "no value." After that he would take them to the bank and turn them in for pennies. I should also mention that my father was not overly fond of coins that bore the head of Lincoln who, according to him, was only a Midwestern commoner.

Before I could extricate myself from my confusion and formulate any semblance of a response, my father continued, "I suppose in all fairness we can't blame your masters at school. For all I know, they simply don't know any better."

Eager to please him and not wanting him to tell that I was a total failure in history, I respectfully volunteered, "I know that the

Americans won their freedom from the English in the American Revolution."

At the mention of the detested word "revolution" my father scornfully proclaimed, "Peter, you should know some of my ancestors were Tories and they fought valiantly on the side of the English. The Americans were commoners and they didn't know how to conduct themselves properly like gentlemen on the battlefield. They would hide behind trees and take pot shots at the English. Some of them dressed in coonskin and buckskin and looked no better than savages. They made a most unattractive spectacle of themselves. The English marched correctly in battle formation, dressed smartly in full uniform, and the soldiers would not fire willy-nilly but only on command, upon the orders of their betters. The Americans, I grant you, carried the day but their tactics were not aboveboard. Individuality is most unattractive. It recognizes no social superior and breeds anarchy."

"Well, Daddy, I can tell you about the Civil War," I politely submitted, "which the Northerners won when General Robert E. Lee surrendered to Ulysses S. Grant at Appomattox in 1865."

"Peter, you should know that some of my ancestors fought gallantly on the side of the South as well as the North. They were officers and gentlemen of the first rank who fought valiantly for their plantations, family honor, and a way of life that they held dear. Some of them went to Oxford and Cambridge."

"General Sherman was an absolute beast," opined my mother. "Neither he nor his army knew how to conduct themselves. They were very badly behaved."

"Excuse me, Daddy, but I'm a little confused about something."

"Confused? Yes, I dare say. You seem to be in a perpetual fog. Doubtless your mind is on higher things."

"Well, Daddy, earlier when you were telling about the American Revolution, you said that Americans were like savages, but some of our ancestors were American as well as English. Does that mean they were savages?"

"Oh, Peter, what an odd question. If I didn't know better I'd think you were a silly Billy. You really should learn to think before you say any odd thing that pops into that mind of yours. You know very well that our ancestors, no matter what their political sympathies, were aboveboard in all respects. I was talking about the common man, the enlisted man who simply didn't know any better, members of the lower class who ate venison with their bare hands and lived in a state of nature without the redeeming niceties of civilization."

Disregarding his aforementioned dislike for revolutionaries, he continued, "General Greene and Colonel Putnam were ancestors of your mother and they fought valiantly against the English. I can assure you that they didn't cavort in raggle-taggle buckskin like raga-muffins. Take it from me, they were at all times impeccably dressed. No coonskin democracy for them." I wondered, did the general or the colonel, like my father, have their clothes custom made at Brooks Brothers or Savile Row?

"Peter, stop fidgeting," scolded my father. "You've got to learn to pay full attention when your elders are talking to you. Aren't you interested in what I have to say? Please pay full attention. Who knows, you might learn a thing or two."

Coming back to his dislike of revolutionaries, my father said, "The revolutionaries in France and the Bolsheviks are in large measure responsible for the sorry state of the world. Your mother and I have no sympathy whatsoever with revolutionaries and that is why we don't celebrate the Fourth of July or Bastille Day. Those who would make revolutions and undermine civilization, not only do they wish to take away from us all that we have but, given half a chance, they'd lay claim to our ancestors as well." After a pause he added, "I'm not just talking about the Communists and free thinkers in general."

"Don't forget the Fascists," spoke my mother, "Hitler was such a tiresome little man. He had such an unattractive lower-middle-class South Austrian accent. Why the Junkers ever put up with him we'll never know."

"I couldn't agree with you more," said my father. "After all, having Hitler at the dining room table or in the drawing room would be like entertaining an Irish kern or a Cockney as a social equal."

"Speaking perfectly frankly, I'm all in favor of 'Cocknese' and all the dialects of the country," said my mother. "They have great charm and are colorful in their proper place. I prefer them to the bland tongues of the middle-class morass. Sad to say, the accents rude and wild of the countryside are disappearing. The richness and wisdom of country sayings will all but vanish, and I'm sorry to say we will be the worse off for it."

"Quite true," echoed my father. "Democracy doesn't raise standards, as modern intellectuals will have us think, but rather lowers them. This leveling process has produced the age of the common man."

I noticed Margaret quietly going about her business, drawing blinds and removing the dogs' empty bowls. Thinking about Ridgemere and its surrounding environs—the horse-drawn carriages (remnants of an earlier age), the gardener's cottage, the pump house, the tool shed, the chicken shed, the greenhouses, the gazebo on the back lawn, and our well-manicured gardens, I felt myself to be an adjunct to the property at my family's disposal, like the maids, and certainly not the heir apparent in training.

My father was attired for the summer evening in lightweight tropical gray worsted flannels, a pullover, a pink Egyptian cotton shirt, his reading-room club tie, and his custom-made Peal shoes. I tried to imagine myself in his shoes, but the thought didn't get very far. Rather, I longed to be in the kitchen with Nora and the maids. However, my father was not finished with my lesson on family history.

"Now, Peter, there's no reason why you can't learn a little something about your family. I'll explain your ancestry to you and try to give you some glimmer of understanding of how genealogy works. On the Boston side of the family, which is my father's side, you are directly descended from Captain James Johnson, who married Abigail Oliver. They settled somewhere in the vicinity of Lynn in 1630. They were your great-, great-, great-, great-, great-, great-, great-grandparents. Their legal issue was Samuel Johnson, who married Phebe Burton, whose father was Edward Burton, who married Margaret Otis, and they would be your great-, great-, great-, great-, great-, great-, great-aunt and uncle."

Continuing in this fashion to the present, he added, "It wouldn't hurt you to know a little something about some of your living relatives. You remember your cousins Ned and Elsie, who live in Milton? Ned has a good eye for photography and is very mechanical. I remember him when he was at Milton Academy before he went to Harvard. He was well spoken and always had some bright idea about something or other. Young Elsie is a brain's trust. She's mad for books." Turning to my mother, my father added, "Uncle Ted was very concerned about her. He told me that when she was at Miss Porter's she developed a penchant for Buddhism. I reassured him that it was only a passing fancy and that she would get over it. As you know, that sort of odd behavior is very Boston."

Listening to my father, I realized that his lineage defined the length and breadth of who he was. There was really no vocation, no hopes or dreams to modulate that definition. There was simply his place in the order of things, a quite high place thanks exclusively to those who went before him.

"Daddy, I remember several people at school talking about their Mayflower ancestors. Do we have any of those?"

"Oh yes. Some of the poorer, not so well-heeled members of our family came over on the Mayflower."

"And how about the richer ones, Daddy?"

"They came over on their private yachts. On my father's side of the family we have several Mayflower ancestors."

My father went on to tell stories of ancestors such as William White and the Vassals. He also pointed out my mother's Mayflower ancestors, including Francis Cooke, John Peabody, and many others who had helped to settle Salem.

Listening to my father, I recalled a paper I had written for my history class in which I was asked to express my preference for living either in the early days of Greece or in the Medieval ages. Rather than writing about myself, I wrote about my father, depicting him as feeling more at home being Sir Lancelot venturing forth on a noble steed than the wily Odysseus, riding unceremoniously on a lowly oxcart. Feudalism with all of its rituals and trappings would have been more congenial to him than early Greek tribal society, where high and low were connected to each other by ties of blood.

"Tell me, Daddy, what Boston families do you admire?"

"Just off the cuff, I'd say the Lawrences and the Forbes family did well for themselves. Old Bishop Appleton Lawrence was a personal friend of your grandmother. She thought the world of him."

"What else did they do," I asked, "besides being friends of the family?"

"The Lawrences? Amos Lawrence, the old bishop's father, and his brother Abbott manufactured and sold textiles. You can see the mills, which still stand in the city of Lawrence. Over the years they have given generously to charities and cultural organizations, not to mention the leadership they have provided through the pulpit."

"I must say the Lawrence children couldn't be more attractive," said my mother. "They are all well-behaved and have beautiful manners."

"Oh yes, there're five of them," said my father, "young Freddy, who is Peter's age; his elder brother, Peter; and the three girls, Marian, Margaret, and Catherine. Now whether the boys will carry on in their father's footsteps and become men of the cloth remains to be seen. Young Freddy couldn't be nicer but he's rather fey, a bit absent-minded, rather like our Peter. After all, can you even begin to imagine our one and only son expounding God's words?"

"Speaking perfectly frankly, I can't," said my mother. "I don't think we have anything to worry about on that score."

I hope not, I thought.

Turning to me, my father said, "I'm glad you are seeing something of your friend Freddy. I hope he's amusing for you."

"Yes, Daddy, Freddy is very clever. He knows his Latin backwards and forwards."

"Good for him. A little Latin won't hurt you. It's good for the soul. My father, grandfather, and great-grandfather read poetry in

Latin and Greek for pleasure. I'll wager that young Lawrence knows a thing or two."

Thus reminded of my friend Freddy, I recalled quite vividly that during the previous Christmas vacation Grandma and I had attended St. Paul's Church in Brookline to hear Bishop Lawrence give a sermon. During the service, after singing a hymn, I heard a peculiar sound emanating from several pews in front of me, which resembled the singing of birds. After the service, Bishop Lawrence and Mrs. Lawrence invited my grandmother and me, along with several other parishioners, to their house for tea and gossip.

The house was modestly spacious but not forbidding. Soon after our arrival, Bishop Lawrence "changed hats," as he put it. He took off his vestments, sat down by the piano, and sang old tunes from the 1920s. One of them was "Smiles," which had a line, "There are smiles that take away the sadness." In the background I heard what sounded like birds chirping, like the ones I had just heard in church. I noticed other people with puzzled looks, craning their necks, looking about, and wondering the same thing as I. Freddy's mother then gently scolded, "Oh Freddy, do hush. You are not a bird, so please stop acting like one."

I envied Freddy's accomplishments and asked him to elaborate on his technique. He modestly explained that on the side of his mouth that turned up into a smile he sucked in air, which resonated with a hole or gap in a tooth between the incisor and molar. Freddy's father, noticing my disappointment at not being able to produce sounds that remotely resembled Freddy's, consoled, "Don't feel bad. Everyone in the family has tried but to no avail. Perhaps Freddy can give you chirping lessons."

"That's probably less challenging than getting laughing lessons from my father," I retorted.

"Your father means well," said the bishop with a barely concealed smile. "Don't be hard on him."

"Laughing lessons, indeed," said Mrs. Lawrence in an amused tone. "I don't think we need any of those. We all laugh at the drop of a hat."

My mother's voice snapped me out of my reminiscence. "You know, Peter, a family, no matter how old and venerable, has more than their share of skeletons rattling around in the closet."

"Quite so," said my father. "There are no families on the face of the Earth without a few black sheep."

"A kindly way of looking at it, Peter," said my mother, "is that they add a bit of character. Take, for example, your father's first Johnson ancestor, who settled in the Massachusetts Bay Colony. He took to getting plastered to the gills and made a career of wreaking havoc in taverns. He was like a bull in a china shop. From what I gather, things got so bad that he was finally asked to leave his domicile and look for other quarters."

"Oh, Lilias," chided my father. "That's very naughty of you. Telling tales out of school, spilling the beans on my ancestors. Such things should not be mentioned in front of Peter. He might get the wrong idea."

"Well, it doesn't hurt to have a sense of humor about one's ancestors," retorted my mother.

"Yes, I suppose you're right. I find it all too terribly amusing that some of my New York ancestors are mentioned in the 'Knickerbocker Sketches' by Washington Irving."

Whether my father's fondness for the sketches was due to their mentions of his ancestors or, conversely, whether his fondness for those particular ancestors derived from their presence in the sketches, I'm not sure. Most likely it was a bit of both, as he and the celebrated author shared a fondness for the past, avoided lofty moral ideas and vulgar controversial issues of the day, distrusted the mob when tinkers and peddlers were meddling in the affairs of government, and felt more at home in moldering tombs than rotten boroughs. Perhaps my father felt comfortable with the lack of depth in Irving's treatment of human experiences.

"Peter, I'll tell you what I'm going to do," began my father. "I will allow you to look at one of my books on family history. I'm going to the ancestor room and will return forthwith with a book of our New York ancestors."

Several minutes later he returned with some leather books in burnished brown that measured three feet high by two feet wide, custom-made in England with the family crest on the cover. These books were accompanied by a large magnifying glass that was made in Germany for such occasions as peering at family ancestors from a standing position. Setting the books down, he generously assented, "I will make an exception and allow you this once to touch and even turn the pages of these books. However, first there is one thing you must do for me. I'd like you to go to the bathroom and perform your ablutions; wash those hands of yours thoroughly. When your hands are clean and dry, report back to me for inspection."

When I returned from the bathroom, I barely passed my father's inspection as he found a tiny bit of dirt in the lower right-hand corner of my left forefinger. We made our way through the books, but the more my father held forth on the accomplishments and exploits of my ancestors, the less I felt a part of the family; I felt more like a stranger who didn't belong.

If anything, I felt a greater kinship with my Austro-Hungarian maternal grandmother, Baroness Olga Von Gillming, than with my father's starchy forebears. When the Communists invaded Hungary in the 1950s, they took over my grandmother's castle and turned it into a place for storing ammunition. As a result of her tragic experience, losing everything but finding her family, she became fanatically religious. In the morning, I'd visit her in her room, where she had written "Jesus loves you" on the windowpanes. She forgave the Communists and even prayed for them. Once while lying in her bed she sang me a lovely Hungarian folk song she had learned from her nurse when she was a child back in Hungary.

In response to my parents' view of history, which amounted to the worship of dead idols, I was beginning to hope that history would be something I could take part in shaping. Perhaps in the future I'd come to understand and appreciate my ancestors in my own way and not just to please my family. Despite my realization that "good form" was a way of denying my emotions, not communicating my wishes, I nevertheless felt some grudging awe for my family's ease in moving through life. In their way they were aesthet-ically perfect despite the fact that, in my mind, their conversation grievously lacked content. In my father's sitting room, I had been taught that laughter, if indulged in at all, must be done correctly to display one's good breeding and station in life. On my own, I was beginning to learn that laughter could be indispensable and nour-ishing, a way to survive and flourish.

⅀ Chapter 11 ⅀
Clothes

Values concerning modesty vary from one culture to another and may change with time. Blissfully unaware of this, and being only four or five at the time, I forgot to put on my bathing suit and dashed naked from our cabana to the beach—Bailey's Beach in Newport. Before I could get to the water, I was seized by Mademoiselle, my governess, brought back to the cabana, and severely scolded for my breach of propriety.

Notwithstanding that abashing experience, I never gave clothes much thought. I remember wearing sailor suits until I reached eleven, when my father gave me my first pair of long trousers. I was so proud that I couldn't bear to part with them and wanted to wear them to bed. Wearing them made me feel terribly grown up, a feeling I concealed lest my family think I was becoming too big for my breeches.

Whenever I needed new clothes, my father would take me to Brooks Brothers in Boston. Brooks Brothers was a venerable institution where, for generations, old Yankee families would reluctantly part with their money and buy their clothes. Facing Brooks Brothers across the street was Bonwit Teller, likewise a venerable clothing store, but for women. Brooks and Bonwit's, bastions of respectability, impeccable in their mien, reminded me of a dowdy dowager and a gent who paid homage to each other but, each assured of their rightful position, did not budge an inch.

I remember one occasion when my father took me to the boys' department on the second floor of Brooks. I looked around and noticed the dark paneled walls, like those in a library. It was quiet but not hushed. Looking around further, I noticed a customer talking quietly to a salesman. No backslapping. There was a proper distance and a nicely handled familiarity between salesmen and patrons.

One elderly gentleman, noticing my father, greeted him. "Good afternoon, Mr. Johnson; may I help you? Is this your son?"

"Hello, Mr. Young. Nice to see you. Yes, this is my boy, Peter." Turning to me, he instructed, "Shake hands and say, 'How do you do, Mr. Young.' I've known Mr. Young for many years. He used to wait on me when I was a boy at Milton Academy."

I did as I was told. My father, getting down to business, said, "I'd like some clothes for this young man." My father bought me polo shirts, socks, underwear, a beige-colored linen Palm Beach suit, knee-length pants, and a jacket. I was ushered into the sanctity of a try-on booth, where my father inspected the fit. In a matter of minutes, my father and Mr. Young concluded their business.

"Thank you, Mr. Young, for looking after my boy. I'm much obliged. Please send me the bill at the Newport address."

My father then asked me, "Peter, do you like your new clothes?"

"Yes, Daddy, thank you," I politely replied. In fact, I had no feelings one way or another about them. As long as my father bought my clothes, I had no say whatever as to my personal preference. I thought about Mr. Young and wondered whether he ever got tired of waiting on people.

It wasn't until years later, as a student at the Brooks School in North Andover, Massachusetts, that I gave clothes a second thought. Gray flannels, khaki trousers, tweed sports coats, and seersucker suits were in order. Clean, white bucks were considered chic, especially if worn with gray flannels and a dark blue school blazer. Dirty, scuffed bucks were worn for casually knocking about. Nearly everyone wore button-down Oxford cloth shirts, and rounded collars with a gold pin under the knot of the tie were also popular. Bowties were in. A few upperclassmen made a fetish of the high art of dressing. They made sure that the polka dots or stripes of their ties, the colored stripes of their cinch belts, and the colored handkerchief that raffishly protruded from the breast pocket of their sport coats were a chromatically correct match.

Being perfectly dressed, but not overdressed, on a dance weekend was considered to have an aphrodisiac effect on girls. Formal attire for dances consisted of a dinner jacket; patent leather shoes or pumps; and black, maroon, or plaid cummerbunds with matching ties. In lieu of cummerbunds, some of us sported waistcoats. Proper attire was almost as difficult as one's studies; it required great effort to appear effortlessly well dressed.

At Brooks School, most of us were educated under the fine tutelage of Charley Davidson, owner of the nearby Andover Shop. He set an example for all of us. He was fond of saying, "Clothes are the badge that shows you are a member of a never-mentioned but well-understood club."

Thanks to my classmates, I learned such subtleties as how wide a bowtie should be, what type of knot to tie for a four-in-hand, the proper length of trousers (no pleats), and what materials were used in various garments. One's hair should be short, neatly combed, and never greasy. Coats and ties were required for all occasions. The dress code for Sunday chapel prescribed dark-blue suits; dark shoes and socks; and a white shirt with a stiff, detachable collar. Our Episcopal deity and his representative at Brooks demanded a strict obedience to the law as well as the spirit of correct dress.

With clothes playing such an important part in our lives, it is only fair to mention one article of clothing that inspired fear and resentment among the students: white silk gloves. Once a week, dormitory prefects, inspecting the rooms for neatness and cleanliness, would pass their white-gloved, silken fingers along the furniture. If dirt appeared, the occupant of the room would be called to task. Those tours of inspection typify the strange blend of elegant and punitive qualities attached to clothing in my world at that time.

* * *

"I'm fondest of some of my oldest clothes," asserted Mr. Waterston, an English teacher at Brooks, in the course of conversation in the dining hall. Also present were Sam Parkman, David Saltonstall, Reginald Sturgis, Bobby Pratt, Mr. Waterston's son, Sam (who became a well-known actor), and his daughter Roberta. "I prefer to make as few choices as possible about what I wear. I simply have more pressing employment for my faculties. I find that old, tried-and-true clothing does the job and, moreover, is more comfortable to have around, like an old friend."

Mr. Waterston, strangely enough, had become someone I looked to for answers, even though he habitually declined to provide them. What he did give me was encouragement to think things through for myself, plus a lively set of ideas to get me on my way. He would tactfully suggest alternative points of view, often several, and leave me the task of weighing them against my assumptions.

On this afternoon, having emptied my plate of Welsh rarebit, I complained that while school dances were fun, I got tired just thinking about all those tasks I had to accomplish: shining my pumps with Vaseline; having my dinner clothes pressed; putting in studs and cuff links; tying my bowtie correctly; making sure I had my suspenders, garters, and a white handkerchief; deciding between a cummerbund and a waistcoat; and checking to see that everything was in order. "Sometimes I'd just like to be a caveman and not have to worry about a thing," I sighed.

Mr. Waterston quietly remarked, "Before you decide to become a caveman, just remember that in many ways his life was probably more demanding than yours. I remember some years back watching a newsreel about the life cycle of an aboriginal tribe living under later Stone Age conditions. Preparing for a tribal dance, they pierced their earlobes and inserted wooden plugs decorated with feathers. They also used heat and tree barks to produce textured scars on their skin. I don't think that is what you had in mind."

When I heard that, my own ordeal with fashion seemed a bit less exacting.

"Really? That's a stitch. I guess we can't get away from it. If you're going to suffer you may as well do it in style, à la Louis XIV," said Sam Parkman.

"If you can afford it, all well and good," smiled Mr. Waterston. "Not many of us can. Some of the French nobility couldn't afford it. The expense of a wardrobe for Versailles or Fontainebleau must have been staggering. For a visit of a week, a lady would have to buy at least fifteen new gowns, two for each day. For fear of appearing déclassé and incurring an imperial rebuke, she would not wear any of those outfits ever again."

"That's funny," chimed in Reginald Sturgis. "From caveman to Louis XIV. Isn't that going from the ridiculous to the sublime?"

"That depends on your point of view," said Mr. Waterston. "Yes, if you subscribe to the traditional hierarchical view that places Western culture at the top of cultural evolution; and no, if you favor the more modern and charitable view that believes in a plurality of cultures, all deserving equal recognition."

"Excuse me, sir," asked Bobby Pratt, "but what point of view do you think best?"

"Putting me on the spot, are you? That's a good question. The traditionalists draw on Plato and Aristotle's ideal of hierarchy and absolute value. This view has fostered the growth of ethics and standards in our society. Seeing ourselves at the top of the hierarchy also has led to flagrant colonialism and the arrogant notion of 'the white man's burden.' For its part, the relativist point of view is more tolerant of other cultures. However, if taken to an extreme, it can lead to anarchy and an erosion of standards where anything and everything goes. I hope I've answered your question."

* * *

One of my classmates, an ardent clotheshorse, went into business for himself with the help of a few of his friends. Indulging his entrepreneurial instincts, he took orders from select members of the student body and went to Chip and J. Press, ordered merchandise, charged it to his father's account, and then sold the goods to his customers for half price. This mutually beneficial arrangement didn't last long, as his father put a stop to it. From him I bought several ties that I have to this day.

≷ Chapter 12 ≷

The Arts

"One doesn't go on stage, Peter," admonished my father, "unless of course one's a professional actor, and for you, or for that matter anyone from a nice family, this is simply out of the question. Actors are not looked upon kindly by polite society. They're fast and racy and not our cup of tea by a long shot."

On rare occasions, he, along with my mother, would go to the Newport Casino to see a lighthearted play directed by Sarah Stamm. The music he enjoyed most was Mozart and Chopin as played by my mother on the piano, or ballroom dance music played by Harry Marchard, Ralph Stuart, or Meyer Davis.

Having a keen eye for painting, my father took pleasure in portraits of his ancestors and seascapes, especially those of Fitz Hugh Lane (now properly known as Fitz Henry Lane), which graced the walls of Ridgemere and Eastcote. In literature, his taste inclined toward books and magazines that had to do with sailing, shooting, gardening, the British Isles, European and American country life, antiques, the China trade, and genealogy. For humor, he read the English magazine *Punch,* which offered light amusement.

My mother's favorite books were royal autobiographies and European novels that she read in their original languages, including German, French, and Hungarian. A capable pianist, she was once told by a musician friend that she was good enough to go on stage, but as she was a lady such exposure was beneath her. Having attended the Winsor School, Miss Spence's, and St. Timothy's, she did not go to college because, in her words, "college was for horsy girls and bookworms. Most nice girls either went abroad or got married." According to my mother, going to college was tantamount to being a bit peculiar.

The daughter of Baroness Olga Von Gillming, a Hungarian aristocrat, my mother had the social connections that afforded her entrée into the polite society of old Europe, where she had family, friends, and relatives. She acquired her fluency in languages by traveling, meeting people, and going to the theater and opera.

At fourteen, my exposure to the performing and visual arts came mostly from schools where students, like it or not, were made to attend symphony concerts, piano recitals, museums, and school plays. My Boston grandmother, who religiously attended the symphony, occasionally would take me there.

"Tell me, my boy," said my father, "you mentioned that you were taking a course in art appreciation. Good for you. That's fine. It should do you good. I'll wager your masters will perforce show you some modern art. Then you'll know what to avoid. But pay close attention to the works of the great masters. They have a good eye, a steady hand, and depict only those things that are deemed civilized. I'm speaking of religious, historical, and classical themes that exercise an ennobling influence on the onlooker. I'm especially fond of some of the Dutch seascapes. You can't go wrong with Van Ruisdael; he had a good feeling for the sea and knew a thing or two about ships. His paintings are restful to the eyes.

"Try to develop an ear for good classical music. Modern music is monotonous, not natural, and doesn't ring true to a gentleman's ears. Once you've heard it you have no good reason to want to hear it again. A lot of self-appointed critics have become too big for their breeches. They spin outlandish theories that contradict one another and don't make any sense, leaving only a residue of confusion. In a democracy such as ours, much of this all-too-new tasteless music and art is made available to the common man. The more of it he sees, hears, and reads, the more he becomes deprived of what is good and the less he is satisfied—but then highbrow art, music, and literature are not meant for everyone. The common man is not up to it.

"*En passant*, I should say a thing about modern literature. Most of it is depressing, not amusing, and it disturbs one's tranquility.

"In the eighteenth and nineteenth centuries the ruling classes, thinking themselves enlightened by these new romantic ideas of freedom and self-expression and wanting to go with the trend, grew soft. They fell short of living up to their time-honored responsibilities. There was no longer a respectful distance between the noble as patron and the artist as servant. Many of the new breed of artists and musicians knew a good thing when they saw it. They played up to the ruling classes, fawned on them, and took them for a ride.

"Your mother and I have a friend, Mrs. Rush, who lives outside Philadelphia. I think you met her son, John. She told us that a French artist moved into a house next to hers. When he was invited for cocktails, he appeared at their doorstep on a horse, which he rode into her parlor, almost knocking down one of the maids. The horse, and I'm not blaming him, left his calling card and the front hall stank for weeks. The Frenchman should have known better. He was, I'm told, from a good family. There's no excuse for that sort of behavior. It's not in the least bit cunning or amusing. Quite frankly, I find it appalling!

"The other day at the Reading Room, Mr. Chanler and Mr. Grosvenor were telling me about an art show in New York where, if you'll excuse my saying so, a toilet was put on exhibition, in public mind you, for everyone to see. Mr. Rhinelander calls it the wretched refuse movement in art. When I heard that, I told them I simply couldn't believe it, but they assured me it was true. I told them outright that I didn't think anything like a toilet, which is not exactly a fitting topic of conversation, is a proper subject matter for art, and they heartily agreed with me on that score."

"That's awful," I said in a sympathetic tone, but secretly delighted.

"Well, indeed it is," echoed my father.

"Just imagine," I said, "if a drunk wandered into the exhibition and, not knowing any better, decided to piddle in the toilet, or the statue of a toilet, whatever it was."

"Oh, Peter. Really. Need you be so graphic?"

"Excuse me, Daddy. I should say, test the facilities or the utilities."

"That's better. That's more like it," said my father. "You may think this is funny, but I assure you full well it's not. It's appalling. In my father's day that never would have happened, but you know if a drunk went so far as to mistake a fake toilet for a real one, then all I can say is that it serves the proprietor right. He had it coming. Anyway, as I told you before, this is not a particularly attractive subject of conversation, so I suggest that we drop it *tout de suite*."

Reluctant to give up the conversation and wanting to milk it for more, I scratched my head, made a little face, and said in a perplexed tone, "I'm sorry. I realize that this is not a nice topic of conversation."

"What's not?" snapped my father.

"Toilets."

"Are we still on that? I thought we decided to call it quits, so please knock it off."

"I'm sorry, Daddy. May I ask you something about art?"

"Of course you may! Ask away."

"You said earlier that you preferred traditional or classical art to modern art."

"Yes, indeed I did."

"Well, last year at school in art history we learned about the different styles. You know, classical, Romanesque, Gothic, and Rococo, that sort of thing. It was very interesting."

"Yes, quite. But what is your point? Don't beat around the bush! Get to the point."

"Yes, Daddy. Well, you know how classical art tries to depict the ideal. According to what you're saying, wouldn't it be better to portray a toilet in its most noble light by depicting it in a classical style, as opposed to the more vulgar modern one? That would make it more socially acceptable."

A look of horror came over my father's face. I knew this conversation would rapidly come to an abrupt halt, but before he could apply the brakes I said quickly, "Or maybe the grandeur of a Baroque toilet, or the spirituality of the Gothic. And then there's . . . "

"Peter," interrupted my father, sounding rather agitated. "Oh, do hush! What are you trying to do, get my goat? Have you gone round the bend completely? What on Earth has gotten into you?"

Then, in a tone of concern, he asked, "Are you feeling all right?"

"Yes, thank you, Daddy."

"Good, I'm glad to hear it. I will not hear another word. We've been through this before and I trust we understand each other. You can call it all the fancy names you want, but a spade is always a spade. Can't you get that through that head of yours?"

At the dinner table my father and I were joined by my mother and Grandma. Resuming our talk on art, my mother said quite matter-of-factly, "Nowadays many so-called artists are full of themselves. They take themselves terribly seriously."

"And the worst part," interjected my father, "is that they insist on inflicting themselves on others."

"I'll have you know," continued my mother, "that we had a family friend whose one passion in life was singing, but if the truth be told, she couldn't hold a note. She would try to sing but it would come out all wrong. She shrieked like a screech owl or a banshee, but not even her best friend dared tell her. She suffered from delusions of grandeur, but then she could afford it. She was made of money and, not knowing what to do with herself, she hired several world-renowned voice teachers, which must have cost a pretty penny. After taking lessons for a year, she decided that she had had enough. Her teachers had flattered her no end, telling her she was God's gift to opera, so naturally they were disappointed when she announced that there would be no more voice lessons.

"Trying to appeal to reason as well as flattery, they told her that as good as she was, she wasn't quite ready. Reason didn't work, but flattery did. All of this praise went to her head, and she became more determined than ever to assume the limelight. Forthwith, she hired the Metropolitan Opera House and an orchestra and spent a small fortune on publicity. She had herself billed as the leading lady of opera. I also heard that she threatened to cut her relatives out of her will if they didn't come to see her make her debut. However, they all came gladly and voluntarily. Her family and friends encouraged her no end. She was known for making many mistakes, singing the wrong notes, sometimes even the wrong words. She made such an amusing spectacle of herself that her friends came to see her not as an opera singer, but rather as a comedienne. They said she had people rolling in the aisles. Given a chance, I would any day much rather hear a primitive ditty, a folk song sung well, than an aria sung badly. At least folk songs have their own peculiar kind of charm."

The woman my mother spoke of sounds much like Florence Foster Jenkins, the subject of the 2016 film starring Meryl Streep, but I have not been able to confirm her identity.

"Do you remember Ruth Draper?" asked my grandmother.

"Oh, Ruth Draper, of course. She's sheer heaven. She couldn't be more amusing."

"I saw her perform in Boston," continued my grandmother, "on a stage with only a few props. She was delightful. You could tell that she understood and liked people. At times she poked gentle fun, but she was always kind. There wasn't a mean bone in her body. Even though I don't know her, I think of her as being like a good friend or even a member of the family. She is a gentle spirit."

I looked at Grandma and noticed that her spectacles, as usual, were perched on top of her head. I remembered how on several occasions she'd announce that her spectacles were missing. With a search party in progress, one of the maids would tell her in a low voice, "Excuse me, Madam, but they're sitting on top of your head." She'd reply, "Dear me, so they are. Thank you, Catherine." I liked Grandma; like Nora, she was plump and elderly and had a kind word for everybody, including me.

"Draper, Draper, the name rings a bell," said my father. "We don't know her personally but we know who she is. She's a friend of some friends of ours."

"Ruth Draper's skit, 'The Italian Lesson,' was very funny," said Grandma. "It reminded me of learning Italian when I was a girl."

"Lilias," said my father, "remember when we went to Italy? You tried to teach yourself Italian."

"Oh, indeed I do. How could I ever forget? I didn't exactly pass with flying colors. Remember that waiter in the hotel? I asked him for what I thought was hot milk but it came out all wrong. I found out later that I had asked him for a hot bed."

"Oh, Lilias, really," said my father, sounding embarrassed. "Yes, I remember. I must tell you that I thought he possessed great presence of mind. He had great self-control. You could tell that he was dying to smile, but he made a great effort not to. My hat is off to him."

"Excuse me, Daddy," I said, genuinely confused. "It's about Ruth Draper. I thought you said ladies don't go on the stage. The nice ones, anyway."

"And so I did, and you have every right to bring that to my attention," my father responded. "Ruth Draper is not just another pretty face in a chorus line. There are many actresses who look glamorous at a distance but who, when they open their mouths, spoil the whole effect. As you can imagine, their English is not the best. There's nothing cheap or tawdry about Ruth Draper. She comes from an old family and naturally never does or says anything to disgrace herself on or off stage. She's a lady and is always in very good taste. She performed for various European crowned heads, including the English royal family, and was well received. That in itself is sufficient to discourage even the sharpest American critics, who get their cues from their betters."

≋ Chapter 13 ≋

The Fair Sex

As a young child without any sisters, I had very little knowledge of the opposite sex. There were only my mother, the maids, Nora the cook, and the various governesses. My mother was very attractive; by comparison, the maids, though pleasant, seemed quite ordinary. Usually dressed in uniforms, they spent most of their time busying themselves about the house. Nora hardly left the kitchen except to walk the dog. Thus, I perceived the difference between my mother and the servants as that between mistress and menials.

From my parents and governesses, I learned appropriate behavior toward the fair sex. At my birthday parties, I was taught how to bow to little girls, who, in turn, would curtsy to me. For older women, usually friends of my mother, I had learned to perform such civilized gestures as opening doors, standing up when they entered the room, lighting their cigarettes, and politely shaking hands. In return, they would say a few courteous words of thanks.

My parents fastidiously defined my relationship to the fair sex in terms of correct social behavior; they said very little else on the subject. Wondering how I came into existence, I was told that little boys came from storks. The matter was not discussed further. I thought about that and, over a period of years, became confused about my origin. If, in fact, I did come from storks, where were my stork parents? Storks bore very little resemblance to humans,

and it was beyond my comprehension how they could mysteri-
ously produce human babies. I even wondered whether my stork
parents ever tried to pay me a visit. If they had, perhaps my family
had excluded them from the premises as they did others who were
socially unacceptable.

By the time I turned fourteen, it seemed questionable that
human babies came from storks. The sad truth was that I didn't
know. My parents declared by verbal fiat the truth of the matter, so
naturally I accepted their word as gospel. Not permitted to look at
my family's books, I paid a visit to Redwood Library in Newport.
There I looked up the meaning of the word "stork" and found that
it was related to the word "stark," which referred to the qualities
of stiffness and rigidity. Perhaps this was the connection. If storks
had stiff and rigid habits, didn't such habits characterize my family
as well? One of the dictionaries I consulted mentioned that storks
were named after their stiff-legged walk, and then I remembered
that my father had given me lessons on how to walk correctly—a
walk that could only be described as stiff. Through further research,
I found that storks didn't live all over the globe. More bewildered
than ever, I wondered who brings storks to people who live in the
prairies. It couldn't be swallows, for they were too small. I thought
of buzzards, but they looked so sinister it occurred to me that they
might eat the babies.

Vexed at my ignorance, when I returned home I went into the
kitchen, a place where I had been forbidden to go, and asked Nora,
"I'm really curious. Where do little children come from? How do
they get born? Is that a silly question?"

"Oh, not at all," she said sympathetically. "Don't you know
God made you? He made all of us." So saying, she put her arm
around me and concluded, "and remember this. God loves you very
much. You're very special."

Fond as I was of Nora, and wanting to believe her, I was still
perplexed and thought maybe God made the babies and the storks
just delivered them.

More curious than ever, while in my third-form year at Brooks,

I decided to consult my French teacher, Schofield Andrews. As he and my parents were friends, having met years ago at the Kimball House in Northeast Harbor, it seemed appropriate that I speak with him on the matter. I chatted with him after Sunday morning chapel. "Good to see you," he said. "My wife and I look forward to seeing your mother and father next summer in Maine. Now tell me what can I do for you? Did you come to see me about your studies?"

"No, sir, not exactly," I said, feeling a bit sheepish. "It's nothing to do with school. It's a personal matter."

"A personal matter, you say? Well, there's nothing like having a heart-to-heart chat to clear the air. Now tell me, what's on your mind?"

In a faltering voice, I said, "I'd like to know where babies come from. I know that God and the stork have something to do with it, but I'm not sure."

"Babies! Good God!" exclaimed Mr. Andrews, quite taken aback by the unexpected question. Regaining his composure, he asked in a paternal tone, "Now tell me, how old are you?"

"I'm fifteen, sir."

"Fifteen. Well, it's getting to be high time that you find out the facts of life. I wish it were in my power to help you. I really do. But it's not my place to discuss this matter with you. After all, I'm not a member of your family. I'm a good friend of your mother and father, and as such I strongly urge you and your father to have a heart-to-heart talk on this matter. I know him well and can tell you that he's a most reasonable man. He'll listen to what you have to say, and he'll be very aboveboard with you. It's better that you hear it from him than from me. Whatever you do, I hope you don't get the wrong idea from your contemporaries in the locker room."

Pursuing the matter further, I decided to speak to some sixth formers—Archie Van Buren and David Warren, whom I knew from Newport. Prior to my coming to Brooks, my father mentioned, "The Warrens and the Van Burens are old friends of ours. I'm sure their boys, Archie and David, will be glad to keep a weather eye on you. Help you learn the ropes, and take you under their wing. Remember, they are older than you, so do pay attention to what they have to say. And try not to bother them with silly questions."

One afternoon in the locker room I engaged David and Archie in conversation. "I know this sounds silly, but I have a question that's been bothering me for several years, and everyone is keeping it a mystery."

"Peter," said Archie cheerfully, "David and I know your mother and father and will try to help you any way we can. Are you in trouble, or falling behind in your studies?"

"Oh, no. Nothing like that. I'm fine on that score. I could pull up my marks in history, but that's not the problem. It's a personal matter. I'd like to know where little babies come from. I'm told that they come from storks and God, but I don't quite understand how."

"Good God," exclaimed David. "Storks!"

"Yes. Mummy and Daddy and my old governess told me that the young come from storks, but Nora our cook said that I came from God. But somehow it all doesn't quite make sense." Shrugging my shoulders, I added, "I don't know what's coming off."

"You're not joking; you are serious," said David, looking concerned. "It seems this is a family matter, something you should talk over with your father. What do you say, Archie?"

"Yes, absolutely. I couldn't agree with you more. It's best that Peter discuss the matter with his father. It's not our place to do that. After all, we don't want to go behind his parents' backs and tell tales out of school. His parents would be far from pleased if they knew it came from us."

"Yes," agreed David. "You're absolutely correct. Archie and I agree that you should know and have every right to know, but suffice it to say that if we told you, we would be doing you and your parents a great disservice."

While at home on my vacation, unwilling to seek enlightenment on this embarrassing topic in the recommended heart-to-heart talk with my father, I sneaked out of bed, quietly slipped into the servants' quarters, peered through the keyhole, and watched Margaret, one of the maids, undress. There, I learned to my surprise that women were physically constituted very differently from men. I was so amazed about my newfound discovery that my first inclination was to tell my parents, but I thought better of it as they would only be shocked and annoyed.

* * *

The first time I kissed a girl was when I was seventeen. The occasion was a party attended by a mix of boys and girls. Tired of playing hide and seek and pin the tail on the donkey, some thoughtful, adventurous soul suggested we play a new game, spin the bottle. Some of us had heard of this game but hadn't played it before. I was terrified at the prospect of being called upon to perform, but not wishing to appear backward or cowardly, I consented.

There were several girls in our group: Laurel Tower, Binky Reventlow, Molly Richmond, Gypsy Altemus, Nina Auchincloss, and Allison and Abigail Adams. I shut my eyes and spun the bottle. A few seconds later, forcing myself to open them, I saw that the tip of the bottle was pointed at Binky. Closing my eyes again, I gave her an amateurish peck on the head and then, mortified and disconcerted by the good-natured ribbing from our audience, ran away and hid in the bushes, where I remained for a good five minutes. Later that evening, my mother, hearing of this, instructed me to write a formal letter of apology to Binky's mother, Countess Reventlow. Thus convinced that I had committed a dreadful sin, I politely declined further invitations to play games of that sort.

* * *

Brooks School is where I became aware of girls in a new way. Previously, I had attended Dexter and Fessenden, where girls were almost an unknown quantity. Most of us lower formers experienced girls vicariously. Upperclassmen talked about girls in much the same way as they would discuss their cars, clothes, or any other coveted possessions. What girls had in common with those objects was that they were desirable. Unattractive girls, pejoratively referred to as "dogs," were held in low esteem, like second-rate golf clubs, boots, or cars.

At a school dance, boys would poke fun at some poor fellow if they deemed his date unattractive. To be on public display on the dance floor with a homely girl was considered laughably gauche. It was on a par with wearing the wrong clothes, driving a tacky car, speaking with a socially unacceptable accent, or having a bad address.

On the brighter side, if a young man was seen squiring an attractive girl to the football game or put her on display at some other social function like a dance, he would rise in status among his classmates. Once, I invited an attractive girl from Foxcroft School for a dance weekend, and some of my friends, who fancied themselves connoisseurs of girls, admired her openly. It was assumed, as a matter of course, that I had at least kissed her, even if I hadn't done so. Admitting failure in this regard would have been a serious blunder. I never admitted defeat among friends.

I remember having kissed that girl chastely on the cheek while bidding her goodnight after the dance. It was a polite peck, nothing more, devoid of feeling. In order to gratify my friends' highest expectations and inchoate fantasies, I exaggerated my romantic feats of valor, straining credulity and leaving everyone well satisfied and my male dominance, pride, and prowess intact. Several of my friends tried to "bird dog" me, that is, to steal her away, but their attempts were futile as she would have none of them.

My classmates would do everything in their power to make themselves attractive to their lady friends. They would accomplish this in a variety of ways. If a fellow were a good athlete, he would display his prowess on the playing field, where his date, in his letter sweater, would admire him from the sidelines.

If a young man were not athletically inclined, all was not lost. He might be resourceful in other ways, such as by cultivating a suave, urbane personality and passing himself off as a man of the world. He might, for instance, spread his savoir faire thickly and display his knowledge of all the places where one goes to socialize in New York, such as Eddie Condon's, Nick's, the Stork Club, parties at the St. Regis, or some posh soirée at a friend's house on Park Avenue.

In this vein, he could also mention all the coming-out parties and other social occasions he attended, going into great detail as to who was there and what they did and said. I remember one fellow telling his lady friend, "I went whipping down to Oyster Bay for Mopsy's coming-out party in the old Jag." He went on to explain with great relish how, due to an excess of alcohol, he had a mild driving accident. He added, "Oh, Christ, it was such a bore. I cracked up the old thing and Grammy's chauffeur had to come all the way from Philadelphia to pick me up. I mean, God, I was just so smashed to the gills. Really bad news." He had been visiting his grandmother, who lived on the Main Line. He also regaled his date with stories of how he had misbehaved and got kicked out of St. Paul's.

While we were conducting these sterile conversations on the dance floor, a teacher occasionally would come over and reprimand us for dancing too close.

* * *

In my sixth-form year at Salisbury, when our regular biology teacher took a brief leave of absence, a female teacher filling in for him proceeded to teach us the facts of life, namely reproduction. She appeared to be in her thirties, was very attractive, and some of us developed a crush on her. Perhaps on account of our adolescent attraction and frustration, several of us decided to play a joke on our beguiling but inaccessible teacher.

Early one evening we crept into the biology laboratory. Locating two wooden figurines, replicas of the male and female bodies, one of the boys quickly removed the numbered but detachable private part from the male body and deftly inserted it into the orifice of the female figurine. Quickly we draped the figurines with the sheet that had covered them and returned to our dormitories. The next day, after bidding us all good morning and taking class attendance, our teacher went over to the figurines. We waited with bated breath for the grand unveiling.

She removed the sheet, stepped back a few feet, and smiled. Pointing a stick at the make-believe Romeo, whose member was still flagrantly violating the female figurine, she exclaimed, "My, someone certainly left in a hurry." From that point on, in our eyes she could do no wrong, and the answer to the mystery of where babies come from was complete.

Chapter 14

Discourse

I recall one summer evening when I was in my mid-teens. It was Nora's night off and, as the maids didn't do any of the cooking, my mother and father decided to go to La Forge restaurant on Bellevue Avenue with me in tow.

After we had ordered our dinners, my mother asked, "Tell me, Peter, do you ever go to the Gardner Museum when you're in Boston?"

"No, Mummy, I haven't gone yet."

"Well, you really should. When I was a young girl, my great aunt took me to see her friend Mrs. Jack Gardner. Mrs. Gardner had white, white hair and wore a long black dress with ropes of pearls hanging down to her waist. While they were having their tea, I was given ginger ale. I drank it by a pool on the patio, which had a little frog. We became great friends. I hated to leave and felt sad at having to say good-bye to my frog. I remember asking my father why Mrs. Gardner wore all that jewelry. He looked at me for a moment and replied, 'Because she is what's known as a "character," an eccentric to the core.'"

Talk turned to a party I had been invited to at the home of my parents' friends. "Peter," my father complimented, "I can't even begin to tell you how pleased I am that you're making an effort to get together with some of the children of my friends."

"Thank you, Daddy, I look forward to seeing them again." Do

I have any choice? I thought. He continued, "It's better that you see something of them than associate with the common herd from the town where you don't belong. Stick to your own kind and you'll be better off for it, I promise you. Take my word."

Feeling that townspeople were friendlier and kindlier than their alleged betters, the summer people, but knowing better than to say so, I replied, "Yes, Daddy, you're right."

"Billy Astor is in town. I'm sure he'd love to see something of you. Why don't you give him a call and see what he's up to?"

Call him? Why can't he call me, I thought. "Excuse me, Daddy, but I thought you said that people like the Astors and Vanderbilts were new money and not socially acceptable."

"And so I did. If you had been listening correctly with your God-given ears, you'd remember what I said: that at one time, not long ago, nouveau riche families were not immediately received by polite society, at least not without some reservation. However, in time—a matter of several generations—some of those families managed to pull themselves up by their bootstraps and become civilized. In this day and age, sad to say, we have to learn to make allowances and be more broadminded."

Yes, Daddy, I thought, that's big of you!

"Oh, I forgot to tell you," said my mother, "I heard the funniest thing the other day. At Bailey's Beach I ran into Maxim Karolik and Jimmy Van Alen. Maxim was talking about the usual thing, his art collection. No sooner had Jimmy left than Maxim asked, 'Have you noticed that Jimmy's mother has dyed her hair blue? All of that blue blood rushing to her hair.'

"Daisy Van Alen is capable of just about anything," said my mother. "After all, didn't she really get married to her butler, who was an impoverished French count?"

"Excuse me!" I gasped, inwardly in hysterics. I was trying to create the impression that I was merely choking on some food.

Hardly looking up, my father continued in his normal tone of composure. "By the looks of it, Peter has swallowed a frog; something went down the wrong throat."

Hearing that brought tears to my eyes, but with Herculean effort I barely managed to suppress a giggle. Realizing that excessive laughter was in worse taste than choking, I opted for the latter. To distract my father, I decided it was time to inject a little fun into the conversation.

"Excuse me, Daddy, but may I ask you a question?"

"A question, you say? Yes, you may. Ask away."

"Thank you, Daddy."

"Not at all, you're entirely welcome. Now tell me what's on your mind."

"You mentioned something about a frog being stuck in my throat, but didn't you once tell me that 'frog' was also a slang term for a Frenchman? Was it a Frenchman or just a French person? That's why I am just a little confused. Did you mean that a real frog or a Frenchman or Frenchwoman was in my throat?"

"Oh, really, Peter. I must say that you really do sometimes say the oddest things. I know that you don't mean to, but do try not to be such a silly Billy. If I didn't know you any better, I'd think you were having me on and pulling my leg. You know full well what I mean; you've heard me use that expression countless times. You're not so dimwitted as you make yourself out to be. After all, you are my son."

"Yes, Daddy, you're right. It's not a Frenchman or a French-woman. It's just plain old Froggy. Just like Mr. Frog in *Wind in the Willows* or that song, 'Mr. Frog Went a-Courting.'"

"Peter, I don't mean to be hard on you, but I must say there are times when your mother and I simply don't know what to make of you. If you had even the remotest idea of how silly you sound, you'd have second thoughts before you blurt out any old thing that pops into that head of yours."

"As I've said before," remarked my mother, "Peter lives in a world of his own. He's very fey, not to mention *contra corrente*, aren't you, Peter?

"Peter," continued my mother, "I don't know whether you recall Mary McCarthy. She remembers you. She was married to Edmund

Wilson, also a writer. She and her son, Ruel, are coming over next weekend and I'd like you to be on hand, so please don't make any plans of your own without checking with me first." Turning to my father, she said, "The last time Mary was over, she cast her eagle eye over everything, took it all in, and didn't miss a thing. She's a cold fish; the only warm thing about her is her cooking. She's a perfectly marvelous cook."

"Oh, I know," opined my father. "She's very *au courant*."

"Well, my dear, the other day at the Beach *en passant* I saw Jackie and Lee Bouvier."

"Very attractive girls," said my father. "The boys must be sweet on them."

"I must say," mused my mother, "they looked terribly sophisticated, as if they've seen and done everything. I remember them when they were little girls; they had perfectly exquisite manners."

"Excuse me, Daddy, but may I please have permission to ask you a question?"

"Yes, you may. Permission granted."

"Thank you, Daddy. I remember at Brooks our headmaster, Mr. Ashburn, once mentioned that he met Sir Anthony Eden. Well, I remember some years ago, I think it was sometime during the war, didn't Anthony Eden, the Englishman, come to Bailey's Beach?"

"Oh, yes, I also remember him. He was very reclusive and bookish. Always reading and writing. Not as much as one peep out of him."

"I also remember another famous person around that time at Bailey's Beach," I continued. "His name was Van Johnson. Actually, it was kind of funny. One of the beach boys told me that Van Johnson was my long-lost cousin and that I should go over and introduce myself and say hello. Well, that's exactly what I did. I went over and introduced myself and told him I was his cousin. He actually called me cousin. He's not really my cousin, is he, Daddy?"

"Cousin? I should say not. Peter, you're too gullible for words. Van Johnson is an actor. I can assure you that we don't have any actors in the family. Not by a long shot. That's unheard of. Van

Johnson is of no consequence. He's just a local yokel with freckles who has made good. Why he was ever allowed on the Beach in the first place, I'll never know. It's a concession to democracy and egalitarian thinking." My father added, sternly, "The beach boy who had the temerity to tell you that had some nerve. Such impudence and impertinence!"

"What an amusing idea," said my mother, barely concealing a smile. "Peter, you'll be interested to know your so-called cousin, Mr. Van Johnson the actor, was born right here in Newport. When I was a girl, I remember, he worked as a beach boy at Bailey's Beach as a teenager. He always gave us good service, always did what he was told, and never complained about a thing. So, bearing that in mind, I will not hear a word spoken against Van Johnson."

"Oh, very well," said my father. "Have it your own way."

"Speaking of relatives," began my mother, "Aunt Elsie tells me that your Uncle Ted is starting some sort of investment business. It's called Fidelity. Something to do with managing people's money. Mutual funds where you don't put all your eggs in one basket, so to speak."

"Oh, yes, I got word of that a while ago. Ted has a good feel for that sort of thing. I'm sure he'll do well for himself. He's got a keen eye, knows a good thing when he sees it. We were both at Milton Academy, but I didn't know him very well as he was a few years my senior. Most likely Ned will go into the business as well." Turning to me, he asked, "You remember your cousin Ned, don't you?"

"Yes, Daddy. Very well."

"Well, good. You should. After all, he is your cousin."

"Excuse me, Daddy, but earlier you mentioned that you didn't approve of actors. If that's the case, why was Errol Flynn invited to the house? I remember meeting him when I was very young."

"Errol Flynn," interjected my mother, "was very dashing. It was sort of the thing to do to have him over. But I must say he had rather unsavory habits. He was mad for girls. It seems he had a one-track mind. I gather that he'd instruct his secretary to go to drugstores to procure anyone in skirts. He was not particularly discriminating, but would settle for anyone who came along and took a fancy to him. However, in all fairness, I'll say this for him. When Errol Flynn came to Ridgemere to see us, he was on his best behavior and couldn't have been more charming."

"You'd think there'd be enough girls in Hollywood without having to resort to drugstores," my father commented. "All very tawdry, if you ask me. He must have been very hard up. I've nothing against him personally. He seemed perfectly pleasant for the short time he was here."

"Well, I must say, it's been a rather pleasant meal," said my mother, who hadn't eaten much of anything. "My steak was not overdone. As far as eating out is concerned, I absolutely adore the Chilton Club. I much prefer it to the Somerset Club, which has seen better days. It has become rather threadbare and gaping at the seams."

"Well, I know how it is," complained my father sympathetically. "Times are hard. The Newport Reading Room is in need of repair and, sad to say, the Bar Harbor Club and the Kimball House in Northeast Harbor are postponing their renovations until next year. The last time I had lunch at the Somerset Club, the service was quite good and I had no complaints whatsoever."

"Ah, but that was several years ago," said my mother. "Times have changed. Last year when I went to the Somerset Club, I saw a sign hanging over one of the doors that said, 'Gentlemen will behave at all times.' Well, I ask you," she said in a lofty tone, "need a gentleman be reminded?"

"In all fairness I should point out that the members of the Somerset Club in Boston, several of whom are our friends, have shown good faith and are men of high principles," my father noted. "Some years back a most unfortunate thing happened. A fire started in the front hall of the club. When the firemen arrived they were made, and rightly so, to enter through the servants' entrance at the back door. If workmen are willy-nilly allowed to come and go as they please through the front door, the floodgates are open and beckon to every Tom, Dick, and Harry."

It all sounded too terribly silly to me.

Turning to my father, my mother said, "I beg to differ with you on one point. A small one. If there were a fire in the front part of Ridgemere—in, say, the *porte-cochère*, the vestibule, or the cloak-room—I would feel loath to make the firemen enter through the back door. After all, they wouldn't be paying us a social call, but would be performing their duty, and form should not be a hindrance or detriment to those it was meant to serve. Having the house burn down is a dreadful price to pay to maintain class distinction."

"You have a good point," agreed my father. "However, one can't afford to be too casual about these things, or you'll let your guard down and the enemy will be quick to take advantage of it." Noticing my empty plate, my father added cheerfully, "I'm glad to see that you've finished everything set before you. Just remember there are plenty of children in the world who aren't as lucky as you and have to go without food, so thank your lucky stars that you are not numbered among the unfortunates."

"Yes, Daddy, you're right. It's so unfair that a few people have everything and many have nothing. It's too bad we can't do something about it."

"Peter, I know your heart is in the right place and that you mean well. You have good instincts, and I don't mean to sound unfeeling or blasé, but hearing about the misfortunes of others doesn't lend itself to pleasant conversation, especially at the dinner table. I grant you that the world may seem unfair, but you mustn't, whatever you do, think that you are personally responsible for the well-being of others and that you have to bear the burdens of the world on your shoulders. Simply enjoy what you have and don't complain, or you'll sound like one of those longhaired, wide-eyed socialists. If you wish to make conversation, keep it light and amusing. I would much rather hear about who shot the first partridge or your croquet score than some gloomy tidings. Hearing about the ills and woes of the world is not particularly consoling or appetizing."

He continued, "I don't mean to sound like I'm lecturing you, but I should tell you to stay clear of controversial issues that don't concern you. Remember, in the course of normal discourse stick to the tried and true and stay away from that which is abstract, obscure, or exotic. These may at the time seem glamorous to you, but take it from me, they're not. Not in the long run, anyway. And whatever you do, stay away from subjects you know nothing about, or you'll be on shaky ground. People who are in the know will find you out, and you'll lose credence in the eyes of others. I may add also, refrain from vulgar, controversial subjects that stir people's emotions; there's no need whatever to bare your soul for all the world to see. Displays of feeling are most unattractive and not in good form. You're not that dreary man Rousseau, who felt that he had to go around confessing everything for all to hear. On that score, whatever you do, avoid talking about yourself. Some people who are overly enamored of the sound of their own voices think they are fascinating, but take it from me, they couldn't be more wrong. Also, avoid talking about your health. People are not interested in your ailments. You keep that to yourself, under your hat." My father paused, looked at me, and added, "What I'm telling you shouldn't be too difficult to understand. It's not complicated at all. It's just common sense."

"Yes, Daddy," I replied, trying to appear alert and interested, which was difficult as I was very tired.

"Good for you," my father continued. "I should also tell you, leave the highbrow gobbledygook to the intellectuals. They talk a good game, but they get too abstract and often haven't the slightest idea of what they're talking about. Remember, anything of value is grounded in the concrete and not in the clouds. I'd like to qualify that. I'm all for empiricism up to a point, as long as we are not forced to look at all the unattractive particulars. The dark side of empiricism is that it may lead one astray and encourage what's currently in vogue among intelligentsia—namely, individualism and relativism. Basically, I'm all in favor of empirical thinking as long as it supports and doesn't contradict the known truths that are laid away in heaven."

There's no stopping him now, I thought.

"I should also tell you that if you're debating a matter and you find yourself *en colère*, never raise your voice in anger or your opponent will have the upper hand. Besides, only truck drivers or sailors raise their voices. Whatever you have to say in making your point will sound more appealing and reasonable to others if, rather than grinding an axe, you take a disinterested view. Also, if you have something to say to someone, wait until he is within earshot. Shouting is for truck drivers or politicians like Roosevelt, currying the favor of the masses, and backward itinerant preachers—enthusiasts who appeal to emotion and not steadfast reason. Don't let your feelings cloud your judgment. Besides being bad form, shouting is hard on the ears. If you're a drill sergeant, that's one thing, but you're not."

"Excuse me, Daddy, but what's wrong with being a drill sergeant?"

"There's nothing wrong with being a drill sergeant if you're from the lower orders," he replied. "In that case, it's probably a step upward from working on the farm or in the factory. Drill sergeants and bosun's mates in the Navy raise their voices because it's the only way they are capable of expressing themselves. Officers, too; more's the pity. In the old days, an officer was a gentleman by birth, but in this day and age democracy confers the title of officer on any Johnny-come-lately who can pass college exams.

"Oh, dear me! I fear I am straying from the beaten path, but I think I've said all I have to say about how you express yourself with others." Looking at me gravely, he continued, "I don't know whether you've gotten to the stage where you notice girls, but when you're older and take an interest in them, never discuss them behind their backs with your friends. That's not cricket. Well-brought-up boys don't do that. Another thing, don't go around telling puerile jokes. You're not a comedian. If you're relating a vignette or an anecdote to your friends, make it short and snappy and you'll never lose your listeners. Otherwise, your friends will give you a wide berth and consider you a bore. Another thing, avoid talking about class or money, and whatever you do, don't brag about your accomplishments for the whole world to hear. No one likes a brag-gart or a boaster; it's most unattractive. When one accomplishes something that is worthy of merit, people will find out about it in good time. You don't have to broadcast it to the high heavens, for if you do, people will turn a deaf ear. Remember, if there are any feathers to be put on your cap, or a medal to be pinned on your chest, it's best that they come from others. Always keep the conver-sation light and easy, and people will seek you out and enjoy your company."

"Oh, dearie," said my mother, "you mustn't confuse the boy by telling him too much all at once. He won't be able to take it all in, and it will go in one ear and out the other. Also, it is getting late and soon it will be Peter's bedtime, so I suggest we think about wending our way homeward and call it an evening."

As if reading my thoughts, my father said, "It's difficult to have champagne tastes on a water budget."

Chapter 15

Democracy

Having finished the dreary task of paying the bills—the Social Register, the Bar Harbor Club, the Newport Reading Room, Brooks Brothers, and the servants—my father looked out the window. "I must say Bar Harbor is lovely this time of year. All the tourists are gone and the leaves are starting to turn. In another few days, sad to say, we'll bid adieu to Eastcote and return to Ridgemere."

Turning to me, he said, "Peter, we've got to get you squared away for Brooks School. It's perfectly lovely up there in North Andover this time of year. How time flies! It's already the middle of the century. Why, it just seems like the other day when I went for my first drive, motoring along the winding back roads of Milton. That was back in the 1920s, when only the right people had cars and we all knew each other and weren't in a hurry to get somewhere. Life was quieter then, less hectic, and we all managed to have a good time. I remember as a boy at Milton Academy singing, 'Time, like an ever-rolling stream, bears all its songs away.' Our old school rector, the Reverend Perry, was fond of a good song.

"Peter, you never knew Bar Harbor in the old days. Before the turn of the century, it was *en famille*, until it became very gay and social with loud and angry parties, with Johnny-come-lately newcomers and their ill-gotten gains putting themselves on display. In the early days, and I'm talking about the latter part of the nineteenth century, nice families from Boston, New York, and Philadelphia would come with just their servants and rusticate. It was a day and age when life was simpler and more pleasant. It was a quiet time. No blaring of angry horns or dreadful tourists raising their voices in public. Everything was more secluded, and privacy was valued more than cheap publicity. Nature was unspoiled. No nasty hotdog signs, billboards, and other eyesores. These days it's a rat race, and we have democracy to thank for that."

"Excuse me, Daddy, but do you mean like what Thoreau wrote about? We read him in school last spring."

"No, Peter. If the truth be told, I'm afraid I can't say that Thoreau was first and foremost on my mind. Don't misunderstand me. I enjoy some of his writing. He was very observant and had a keen eye for everything around him. However, he did make a fetish out of simplicity; as you very well know, carrying anything to an extreme is not particularly attractive. Far from it. Roughing it without the benefit of civilized amenities, such as servants, is hardly my idea of relaxation. Going primitive does not guarantee personal salvation as the romantics would have us believe, but is, rather, a sign of decadence and weakness. It may temporarily harden the flesh, but in the long haul it will soften the spirit. Thoreau opposed slavery and entertained all sorts of peculiar notions about democracy and the perfectibility of man—the common man, at that.

"Perhaps he was a bit deranged or demented. Peter, let me put it to you this way. If your mother and I took it into our heads to go waltzing off into the wilds, cavorting with the animals, what would you think? If I may be so bold as to speak for you, I dare say you'd be hard put to make head or tail of our behavior. You'd be well within your rights to consider us mad as March hares."

"Excuse me, Daddy, for asking," I said in a deferential tone, "but if animals are so far beneath us, then why do you and Mummy carry on long conversations with Mr. Putnam, Mr. Peabody, Miss Phipps, and the rest of our dogs? And why do you have their portraits painted, and why are they named after some of our ancestors?"

"Oh, Peter, you do manage to ask the silliest questions when the answers are so very obvious. In the first place, Pekinese are not your ordinary run-of-the-mill dog. They are well-bred, thoroughly domesticated creatures, intelligent, brave, loyal to the end, and highly refined. They have all the right instincts, very aristocratic. Democracy's common cry of cur they are not. There's all the difference in the world between talking to our dogs and to some wild and woolly woodchuck that smells to high heaven. Whereas our Pekinese are simpatico, Thoreau's woodchucks are dense. They wouldn't have the faintest idea of what you're saying; nor, for that matter, would they care. You could talk to them to your heart's content, until you're blue in the face, and I'm afraid it would be in one ear and out the other. In all fairness, you can't blame them. They don't know any better. It's the way God made them. In days of yore, Pekinese weren't just lapdogs, useless but ornamental. They were known as lion dogs, used by emperors of China and their court for hunting. They enjoyed great popularity, from the Manchu courts to the monasteries and tents of the Tibetan steppes."

"Indeed they were," said my mother, having recently entered the room. "I remember seeing Pekinese depicted in jade, amber, lapis lazuli, and other stones as well. They were displayed in specially designed lighted cabinets."

"So you see," said my father, "there is a great deal of difference between our Pekinese and Thoreau's lowly woodchucks."

"Nary a word," scolded my mother in a tone of feigned and wounded indignation, "will I have a word spoken against woodchucks. As a child I absolutely adored them. My governess used to read me the Thornton Burgess books with all their heavenly animals. I remember Johnny Chuck and Billy Mink. They were sheer heaven. Even today I feel like they're old friends. They are absolutely enchanting and it's not fair to them to speak behind their backs. I'm very sentimental that way."

"Of course you are," said my father in a sympathetic tone. "My governess also used to read Thornton Burgess to me. I was merely trying to get the point across to Peter that Thoreau and people like him, camping out like gypsies, are not worthy of emulation and should not be taken seriously."

Turning to me, my mother said, "I don't know whether you remember our friend Mrs. Sherman, who recently painted the portraits of our dogs. She captured their personality and she tells me that she understands them. I wouldn't be at all surprised if Mrs. Sherman had been a Pekinese in another lifetime."

Looking up at the wall I noticed, next to the portrait of one of my great-grandfathers, the recently painted portrait of Miss Phipps and Mr. Putnam with eyes popping out like saucers. For a moment I thought they were something out of the Mad Hatter's tea party. With a look of feigned admiration, I dutifully replied, "Yes, Mummy, I see what you mean."

She continued, "In the old days in China, as your father mentioned, Pekinese were very loyal to their master. They reflected his every mood. When he was sad, they were sad; when he was cheerful, they were cheerful. It's too terribly touching for words."

At this point I wasn't sure whether I was confused, bemused, or amused, but since any of these reactions would have elicited my father's displeasure, I wisely refrained from saying anything. I could only wonder why Thoreau should be considered mad for talking to woodchucks, but not my father for carrying on long-winded conversations with our dogs. In retrospect, it stood to reason that because my father considered himself and our dogs as belonging to the same social sphere, above that of Thoreau and his woodchucks (not to mention the working and middle classes), then the dogs would be worthy to converse with him.

"Now, where were we? Ah, yes. Thoreau. Emerson was more my cup of tea. Not so hard to take. He wasn't quite so bohemian or eccentric and didn't feel, as Thoreau did, that he had to wallow in the woods for 365 days of the year or glamorize it, but rather could set pen to paper from the comfort of his library. It might interest you to know that Emerson, in some shape or form, is related to us. Let's see. Samuel Wheeler, one of my great-, great-, great-, great-, great-, great-, great-, great-, great-grandfathers, married a certain Joanna Wolcott in Concord at the beginning of the eighteenth century. She was the daughter of John Wolcott and Joanna Emerson. It would not be at all surprising if Miss Emerson were an early ancestor of Ralph Waldo Emerson.

"Emerson, I fear, went a trifle overboard with his transcendentalist hocus pocus. He meant well. His heart, if not his head, was in the right place. I don't mean to be hard on him, but he was generous to a fault. He endorsed that perfectly dreadful man, Whitman, who was overly enamored of the sound of his own voice. Whitman behaved like a young child who doesn't know any better but, unlike the child, he disregarded the dictum that little children should be seen and not heard. The man was an absolute horror. He put the common man on a pedestal, being common himself and revered by the masses. It was a case of mutual backslapping. Since then every nut, bolt, and screw; starry-eyed poet; and the disenfranchised have ridden on his coattails.

"Democracy, the source of all our ills, found a champion in Walt Whitman. He had democracy on the brain. Couldn't get enough of it and wanted to push everyone else's face in it. Perhaps Emerson, in endorsing the man, was momentarily caught off his guard. He didn't have his thinking cap on."

I doubt that my father ever read anything by Walt Whitman. Mostly likely he had heard about him from others who themselves knew about Whitman only from what they had heard from others.

"Don't misunderstand me, Peter. I needn't tell you that generosity in and of itself, when tempered by wisdom, is a most admirable quality. I believe in it wholeheartedly. However, that's not to say that altruism should not be without limits.

"Thomas Jefferson, in this regard, went overboard. Can you imagine, he went so far as to borrow money to give to beggars. What got into him, we'll never know. Most likely he was unduly influenced by his father, a self-made man. He should have paid stricter attention to his mother's side of the family, who were legitimate landowners, very aboveboard, and on the up and up."

In that case, I thought, we might never have gotten the Declaration of Independence.

My father continued, "Where would we be if we gave our money away to ne'er-do-wells, laggards, and layabouts, I ask you? Need I tell you, Peter, that I'll take it on good faith that you will never dissipate your future inheritance upon the poor, and all in the name of philanthropy?"

"Yes, Daddy, I promise you that."

"Good for you. See that you don't. Jefferson believed in suffrage for the multitudes, but remember, 'a little knowledge is a dangerous thing, drink deep or taste not the Pierian spring.' I'll take Jefferson's gentleman farmer any day over those Johnny-come-lately robber barons. Sad to say, the way of life of the patroon, landed gentry, and the Southern plantation owner gave way to industrialism. I don't mean to fill your ears with tales and tidings of woe, but perhaps we would all be better off living under a king."

Then perhaps the Magna Carta should be repealed, I thought.

He continued, "Prior to the sad conclusion of that nasty affair—the war with England—we were true blue Englishmen and not wild and wooly, buckskin-clad Americans who had nothing better to do than spend their entire lives trying to discover who they were. Can you imagine anything more tiresome?"

"No, Daddy."

"Neither can I. Thomas Jefferson meant well, but entertained queer notions about democracy and the common man. He didn't know a good thing when he had it. After all, he had a perfectly good plantation and slaves to work it. Why he would want to give it up is more than I'll ever know. Also, Jefferson was known to be overly permissive with members of his own family. I've heard he allowed his grandsons to cavort about Monticello in bare feet. Can you even begin to imagine such a thing? Peter, I hope I'm not putting any naughty ideas into your head. Whatever you do, don't let me ever catch you gadding about Ridgemere with bare feet."

"Excuse me, Daddy, may I ask you a question? Do you prefer Alexander Hamilton to Thomas Jefferson? After all, he was more conservative."

"I'll put it to you this way: Alexander Hamilton had the right

idea about having a strong central government. He was sound polit-
ically. I can't take anything away from him there. However, that's
not to say I'd trust him as a man. After all, he was a Johnny-come-
lately, born out of wedlock somewhere in God-forsaken Barbados,
where he learned exotic dances from the heathen natives, which he
later performed for polite society after he came to this country.

"What Jefferson and Hamilton had in common other than being
representatives of their times, the Enlightenment, was that both had
good blood from the maternal side of their family. Hamilton suppos-
edly was descended from Scottish nobility on his mother's side, and
Jefferson's mother was from an old aristocratic Virginia family, the
Randolphs. And they both married ladies from old families who
were socially above them.

"Getting down to brass tacks, I can safely say that Jefferson and
Hamilton, each in his own way, meant well, but the rising tide of
democracy was their undoing as well as ours."

I blurted out, "Excuse me, Daddy, may I have permission to ask
you a question?"

"A question, you say? Yes, you may. Ask away."

"Thank you. Do you mean to say you don't believe in democracy at all?"

"Peter, you should know by now what my feelings are on that
score. My answer to you is let the masses dream their dreams to
their hearts' content, just as long as they know their place when
they wake up and see the light of day. In the old days, the Catholic Church performed a great service when it encouraged the poor
to dwell on their future in the great hereafter. The only recourse of
the old guard, what's left of them, is to court the masses, allowing
them to think they hold the cards. If the denizens of the gutter can
be hoodwinked into thinking their vote can change things, then I'm
all for it. Give them tidbits from our table and let them think it's
a banquet. Society has all gone to hell and back. The last civilized
century was the eighteenth, when Dutch patroons and Southern
plantation owners ruled their fiefdoms with an iron hand and not
kid gloves. In those days there was a *consensus gentium* of values

where good form and hierarchy were the order of the day."

"If I may intrude," volunteered my mother, "I have no desire to confuse Peter any more than he already is. However, I should say that not all forms of democracy are unattractive. While at St. Tim's we had a perfectly marvelous history teacher who kept us hanging on her every word. She talked about early Athenian democracy, which, if I recall, was rule by the few, not the many. They were the oligarchs. There were Greek plays, poetry, and some philosophy. All very highbrow. All of which I've forgotten."

"Yes, by Jove. Your mother couldn't be more right in this matter. If you'll forgive the dreary expression, she's hit the nail square on the head."

Oh, I see, I thought. Democracy is all well and good safely when it's buried twenty-five centuries in the past.

"Pericles' Athens was *sine qua non*, the beau ideal of the known world. In eighteenth-century England, Tory oligarchs were at the helm. They called the shots and ruled according to the right of reason. Not *vox populi*. Now, Peter, whatever you do, don't get the wrong idea and think me stodgy, but for your own future well-being do heed my advice. By all means read your romances and popular fictions, but don't live your life that way or you'll rue the day. Take my word for it. Factions and political parties have brought this century to rack and ruin. These days people no longer feel confidence in their God-given reason, but rather consult moonstruck, starry-eyed theorists, professional thinkers who confuse issues at hand with their unattractive and meaningless jargon.

"Nowadays there's no longer a right way to look at things, but many ways. No wonder people don't know whether they're coming or going. In another few generations, we're all going to become terribly middle class. I hope I won't be around to see the day when we all look and sound alike and speak midwesternese. The young make common cause with people like Oscar Wilde, Baudelaire, and other dregs of society. Need I say more on that score?"

"No, Daddy, you needn't say more on that score," I said, emphasizing the words "more" and "score" to bring out the repetitious rhythm. That was the extent of my rebellion.

"Peter, you needn't parrot my every word. You're not a parrot, are you?"

"No, Daddy, I'm not a parrot."

"What hath God wrought?" my father complained. "My one and only son. Where have I gone wrong?"

⅜ Chapter 16 ⅝

Good Form

In my fourth-form year at Brooks, I attended my first school dance, which was held in the evening in the dining room. I had arrived late and, like most nervous latecomers, was mesmerized by the whirling spectacle. The big band was in full swing. The patter of shining black pumps mingled with the rustling of dresses: organza, satin, taffeta, and chiffon radiated their plenitude of solid hues—deep burgundy, bright yellow, dark green, black, white, and blue. The dresses were strapless with full skirts that billowed out from the waist. This carnival atmosphere stood in bold relief to the sedate behavior of normal school routine.

From a nearby corner of the dance floor a delicate scent of perfume wafted my way. A flush of excitement tingled the back of my neck. There to the right of me, dancing and lost in animated conversation was a classmate of mine, Reginald Sturgis, was a pretty girl. Her strapless dress was burgundy taffeta. She had short hair, sable in color, in a Joan of Arc style, and her face reminded me of Ingrid Bergman's in shape and expression. By some inexplicable impulse I tapped Reginald on the shoulder and asked permission to cut in. With a half-smile she accepted and Reginald retired.

I had mixed feelings about all of this, both exhilaration and trepidation. Having just asked her for a dance, I couldn't very well renege on my request. Resigned, I took her right hand in my left, put my left hand behind her waist, and awkwardly and mechanically managed to commence a box step. The world did not cave in. Terribly nervous, almost frightened, I was convinced that I would commit some faux pas like stepping on her foot or breaching some other principle of good form.

The band played a foxtrot. That wasn't too difficult. After all, I had been practicing it for a week. "Hello, my name is Pierrepont Johnson but I'm known as Peter," I managed. "What's your name?"

"I'm Mopsy Phipps Suckley. It's nice to meet you."

Feeling a resurgence of courage, I replied a little more forcefully. "It's nice to see you. Where do you go to school?" The palms of my hands were slightly moist. She was pretty, and that was unnerving. Unprepared for this, trying to pull myself together, I sought refuge in the fact that I was impeccably dressed in my new Brooks Brothers dinner jacket, pumps, waistcoat, gold chain, silk socks, and a stiff collar that pinched my neck.

She replied, "I go to St. Tim's. Have you heard of it?"

Thank God I had heard of it. Feeling I was being interrogated by the Grand Inquisitor, I found some small comfort in the fact that I would soon go on the offensive. Affecting bored disdain, I quickly replied, "Why, of course. Who hasn't heard of it? Mummy went there after she left Beverly."

Aside from my mother having gone there, I knew very little about it; nor did I care, except in this one instance. The difficult thing about this charade was trying to do two things at once: synchronizing our polite, tedious, and terrifying conversation with the correct movement of my hands and feet. Remembering the reassuring voice of my dance instructor ("Side step front, side step back"), I tried to do everything I had learned in the last dance class. Mopsy's voice broke my reverie of silent confusion with some little boast about St. Tim's, the gist of which in my distracted state I didn't quite catch. At a loss for words, I blurted out, "Gosh, Mopsy, that's terrific." I blushed as I remembered my father's admonition, "Don't say, 'Gosh'; it's not becoming." I wasn't doing too badly. So far, I had answered all her questions to our mutual satisfaction, countered with several of my own, and managed to avoid stepping on her feet.

As far as I knew, "gosh" was my only faux pas. Pretty soon I'd be an old hand at this.

Feeling braver, I decided to go on the attack by converting the box step into a turn, and I succeeded in making a complete revolution. Pleased as Punch at my daring accomplishments, I mounted an offensive by asking her where she lived. Only seasoned boys could have asked such a bold question. With renewed confidence I continued my daring moves, and in a few terrible seconds my box turns were a fait accompli. Mission accomplished, I thought. Authority emanated from my left hand as I pumped it vigorously up and down in imitation of all those other flailing arms on the dance floor.

Mopsy, taking up the challenge, answered briskly, "My family is from Philadelphia and we go to Maine in the summer."

"You go to Maine; why, that's terrific. Where do you go?" I asked with forced enthusiasm.

"We go to Northeast Harbor. Have you been there?"

"Oh, Philadelphia on the rocks. God, yes." So far so good, I thought. I'm on familiar territory. I was beginning to feel awfully important as, most assuredly, I was answering her questions correctly and, furthermore, there was a pretty girl in my arms following my lead on the dance floor. "Northeast Harbor is great. Damn good fun. I go to the Kimball House all the time."

I was getting carried away; after all, I had been there only once or twice in my life. "The dances are terrific. The Harry Marchand Band is really good, but Ralph Stuart and Meyer Davis will do in a pinch." She seemed quite pleased that I was au courant. "Were you visiting friends?" she asked.

"Oh no, not friends. I visit Grandma, who has a house in Bar Harbor." She continued to look pleased and was beaming. "You go to Bar Harbor. That's nifty. Do you know Potter Palmer and Oakley Thorn?"

"God, yes," I said in my best Locust Valley lockjaw accent. "Potter and I play tennis all the time."

"You do?" she perkily responded. "You must be pretty good.

Potter is a terrific player. He was on the St. Mark's tennis team."

I exaggerated my tennis playing a bit, for in fact Potter was several years my senior and was a much better player than I. He had been kind enough to give me a few tennis lessons, which perhaps I interpreted as meaning that we were on a par with each other. However, I didn't want to disenchant my companion by letting her know that I wasn't on top of my game.

Mopsy and I were enjoying ourselves, or so it seemed. In truth I was feeling a bit frustrated. We were dancing two feet apart in the prescribed fashion, and I wanted to get closer to her but refrained for fear that one of the masters, acting as a chaperone, would come over and remind me to keep my proper distance. Erotic, confused, and naughty thoughts danced in my mind, sublimated into socially acceptable fantasies like driving a racy-looking sports car, smoking a cigarette with Mopsy at my side, and perhaps stopping along the way to share a drink with her from an onboard silver flask of gin and tonic. Momentarily at a loss for a suitable question, I asked, "Do you know Posie, Potter's sister?"

"Of course I know Posie. Didn't she graduate from Dobbs Ferry? She gave a terrific party last summer. Did you go?"

"Oh, that party. Yes, I heard it was terrific," I fibbed. "I couldn't make it as I had to go to another party in Newport." At the mention of Newport her face lit up. It occurred to me that although we were saying the right things in the right way, everyone on the dance floor was also saying all the right things. Everyone was taking it so seriously, yet with so little to show for it, not even a kiss.

"Whose party did you go to?" she asked with enthusiasm. Making up a name, I said, "Binky Throckmorten."

"Binky Throckmorten. Oh, that name sounds so familiar," she fibbed. "Doesn't she go to Foxcroft? Or was it Garrison Forest?" Continuing the charade, I answered, "Yes, she's at Garrison Forest."

"Don't you just adore Newport?" she asked me in a rhetorical tone.

"Well, it's all right. I'm so used to it," I said nonchalantly. "After all, I live there." She stepped back with a gesture of pleased amazement. "My God, it's one of my favorite places. Bailey's Beach is sheer heaven and I'm mad for the Casino. Do you know Minnie Cushing?"

"I certainly do. I'm a great friend of her brothers, Howard and Freddy."

"Don't you just adore them? They're divine."

"Yes, they couldn't be nicer," I agreed. "What dances are you going to this vacation?" I couldn't have asked her a better question. I looked at her, and she was in seventh heaven.

"I'm going to Cassandra Van Alen's party in Philadelphia," she answered, "and Noni Van Rensselaer's party in New York, the Groton St. Mark's dance, and the Grosvenor Ball. What parties are you going to?"

Running out of ammunition and seeking to hold my own, I countered, "My family and I are invited to a ball at Buckingham Palace. They say London is very gay during the holidays." I wondered whether she believed me.

"Oh, you lucky thing," she commented. Mercifully the dance came to an end and I politely shook Mopsy's hand. "Thank you so much. It was such good fun and it was so nice to meet you."

"Awfully good fun and it was so nice to meet you. Perhaps we'll run into each other at Newport or Bar Harbor."

"Or perhaps Locust Valley or Oyster Bay or Fishers Island," I shot back. She volleyed, "Or maybe the Piping Rock Club." Still on the attack, she asked, "You know Livingston Fish, don't you? Everyone knows him."

Letting loose with the heavy artillery, I fibbed, point blank, "Why, of course I know him. Who doesn't?" Fully erect in the grand manner of my father, I confabulated, "He's a second cousin three and a half times removed from Bartle Bull Byrd of Virginia. The Byrds, Bulls, and Fishers are all related."

"Oh, I'm mad for it. You sound like my elder brother, Chauncy. He loves genealogy. He can recite the family tree by heart. You know that name sounds awfully familiar, Bartle Bull. I've heard it somewhere. I think he is a friend of Pete Bostwick, who is a friend of my brother's."

"Mopsy, it's time for the next dance," spoke up a voice. With a gesture of farewell, she raised her hand in parting.

"Well, Peter, I see that you're in good form tonight." I looked up and there was Ian Laskaris, a friend of mine. He was a senior, several years older than I, and he always seemed to find the time to say hello or to offer words of encouragement to lower classmen. Most of the time, I managed to stay on the side of good form, as my father incessantly reminded me to do, but not always.

⧫ Chapter 17 ⧫

Folk Music

The only persons in the household who sang were Nora and myself. She was usually in the kitchen and I was either in my room, where I wouldn't disturb anyone, or taking solitary walks in the garden, the woods, or by the sea. Nora's songs somehow connected me with the past in a more vital way than those histories related to me by the official culture, at school, or by my parents.

Nora's songs opened up a new world to me, as did the music and surroundings I later encountered on trips to Greenwich Village. They were an antidote to the insular views held by my parents, teachers, and friends. There were days when I didn't get to see Nora, but the sound of her voice reminded me that she was there, and reminded me as well of her affection and love that had been my sustenance during childhood. Thinking about Nora, I wondered about Ireland (her homeland) and imagined it to be a very special, magical place full of people, young and old, who could enchant and comfort with their songs. I thought, "Someday I'll go there; maybe I'll meet a girl and we can sing sad songs of long ago."

During my middle teens, my father gave me some Burl Ives records. In a matter of weeks, I learned several songs: "Jimmy Crack Corn"; "Mr. Frog Went a' Courting"; and a lovely, sad ballad, "Edward." I sang several of these songs for Nora and was surprised and delighted that she had heard one of them in Connemara. About "Edward" she said, "I heard that when I was a girl. All I remember is the first verse. It's a little like the one you sing. You sing, 'How came that blood on your shirt sleeve?' but I remember it as 'Who put the blood on your left shoulder?' Isn't it interesting? I guess there's no right or wrong way to sing it. If you forget a word or the tune, just make it up."

"No right or wrong way! Really?" I exclaimed, surprised by her allowance for personal preference. "Are you sure?"

"Oh, I'm sure of that," she said kindly. "It doesn't matter whether you learn songs from people, the radio, or books. It's all music." Putting her hand on my shoulder, she said, "You're a very fine singer. Good on you, a fine singer you are." Hearing that, I felt proud and grateful for her compliment, but still found it hard to accept, as I was more used to receiving criticism than praise from my family.

While on summer vacation from the Brooks School, I joined my parents in the living room after dinner. "Huntingdon Fish is coming for lunch at the Reading Room," my father mentioned. "He tells me he is a cousin of Bartle Byrd. We'll have him for drinks." Hearing that a Fish was related to a Byrd reminded me of my recently learned folk song, "Mr. Frog Went a'Courting," and his marriage to Miss Mousie. I recalled the words:

Mr. Frog went a'hunting and he did ride
He went up to Miss Mousie's side
He went up to Miss Mousie's door
Where he had been many times before.

I chimed, "Excuse me, Daddy, I don't mean to interrupt, but I couldn't help overhearing what you said about your friends Mr. Fish and Miss Byrd. Forgive me for saying so, but that reminds me of a folk song, 'Mr. Frog Went a' Courting,' where he married a mouse. Wouldn't it be something if there were a song about a fish marrying a bird? Do you think there are any songs like that?"

"Oh, Peter," snapped my father, "how you do prittle prattle. I do wish you'd learn to think before you blurt out any old thing that pops into your mind. You have no idea how silly you sound. But I must say, I'm glad you've taken the time to listen to the folk music records I got you. If you spend more time learning songs than asking silly questions, you'll be on the right track and better off for it. While we were traveling, your mother and I got to hear folk songs, the real thing. When I was in England, I remember going for walks with Cousin Laurie in the gardens at Hidcote in Gloucestershire and hearing one of the gardeners singing a lovely folk song. I confess that I had to stop and listen. The song was something about bushes and briars. Cousin Laurie explained that some of these songs were very old and were handed down from generation to generation. All very romantic." He didn't realize that many of the songs were complaints about injustices at the hands of the nobility and gentry.

"And the Irish have folk songs, too," I said, thinking of Nora.

"Oh, indeed they do," replied my mother. "Last summer when you were in camp, your father and I paid a visit to Lord and Lady Inchiquin. I'm told there's a tune composed in honor of the family. We heard one of the scullery maids singing in Gaelic. I can't even begin to tell you how lovely her voice sounded, so pure, unaffected, and natural. I held my breath."

"Thank goodness for folk songs. It keeps the kerns and cock-neys in line," said my father, using an archaic word for Irish peasants or soldiers. "Those songs have a soothing influence on their rebellious and stubborn nature. I'm all in favor of folk songs, as long as they help people bear the rigor of work and don't unduly incite them." Looking at me sharply, he added, "Peter, just as you know better than to sing at the table, see to it that you don't go around singing folk songs in public or your friends will think you're quite mad and won't know what to make of you. Unless, of course, you're seated around a campfire. That can be very cozy and is not considered going on stage."

"Excuse me, Daddy. I don't mean to interrupt you. May I please ask a question?"

"A question, you say? Yes, you may. Ask away."

"What do you mean by folk songs keeping people in line? I don't understand."

"Of course you don't. In peasant communities, such things as folk songs, folk tales, riddles, proverbs, and the like play an important role in education, in tempering their lives. Look at you! Whether you realize it or not, folklore played a part in your upbringing. Remember Fräulein, your German governess? You may have forgotten, but she used to tell you stories, some of which were rather scary. They were meant to be. They kept you on the straight and narrow path.

"I remember one story she used to tell you. It was about Strupal Peter, Dirty Peter, and what happened to him. He was always a mess, dirty and raggedy. So the bogeyman cut off his fingers with a long pair of scissors. The book had marvelous illustrations. What you learned is that's what happens to little boys when they don't toe the line, listen to their governesses, and make themselves presentable.

"I don't know whether you've studied the Enlightenment in history class, but I can tell you that one of its thinkers made a great mistake when he proposed ridding peasant culture of its folklore education. Nothing could have been more off the mark. It led only to a leveling off of the classes. I dare say that the Catholic Church did a better job of controlling its peasantry than did the Protestants. They were savvier. They had a better grasp of their own class than their betters did. The peasants, in short, left to their own devices, would control themselves through their folklore.

"Their stories and tales threatened punishment to those who wouldn't behave properly. In many ways Protestants were more responsible than the Catholics for the evils of democracy. Even under Puritanism, the sway of reason gave way to the evangelicals' vulgar emotions. In more recent times the middle classes, feeling a void in their dreary lives, turned to folk music, arts and crafts, and back to nature as panaceas for the emptiness of their lives. They romanticized the rustics and the days of yore, but they didn't under-stand the peasants any more than the man in the moon.

"In the old days, the upper and lower classes had more in common with each other than with the middle classes. They under-stood and depended on each other, and their relationship inspired mutual loyalty. Perhaps I'm barking up the wrong tree and I'm loath to say it, but in an odd sort of way it seems that folklore is good for the economy. When middle-class followers of Thoreau and his ilk return from a week of camping, roughing it in the woods, playing noble savage, and singing songs of protest to their heart's content, they feel rejuvenated and become more productive in the market-place. For them, it's good therapy. If that is indeed the case, then I say let them raise their voices to the high heavens and sing away.

"Everyone uses folklore in one way or another. Even those perfectly dreadful Communists and Fascists. They all have an axe to grind. In the old days, agrarian festivals enabled the hayseeds to release their frustrations. This, in the long run, may have prevented revolutions. Folklore, if used judiciously by the powers that be, may go a long way to maintaining the status quo. These days, pinko intellectuals would take a perfectly simple song like 'Mr. Frog Went a' Courting' and say something preposterous like Mr. Frog and Miss Mouse were proletarian heroes exploited by their masters. Why can't they leave well enough alone?"

"Oh, fiddlesticks and fiddle dee dee," exclaimed my mother. "Sheer, absolute, and utter nonsense. All this fuss and feathers about folk songs. When I was a girl at camp, my friends and I sang folk songs and enjoyed them for what they were. We didn't weary ourselves with long-winded explanations. That would have taken all the fun out of it. By all means sing the songs, but why bother to give them a second thought?"

"You couldn't be more right," agreed my father. "One can go on endlessly, *ad nauseam*, about these songs until one's blue in the face, but to what avail? Folk songs are simple and direct, the province of the heather and glen and hedgerows."

* * *

In my sixth year at Salisbury, my father presented me with Francis James Child's five-volume collection of *English and Scottish Popular Ballads* and Cecil Sharp's *English Folk Songs from the Southern Appalachians*.

"When you first expressed an interest in folk songs, I didn't know if it was a passing fancy, but I see that you've stuck to your guns, so I'm giving you these books," my father commented. "Cecil Sharp was an Englishman who came to America to collect folk songs from delightful hayseeds in the remote areas of the southern Appalachian Mountains. He had no axe to grind. I've never read him, but I know about him. I dare say some of those old songs are quite lovely. If you ever learn to play the piano, you can accompany yourself and sing one of his songs for your mother and me.

"However, it's only fair to caution you that Professor Child should be taken with a grain of salt. Don't misunderstand me. He's topnotch in his field and I can't fault his scholarship. He knows much more than I will ever know about ballads and folk songs. That goes without saying. However, there are times when he gets carried away in a way that an historian shouldn't.

"I'll furnish you with an example. Years ago, when I was a boy at Milton Academy, I read the 'Battle of Otterburn.' The good professor saw fit to praise the English, pinning medals on them and putting feathers in their caps, but doesn't say one word on behalf of the Scots who carried the day."

"Excuse me, Daddy, may I please ask you something? It's about Professor Child's favoring the English over the Scotch."

"Yes, of course, ask away. But first let me remind you that it's not Scotch; it's Scots. We drink Scotch."

"Thank you, Daddy. Were you objecting that Professor Child was being too chauvinistic?"

"In a word, yes. A mark of a good historian is to be neutral in such matters, unless, of course, he's writing about battles between the classes, in which case it's his duty to support the upper classes and monarchy over those who would seek to overthrow them. In the past, nationalism was one thing, but in the nineteenth century monarchies were toppled thanks to romanticism, nationalism, and this new thing—democracy. There are no more kings and emperors in Germany and Austria. The Czar has fallen. In England, the monarchy is but a figurehead. In America, there are no more statesmen, just politicians, common or ordinary, with no background or breeding to speak of. Some of these politicians chew tobacco, get drunk, use perfectly vile language, consort with the lower orders, and go as far as to put their feet on desks, call their betters by their first names, and mangle the King's English. Need I go on? It's not a pretty picture. Most unappetizing. With every Tom, Dick, and Harry at the helm, we're all left in a bad way. Let's talk about something more pleasant."

Chapter 18

Riding, Sailing, Flying

I enjoyed listening to my mother tell about her horseback riding days at St. Tim's (one of her boarding schools); at the Myopia Hunt Club in Hamilton, Massachusetts; and later at Twickenham, Uncle Bob and Aunt Dorothy's plantation in South Carolina. Upon reaching the age of nine or ten, I was put on a horse. I was terrified of falling off and also of criticism for not exhibiting good form. Not succeeding at horsemanship, I did, however, manage to strike up a one-sided conversation with one of the horses.

My father, hearing of this strange and unprecedented behavior, asked, "Peter, would you mind telling me what on Earth you think you are doing talking to horses? And, if I'm not being too personal, would you tell me the nature of your conversation?"

"Yes, Daddy. One of the horses, I forget its name, a brown one with white spots and a nice smile, was a tiny bit sick. And one of the stable boys told me that if I told the horse a few jokes, it would cheer him up and make him feel better."

"Oh, Peter, really! I've never heard of such a thing. You're being a silly goose! A stable boy told you that? Such impudence! He should know better than to be overly familiar with his betters. Get that smile off your face. I'm not the least bit amused."

"His betters?" I said, not knowing what he meant.

"Yes, his betters. After all, you are my son and he is only a menial. I will not have you talked to this way by minions. Besides, what will our friends think? The other day Mr. Whitney reported that he saw you engrossed in a conversation with one of the horses, and he told me you looked like a lost soul and he felt sorry for you. I won't have you behaving this way. It reflects badly on your mother and me. Have you gone off the deep end?"

Almost on the verge of tears, I asked, "But what is wrong with talking to horses? Don't you and Mummy talk to our dogs? When you scold Mr. Pims and Mr. Percy, you sound like you're talking to me."

"Oh, Peter, really," sighed my father in an exasperated tone. "There's all the difference in the world between talking to dogs and telling asinine jokes to strange horses. Besides, gentlemen don't go around telling jokes, even if it's only to their friends. We do talk to our dogs, but they know what we're talking about. After all, they are members of our family.

"Now, Peter, who knows, when you outgrow your childish behavior, you might take an interest in horses. You should know that some ancestors of ours were topnotch polo players. I'm speaking of Larry and Monty Waterbury, who rode for an international team called the Big Four. The other two players were Harry Paine Whitney and somebody or other Millburn. I can assure you full well that they didn't make a dreary spectacle of themselves by conversing with their horses. One issues commands to horses and that's it. By and large, our family interest lies more in boats than horses, but that doesn't mean that one is better or worse than the other."

What would Daddy say if he heard me telling jokes to his boats, I wondered. I decided I'd better not ask.

* * *

My father was a yachtsman—and a serious one at that. Every summer he went on the Bermuda Race of the Blue Hill Cruise in Maine. When not competing, he would go for a leisurely afternoon sail around Frenchman Bay. Though a member of the Ida Lewis Yacht Club in Newport, he much preferred the more rugged waters of the Maine coast. When I was in my early teens, he took me sailing for the first time. At that time, he had two boats, a fifty-eight-foot yawl, the *Flying Cloud*, and an MDI (Mt. Desert Island) class, a much smaller boat.

I remember going for a sail with my father on the *Flying Cloud* with several of his friends: Charley Adams, Atwater Kent, Sarge Collier, and Bobby Ayer. During our sail, my father instructed me with such commands as "Ease off on the main sheet; you're pitching," or "Stand by; we're coming about," and "Look lively! Take a turn at the tiller." Seeing my confusion, my father complained, "Peter, you're too slow on the uptake. Go below until such time as I call for you."

He would then bark orders for my benefit. "Get up on deck. Get cracking, best foot forward. Here, take this line and stow it. Make yourself useful."

"You mean the rope, Daddy?"

"No, Peter, I don't mean the rope. I said nothing whatsoever about a rope. Whatever you do, get this straight. On a ship or boat, what you call a rope is correctly referred to as a line. Only landlubbers who don't know any better would call a line a rope. Remember, you're here to learn something about sailing and not just to admire the scenery. You can't expect people to mollycoddle and treat you with kid gloves; otherwise, you might as well stay ashore. Someday you're going to be on your own, and you can't ride on my coattails forever."

Try as I did, learning the ropes, or lines, was not easy. I desperately wanted to do the right thing so I could please him.

Besides sailing, both my parents knew how to fly a plane. My mother in her early twenties flew her Piper Cub around the North Shore of Massachusetts. Indeed, before she married my father she had been married briefly to pioneering aviator Crocker Snow. Their "aerial honeymoon" was reported in the January 1932 issue of *Popular Aviation* magazine. "Unfortunately," as noted in Snow's profile on the website wikitree.com, "their strong personalities clashed more than they meshed and they divorced after less than a year of matrimony."

When I was home on my summer vacation, my father would

take me up in his plane. I'd shut my eyes and imagine that I was alone at the controls and completely in charge of my destiny. I'd execute flawless spins, rolls, turns, loops, and dives, nonchalantly waving to the crowd of onlookers below. My father, noticing my beatific expression, would chastise me. "Peter, for God's sake, snap out of it. Get that dreamy look off your face. You look as if you're lost in a fog."

⊰ Chapter 19 ⊱
Philosophy

My father, disdainful of the modern intelligentsia and not au courant with modern thought, took more than a passing interest in Plato. For him, Plato provided the rationale for things that mattered—the monarchy (not constitutional) and the aristocracy. Democracy, the least attractive form of government, rested rudely at the bottom of Plato's and my father's esteem.

During my time at Salisbury, my father presented me with a leather-bound edition of Plato's *Republic*. I paid close attention to Plato's advice to his contemporaries regarding all that was comme il faut. It struck me that my father had been explaining Plato to me all my life without mentioning his name. Having spent the better part of a month reading *Republic*, I was given the benefit of several paternal monologues on the subject. He covered such weighty issues as the Platonic forms; the nature of justice; epistemology; meta-physics; aesthetics; political, social, and ethical theory; and how these branches of philosophy reflected my parents' views.

After several of these tutorials at my father's knee, I was allowed to speak and ask a few questions. He also instructed me to write a brief summary of his remarks on the *Republic*. In his words, "Now I know you have a vivid imagination, so whatever you do, make your point logically and plainly. Stay the course, and don't let your mind wander where it doesn't belong. Curb your passing fancies and you'll do fine. These days too many people let their imagination run away with them; little do they know that it will only get them into trouble. You're not a poet! If there's something you don't understand, don't try to cover it up by beating around the bush. All I want from you is plain talk—the facts, nothing more, nothing less."

Attempting to show that I had some grasp of the reading and lectures, I wrote an essay dedicated to my patron, my father, in which I demonstrated the Platonic forms by illustrating themes in the realm of humor and laughter. It read as follows:

> Plato, like Mummy and Daddy, stratified the world such that everything had an ideal form which was above all mundane others. For example, consider a chair. There is an immense variety of chairs in the world; all sizes and shapes, ranging from the familiar Queen Anne, Chippendale, and antique French chairs to lowly stumps. Blithely, effortlessly, and secure in their citadel of seclusion and cliquishly shunning all lower forms on Earth are the heavenly forms. Just as Mummy and Daddy would refuse to sit in anything less than an ideal chair, so would they insist on cultivating the beau ideal of laughter as ideally suited to establishing order and decorum in response to a confusion of social situations.

> It stands to reason that if laughter becomes the ideal form for defining what is humorous, then one knows how and when to laugh in the proper and correct manner. This, in fact, defines what is and what is not humorous. Clearly, then, the ideal form of the laugh, the good upper-class titter, is a metaphysical category designated from Olympian heights. This leaves me that epistemological task of separating humorous from non-humorous situations based on whether one's natural inclination is to laugh properly. The paradigmatic and proper form of Platonic laughter eliminates the necessity of responding to a series of situations on account of their not being Platonically humorous.

After several years spent in dedication to the perfection of my laugh, it is worth noting that the guffaw, snicker, chortle, cackle, and chuckle lack proper Platonic status and indicate such a want of physical and social grace that no one of good breeding would permit them.

On reading my brief essay, my father commented tersely, "Good for you! You finished it. Thank you for mentioning your mother and me, but that wasn't really necessary. You appear to grasp what you've read and everything I've told you. However, your flippant attitude shows that you have an imperfect knowledge and respect for the material. But I'm glad to see that you're taking an interest in family furniture. Some day it will be yours."

Chapter 20

The Experiment in International Living

A t the end of my fourth-form year at Salisbury, I took part in The Experiment in International Living, a program in which high-school students lived for several months with a host family in another country. I went to Salomé, France, near the Belgian border.

For me, part of the fun of The Experiment was getting to France by boat. I have fond memories of some of the other students I met while crossing the Atlantic, the briny deep. Those were good times, singing and dancing and playing card games into all hours of the night. I enjoyed the camaraderie. My only bad experience on the boat was when a bunch of us had too much to drink and had god-awful hangovers the next day, but if you'll forgive the pun, we were all in the same boat. I was underage, but got served anyway.

When I arrived in France, my new French family and I hit it off right away. I felt very welcome, with no need to go out of my way to make a favorable impression. I felt more relaxed and at home with them than I did with my own family.

My French family's last name has slipped my mind, but the father owned a cheese factory. The son, Jean, who was several years my senior, was on leave from his university. The daughter, Gilberte, was about my age.

Each day was different and there was always something to

do—walking in the countryside, going shopping or to the beach, and sharing thoughts and observations. Several days after my arrival we all went to a country club with a pool. Silly me, having forgotten my bathing suit, I borrowed one from Jean, one of those god-awful, tight-fitting, skimpy things, but no matter. Displaying my athletic ability—or lack of it—I dove off the diving board and guess what? My bathing suit fell off, but I managed to retrieve it. We all had a good laugh. Another time, after several sets of tennis, the host father served us all champagne. As you can see, my French family was very welcoming. Everyone was included in what was going on, unlike in my own family, where I was to be seen but not heard.

On occasion, after dinner, my French family and some of their friends would chat, sing folk songs, and put on skits, in which I enthusiastically participated. I was in my element. I did imitations of my parents; the maids with their Irish accents; and my own shy, retiring self, walking pigeon-toed, stuttering and stammering—all of which amused my new family to no end. They told me I had the making of an actor, which I took to heart as, years later, I did take to the stage.

At first, my French family had a hard time believing I was American. They were quite astounded and amused when I told them about my father giving me laughing lessons, requiring me to laugh in the correct manner, which was a serious undertaking. Their minds were boggled when I told them about the fire in the front part of Eastcote, my grandmother's summer house in Bar Harbor, Maine, and my father instructing the firemen to enter through the servants' entrance at the back door to put out the fire in front, with the same instruction as in the Somerset Club fire in Boston. They thought America was a more or less classless society. My French family was modern and progressive in their thinking; my family was the opposite—cool, aloof, and basking in class privilege.

I also learned a thing or two from this French family. They taught me photography, helped improve my tennis game, and introduced me to Impressionist painting. I'm glad to say that it wasn't a one-way street. I showed Gilberte some chords on her guitar and taught the family the rudiments of poker. When they saw that I enjoyed singing and listening to folk songs, they gave me a wonderful little book, *Les Jeunesse Qui Chantent*, which contained the words and music of traditional French folk songs. Together we sang "Auprès de ma blonde" and "Chevaliers de la table ronde," with everyone joining in the chorus. I taught them "Clementine," "Down in the Valley," and "Drunken Sailor."

I especially enjoyed my last two weeks in France, when I took a bicycle trip with other Experiment members to Provence, where the scenery was like something out of a fairy tale with castles, farms, horse-drawn carts, and sheep and geese crossing the road. Rarely encountering cars, we could hear the sounds of animals and smell the salt air and heather. It was picture perfect. We visited the Gorges du Tarn, with its magnificent cliffs, and the Caves of Lascaux in the Dordogne region, with their painted animals racing across walls and ceilings—some outlined in black, others in bright earth colors, looking very alive. Those pictures, as I recall, were not at the mouth of the cave, but only in the darkest part. They were part of a magic ritual to ensure a successful hunt.

Living with my French family, meeting their friends, discussing politics and regional issues, and taking part in their household chores and recreations took me out of myself. I learned to appreciate and enjoy the riches and diversity of their lives, including their literature and history—sometimes bloody, but always interesting. Not only did they sing old French ballads; they also discussed their history and outlook on life. In some cases, those songs and tales expressed ancient pagan beliefs that were preserved and perpetuated down through time. Folk songs, vestigial remnants of the past, also reflect the present, making them simultaneously old and new.

Meeting French people on their home ground, participating in their daily lives, and learning their culture and customs—that was a uniquely precious opportunity, a meaningful rite of passage. I was sad but grateful when I had to leave my adoptive family to go home at the end of the summer. Although I was no longer with them, I felt they were still part of me.

≷ Chapter 21 ≶
Discovering Greenwich Village

After several years at Brooks, I went to Salisbury, where I completed my grand tour of boarding schools. Salisbury School, located in Salisbury, Connecticut, was another church school run by the Reverend George Langdon. The dress code, though strict, was a little more relaxed there than at Brooks. Several of my new classmates—John Galey, Richard Dolittle, and Dick Matthews—were fond of modern art and jazz and occasionally wore dungarees, a work shirt, and boots in their free time. In the beginning, I had fantasies about dressing that way, but I didn't risk it.

In my fifth-form year at Salisbury, Barry Titus and Henry Schrady gave me a tour of some of their haunts in Greenwich Village. Dressed in a seersucker suit; a button-down, Egyptian-cotton Brooks Brothers pink shirt; and my old Brooks tie, I felt well furnished while en route but oddly out of place when I arrived.

Hearing musicians play folk music outside a cafe, smelling the aroma of freshly brewed espresso, and watching people enjoying themselves made a pleasant contrast with Park Avenue, where officious-looking people seemed too busy to enjoy the pleasures of the moment. I'm in another world, I thought. Checking to see whether anyone was watching, I quickly removed my tie and quietly stuffed it in my pocket.

"Taking off your tie?" laughed Barry. "A small concession to art. A mark of the anti-hero."

"Yes," joked Henry. "I'll bet you wouldn't take it off on Park Avenue."

"I'm just being diplomatic," I said sheepishly. In a sly tone I added, "You know what they do in Rome, don't you? I'd hate to be accused of bad form."

My friends took me to Café Rienzi, a crowded coffeehouse. I was pleasantly startled by the air of lively disorder. Somehow, I got the feeling that there was something at stake here; things mattered and something was being created. Everyone there seemed so absorbed in what they were saying to one another and oblivious to their colorful surroundings. The occasional emotional flare-ups that erupted here and there bespoke involvement. Even the clothing—the sandals rather than patent-leather pumps, the blue jeans and work shirts rather than gray flannel and tweed coats, the beards and uncultivated hair—said to me that these people cared more about what they were saying and doing than how they appeared.

Smoking one of Barry's Russian cigarettes, sipping my espresso, and feeling like a fledgling man of the world, I found an excuse to talk to a girl at the next table whose eyes had met mine. She looked to be about eighteen, had long brown hair, and wore a leotard and sandals.

"My parents have regular jobs," she told me, "but they're really musicians. I'm studying theater at Performing Arts." She asked me, "Why are you wearing a suit? You're not from the Village, are you?"

I fibbed, "No, I'm not from here. These aren't my real clothes; I borrowed them. I'm in a play."

"A play. That's wonderful," she beamed. "I'm also trying out for a play. What's the name of yours?"

"It's called *A Laughing Matter*."

"That's a catchy title. Who wrote it and what is it about?"

Dying to tell her that I wrote it, but affecting modesty, I replied, "No one important or anyone you'd know. It's about an upper-class American family that tries to bring up their son to be a gentleman. Everyone means well, but the boy is just a little slow on the uptake and he and his parents give each other a hard time."

"What a sketch," she said. "What part do you play?"

"I'm not sure. The director's trying to make up his mind whether I'd be best as the father or the son." I ad-libbed a few lines, impersonating my parents and myself in a typical afternoon at Ridgemere.

"Oh, that's funny. You really have it down. The stilted way they talk. You make it seem so real. Where is the play?"

"It's just a small play at my school." The girl and I continued our sporadic conversation until Barry and Henry decided to take me to another coffeehouse, the Figaro, and then into a sandal shop.

The owner, a pleasant man in his twenties, was sitting on a chair, playing dance tunes on the fiddle. He nodded hello and we listened in appreciation. A few minutes later he came over and introduced himself as Allan Block. Several other musicians walked in, and in a matter of minutes they were all playing. I had never heard music like that before. I stood there mesmerized. In a way, I envied the musicians. Having taken a break from playing, Allan introduced his friends as Ralph Lee Smith and Andy May.

I ordered a pair of sandals. I was keen to take them with me, but there was a one-week wait. Allan Block consoled me. "These custom-made sandals will fit better than anything off the shelf. I'll try to have them ready within the week. Before you go, I'll have to measure your feet."

"Really, Peter," scolded Barry playfully. "You of all people. Ready-made sandals. How tacky!"

Our final destination was the Folklore Center, which served as a record and instrument shop, a meeting place for musicians, and a site for small concerts. The room was filled with people, some humming, some chatting. One girl caught my eye as she played the guitar and sang a pleasing Appalachian ballad. She was later introduced to me as Ellen Stekert. A large fellow played his banjo and drowned everyone else out. Someone bought a record and remarked, "Kenny Goldstein did the notes. Great!" On the wall in one corner of the room were photographs of musicians who had played at the Folklore Center. There was also a large photograph of the proprietor, Israel (Izzy) Young, in which he was clothed only in a contemplative look and a beard that covered little more than his chin. I thought, "How revealing."

I bought a record on the strength of its cover, which featured a beautiful woman, Robin Roberts, singing Irish street songs. Her eyes met mine and it was love at first sight. I asked Izzy's permission to play my new record and he graciously assented. Robin's beauty, her lovely voice, and the haunting melodies filled me with longing for her and the music.

Three weeks later, while at home in Newport, I received an invitation to a coming-out party in Oyster Bay, Long Island. The trip would afford a tailor-made opportunity for an unscheduled stop in Greenwich Village. On the day of my departure, my mother, spying my open suitcase, noticed that packed with my dress clothes were my new sandals, faded blue jeans, and a crumpled blue denim work shirt.

"Peter! Just what is the meaning of this?" she asked crisply. "Do you propose to wear those things to your dance?"

"Well, yes, of course I plan to wear them. I'm sorry, but it's the best I could come up with. They are rather dreary, aren't they? Not very flamboyant. Perhaps I should have checked with you first."

With a look of incomprehension, my mother said flatly, "I beg your pardon?"

I fibbed in an affected tone, "Oh, Mummy, don't give it a second thought. I forgot to tell you. I've also been invited to another party, a masquerade in New York. Don't worry; the costume is not mine. Heaven forbid. I just borrowed it for the occasion."

"Oh, well," said my mother in a tone of relief. "That's different. If it's a masquerade, that's fine. Frankly, in my wildest dreams I couldn't imagine you wearing those rags in public and making a perfectly ghastly spectacle of yourself."

"Oh, darling," said my father firmly, "now you know very well that Peter wouldn't do that. He's got more sense than we give him credit for. He's no more going to go nipping and gadding about in that getup than the man in the moon." Inspecting my suitcase, he remarked, "How disappointing. There's nothing exotic about Peter's costume. It's rather ordinary. Peter, can't you do better than that for a masquerade? I'd thought you'd have more imagination. Why don't you go as a king or emperor, something with style? Just what are you supposed to be, anyway? A vagabond or something out of *Tobacco Road*?"

"I'm going as a bohemian artist. You know, something out of Greenwich Village," I replied.

"Greenwich Village," snapped my father. "How do you know about Greenwich Village? You can't possibly know about Greenwich Village. You've never heard your mother or me mention it. To whom have you been talking?"

Sounding vague, I said, "I'm not sure, but I think I read about it somewhere. Maybe Henry James. Of course! I remember, I heard some of my friends mention it. They said it's not a place one would want to go."

"Well, they couldn't be more right," agreed my father in a vehement tone. "Why anyone in their right mind would want to go there is beyond me. Take it from me, if you went there you would be sorely disappointed. It's not as romantic as it sounds. It's just sordid. All you'll find are long-haired types: anarchists, people who take opium, laggards, layabouts, and inky-stained Jewesses who write poetry—people who are persona non grata in society.

"Now when you go to New York, why don't you visit your friends on Park Avenue, some of the children of our friends? Don't ever let me catch you going to Greenwich Village, where you don't belong. Now don't get the wrong idea. I'm not knocking New York. Your mother and I couldn't be more fond of the Westbury. We've been going there for years. Some of my ancestors were from New York. They played a prominent part in its history. It's probably just as well that they're not alive today. They'd roll over in their graves."

"Don't worry," I placated him. "I haven't the slightest urge to go to Greenwich Village. It sounds all too terribly unattractive. Not my cup of tea."

"I should say not," said my father, somewhat mollified.

I continued, "I promise that when the masquerade is over, I'll change back to my regular clothes."

"Well, see that you do. You have no business going around in public wearing a costume. It's just not done. When your social engagements are over, I want you to come directly back home. No dilly-dallying or shilly-shallying."

He added, "When you go to Long Island, you undoubtedly will run into some friends of ours. I expect you to be on your best behavior and, whatever you do, don't take more than one drink. Drinking at your age is not attractive; furthermore, you're too young to become an alcoholic. Remember, you're representing us. I'll be checking up on you, and I want nothing but good reports from our friends who will keep an eye out for you. We've brought you up properly to do the right thing, and we want you to be a credit to the family."

"Oh, darling," said my mother to my father. "You know Peter. He means well, has a heart of gold, but he's very absent-minded. I do hope he doesn't get mixed up and wear the masquerade clothes on Long Island. Let's hope he can keep it straight."

"Peter, we love you dearly," said my father, "but I have to tell you, you are in a fog most of the time. You've got to get with it and get on the *qui vive*. Get your head out of the clouds. You can't be a dreamer all your life."

"He's just going through a stage," said my mother, "when the young feel they have to shock their elders."

In a concerned tone my father concluded, "I'd feel better if Peter had a chaperone to keep him on the straight and narrow path."

It occurred to me that the story I told the girl in the Café Rienzi about wearing a costume because I was acting in a play hadn't been such a fib after all.

Chapter 22

Big Piney, Wyoming

In the summer before my last year at Salisbury, at the instigation of headmaster George Langdon, my family sent me to work for the summer on a ranch in Big Piney, Wyoming. Pitching, stacking, and baling hay; driving a tractor; and performing other farm-related chores were not my customary summer routine. However, after several weeks, I got the hang of things and managed to pull my weight.

One time while having trouble starting the tractor, I asked one of the hired hands for help. "All you gotta do," he said with a poker face in that dry tone reminiscent of a Maine fisherman, "is to throw a match in that gas tank and she'll start up real purty."

"Oh, thank you," I said appreciatively. "I didn't know it was as easy as that." So saying, I walked over to the tractor, pulled out a match, lit it, and made as if to throw it in the gas tank. With a look of horror, the cowboy lunged in front of the gas tank and yelled, "Hey, you damn fool. Do you want to blow us to kingdom come? Ain't you got no sense? Where the hell were you when God passed out the brains?"

"When God made me, he broke the mold," I quipped. "I was only kidding."

"Kidding? Sure had me plumb fooled. That ain't no way to kid. You scared the living Jesus outta me."

Serves him right, I thought.

Our recreation consisted mainly of going into town for the evening and drinking at the local saloon. The bartender overlooked the fact that I was underage. Apropos of this, Zeke, one of the ranch hands, informed me, "Hey, ol' buddy, you and me and some of the boys is going to have some fun. We'll git to town, git drunk, and have a good fight. I'll whup you. You kin whup me. We'll tear that saloon apart."

Barely disguising my distaste for and apprehension at this proposal, I asked, "Why do you want to do that? Someone might get hurt, probably me."

"'Cause you and me are buddies, old pal," he announced cheerfully. I politely but firmly declined on the grounds that I had to write to my poor aging grandparents. I further fibbed, "I'm a Quaker. Fighting is against my religion. You wouldn't want me to go to hell, would you?" Fortunately the prospect of fighting was never mentioned again.

Some of the cowboys and cowhands sang songs about cattle drives, gunfights, Indians, and loneliness on the frontier. Like the old Gaelic songs Nora had sung, those down-to-earth cowboy songs spoke to the heart. Hearing them broadened my knowledge and appreciation of folk music.

In the second week of August, my job came to an end. My employers, husband and wife, paid me my wages, wished me good luck, told me I was a good worker, and said they were sorry to see me go. Zeke volunteered to drive me to town to catch the bus for the airport. On the way there, he said, "You know what you gotta do? You gottta git yerself some ginch."

"What the heck is that?"

"You know. Some pussy."

Confused at his terminology, I replied, "Why are you talking about a cat? I can't bring any kittens home. My family already have Pekinese, and I don't think they'd appreciate more animals."

"Damnation!" he exclaimed with feeling. "You city fellas don't know diddledy dick. I'm not talking about any animals. I'm talking about a woman. You know what that is, don't cha?" I nodded apprehensively. "Wal, good. I know an ol' gal who lives at the top of the saloon. She'll fix you up good. Don't worry none. Just tell her ol' Zeke sent you and don't worry about nothing. She'll make a man outta you."

Fortified by a beer at the saloon, I went upstairs as instructed and entered a small, dimly lit room with sparse furniture and walls bare except for a small painting of the Virgin Mary. Standing by the window was an attractive woman with red hair, appearing to be in her mid-to-late thirties. I felt attraction, repulsion, embarrassment, curiosity, fear, and helplessness.

Wondering what I should do now, I announced, "Hello, you must be Jo. Zeke said I'd find you here." I quickly added, "My coming to see you was Zeke's idea, not mine."

"It was, was it?" she replied in a soft-spoken Southern accent. "That figures. I'm Jo. That's short for Josephine, but you can call me Jo. Everyone does."

Not knowing what to do or say next, I fell back on the way I had been taught to introduce myself. I approached her, shook her hand, and said, "My name is Peter. How do you do. It's nice to meet you." I thought, "That sounds dumb. Get hold of yourself."

Sensing that I was ill at ease, Jo said, "Get a load off your feet and pull up a chair. There, that's better. Don't worry, I'm not going to bite you."

Reassured that she wasn't going to jump on me, I realized that I was beginning to like her. She continued, "I've known Zeke for a long time; he's been a good friend. He doesn't mean any harm. He's just trying to be helpful. He's helped out lots of times. He got me this job."

Looking at me in a maternal or sisterly way, she said, "Don't worry. You don't have to do anything you don't want to. We can just talk." Seeing the depth of my discomfort, she added in an apologetic tone, "Goodness gracious, I'm sorry. Can I get you something to drink? All I have is whiskey and ginger ale." Accepting her offer, I smiled as I remembered my father telling me, "Gentlemen don't drink whiskey and ginger ale. It isn't done. Bad form." She continued, "Tell me about yourself. Where do you hail from? Do you have brothers and sisters? You sound kind of educated. I reckon you're not from these parts."

We spent an hour or so talking. I began to enjoy it and all but forgot where I was. Jo said, "Our experiences are so different. You sound like you're someone in a book."

"Well, thank you. I enjoyed hearing about your family in the theater and the traveling shows. It must have been fun."

"Oh, yes, we didn't have much money, but we had our share of good times. A few laughs, too. We were always on the move. When I was seventeen, I got hitched to a fella, but he ran away and I just kind of drifted and here I am."

As our conversation concluded, she said, "If you ever come back to Big Piney, come and say hello. I'll be here." With a wink she added, "And you can buy me a drink." Putting her index finger to her lips, motioning for quiet, she said in a conspiratorial tone, "Just tell Zeke you had a good time and that will make him feel good."

Sorry at having to go, I said, "I'd love to have a souvenir to remember you by. You know what I'd like?"

"No, what's that? I don't have much, but take what you like."

"I'd like one of your freckles," I kidded. "They're beautiful."

"One of my freckles," she exclaimed with a smile. "I wish I could but I can't."

"Why not?"

"'Cause they're stuck."

"Oh, that's too bad," I said, sounding disappointed. "Here, take this. It's not much but a little something to remember me by." So saying, I handed her my Ronson lighter. "It's got my initials on it." She gave me a kiss on the cheek and I went downstairs and found Zeke by the bar, surrounded by several girls and shots of whiskey.

"Thank you, Zeke," I said in a tone of forced cheerfulness. "That was one heck of an experience. May I stand you to a drink?"

"Hell no, boy. It's on me. We gotta celebrate. You done good. What wuz she like?"

"She was wonderful," I replied, feeling a bit uncomfortable.

"But you know what they say, gentlemen should not talk about their ladies."

"Hell's bells, that's okay, kid. I reckon you're just kinda shy, bein' the first time and all."

Half an hour later, having said goodbye to Zeke, I took the bus to the airport and soon was flying home. I thought of Jo and missed her. On first meeting her, I had felt vulnerable and awkward, but she tactfully managed to put me at my ease. Jo, with her down-to-earth smarts and sense of humor, had encouraged me to talk about myself in a way that I couldn't with most people, with the exception of Nora. For that I was grateful. Wish I was rich, I mused. I'd give her some money so she could get out of there, but where would she go?

Arriving the next morning in Ellsworth, Maine, I was met by Dwight Stevenson, Grandma's chauffeur. I confided to him about Jo. He exclaimed in his laconic, Down East way of talking, "I'll be hornswaggled. You did that? Don't tell your Daddy. He'll have a fit."

"But you don't understand. We didn't do anything. We just talked."

"Don't matter none. A prostitute is a prostitute any way you look at it. Iffin you tell your Daddy, you'll never hear the end of it." He shook his head and muttered, "Glory Day," and spat out the window.

Forty-five minutes later we arrived at Eastcote in Bar Harbor. My father gave me a sturdy handshake and said, "Good to have you aboard. It's nice to see you. I like the look in your eye. I see that country living agreed with you. You seem to have acquired a bit of a tan, or is that dirt? Come on and say hello to your mother and your grandmother. It's been some time since they laid eyes on you. They're dying to see you."

Later that afternoon, my father took me out for a sail in Frenchman Bay. Despite feeling nervous about making mistakes of a nautical nature, I seemed to know what I was doing. "Good for you," my father beamed. "It seems that you learned a thing or two at that sailing camp of yours." Torn between wishing to savor the unsullied memory of Jo and wanting to confide in my father, I told him about her.

"Oh, Peter, there you go again," he said, not angrily but condescendingly. "Now you know as well as I do that you have a vivid imagination. You may think you talked to her, but you didn't. Consorting with prostitutes! I never heard of such a thing, not even in my wildest imagination."

I winced at hearing Jo referred to in that way. "It's all in your mind," he went on. "You allow yourself to get carried away, listening to cowboys and hayseeds spinning their racy yarns. You're very impressionable, and you let yourself get taken in by fast talkers. All this loose talk is nothing new. It's old hat, *vieux jeu*. Now, Peter, whatever you do, don't breathe a word of this to your mother and grandmother. Remember, your grandmother is elderly and she wouldn't have the slightest idea what you're talking about. You're no longer living in the wild and woolly west, but here with your family, back in civilization where you belong. So please conduct yourself accordingly. Need I say more? I hate to think that sending you to terra incognita was a great mistake."

⅜ Chapter 23 ⅞

Weeping Willow

While on Christmas vacation during my last year of boarding school, I was invited by some friends to go to the movies. My parents granted me permission, with the stipulation that I get back by ten o'clock.

In the words of my father, "I want you back by ten o'clock on the dot and not a minute later. Just because you're on Christmas vacation is no reason why you and your contemporaries can come and go at all hours as you please, gadding and cavorting about the countryside. Remember, if you get back after ten there will be no one to let you in.

"Furthermore, you cannot go to the back door, ring the bell, and wake up the maids. That would be most unfair to them. They go to bed early and need their sleep. You know full well that we can't give you the key to the house. That's absolutely out of the question. In compliance with my wishes, may I suggest that rather than waiting for the last minute to beat the deadline, you allow ample time to get back by the appointed hour? Consider yourself on trial. I'm giving you responsibility. Let's see how well you handle it."

If responsibility is trust, I thought, I'm given none!

"Yes, Daddy," I murmured. "I'll do my best."

"Your best is good enough only as long as you fulfill my commission," my father responded. "Honoring my wishes shouldn't be that difficult a task. The movie gets out at 9:30. Perhaps you should come straight home and not dilly-dally for refreshments. Your friends will be here shortly to pick you up. Without any further ado I'd like you to put on a coat and tie. I won't have you going around in public looking like a ragamuffin. You're not a townsperson. Now that all that is said, I do hope you have a good time and remember us to your friends. Your mother and I send our warmest regards to their families. Again, I counsel you, don't be late. It's high time you learn to do things right."

After the movie—some sort of war movie, I think—my friends Bobby Grosvenor, Gay Firestone, Hope Blakely, and I went for Coca-Cola and ice cream. Then Bobby dropped me off at my door. Finding the door locked, I looked at my watch. It was ten minutes past ten.

Not sure what to do, I contemplated my possibilities, none of which seemed very promising. As I was cold and had to do something quickly, I walked to the cars that were parked nearby on the driveway, hoping to gain admittance. The car doors were frozen. I trudged wearily through the newly fallen snow down the driveway to the gardener's cottage. Noticing that the lights were out, I thought better of ringing the bell and waking Norman and his family.

After passing the pump house and the tool shed, I reached the carriage house. In the moonlight I was able to locate the great sliding door, open it, and make my way in. As lady luck would have it, none of the three carriages—the victoria, the landau, or the phaeton—was wide enough for me to lie down. Tired, cold, and depressed, I lay on one of the seats with my feet tucked in, but couldn't get comfortably settled. I got out of the carriage and, despite the darkness, found the entrance to the stables next door. There I found a place to lie down in one of the horse stalls.

I found old newspapers, burlap bags, rugs, and straw, cleared away some cobwebs and dirt, and made my place for the night. Lying down on my makeshift bed, which to my pleasant surprise was comfortable, I gazed upward and noticed streaks of dim light that filtered through the bay window, a flickering, dancing play of light and darkness.

I heard myself speak, sounding rather like my father, "I'll wager that I'm the first member of my family ever to lie here on a cold winter's night." I chortled for about five minutes when, all of a sudden, I felt empty and forlorn, not just about being locked out but from reflecting on my life. In my father's words, I was "on the outs."

Out in the cold at Ridgemere, there was no one to bail me out. I got up, left my bed of scraps, and retraced my steps until I passed the gardener's cottage. Then I turned off to the right and continued through some bushes and trees until I reached a clearing. There stood the weeping willow tree, solemn in the middle of the front lawn. It was almost midnight as I stood shivering under some drooping branches, gazing through their tears turned to icicles at the ghostly presence of Ridgemere. Watching the moon's pale yellow light, I felt a premonition that my life in the future would bear little resemblance to anything I then knew. I felt the chill of snowy branches pressed against my face.

"Will I be all right?" I wondered. "What will I do?"

I took a few steps forward, stood in the moonlight, gazed up at the tree—my cathedral—weeping its long sorrow, and hoped for some promising word of the future. I recollected Cousin Laurie talking about ancient Finnish shamans, Celtic druids, and pagan Saxon poets writing in runes. He had recounted the wondrous deeds of Väinämöinen, the hero of a Finnish epic, the *Kalevala*, who sang magical songs so beautifully that all living creatures—animals, birds, and fish—gathered in silence to listen. Old Väinämöinen, moved by his own singing, shed tears that rolled down his cheeks, fell into the ocean, and formed tiny blue pearls.

I then thought of a Celtic nature poem that I had committed to memory the previous year:

What snow on the cold hills has blinded me and soaked my clothes?
By the blessed God, I had no hope that I should ever get there.

I also remembered lines from an Anglo-Saxon poem, *The Seafarer*:

Prosperous men living on land do not begin to understand
How I, careworn and cut off from my kinsmen,
Have as an exile endured winter.

Mr. Herrick, one of my teachers at Salisbury, had told me that in these ancient poems the images of wind, winter, cold, ice, darkness, desolation, and dawn were sources of joy, not despair.

The next morning my exile in the stables ended with a whimper or, more correctly, with a lecture. I awoke at sunrise and entered Ridgemere through the servants' entrance. At breakfast, my father registered his jaundiced view of my escapade.

"Just who do you think you are, behaving in this fashion?" he demanded. "What are you, a gypsy or some sort of guttersnipe that can camp on our doorstep? This is not the Left Bank, where you sleep under bridges like some starry-eyed bohemian. What a ghastly performance. It's simply appalling. I won't have this behavior in my house. . . Not cunning by a long shot."

The movies or any other evening entertainment became off limits to me for the duration of my Christmas vacation. For the rest of the holidays I spent my afternoons in the Redwood Library immersing myself in folklore, literature, and philosophy, including an essay on humor by Bergson, which proved to be enlightening and, in an odd way, consoling. I also memorized a poem by William Blake, which I would say to myself before going to sleep.

To see the world
In a grain of sand
And heaven in a wild flower
Hold infinity
In the palm of your hand
And eternity in an hour.

Sitting in the library, reflecting on the eighteen years of my life, I contemplated my mother's words, "What's yours is yours, and what's mine is mine." I was coming to understand these words more deeply. I dared hope that in the future I, and those who would matter to me, could all be made richer by sharing.

Chapter 24

Naughty Nauticals

I took a couple of stabs at college—at Princeton and in summer school at the University of Virginia—but my days there were rapidly numbered as I became less and less interested in academic pursuits and all the intellectual and social regimentation of college life. In 1956, I decided to join the Navy and let my sensibilities be leavened by the real world out there, somewhere.

My first night at boot camp in Bainbridge, Maryland, was a novel experience. I vaguely remember stepping off the bus and being marched, single file, in the snow to a neon-lighted building with a sign, Welcome Recruits. The rise and fall of voices created an almost hypnotic effect, which was broken when I reached into my pocket for one remaining cookie, the taste of which brought back memories of that morning when I bade goodbye to my parents. Once inside the building we were instructed by a boson's mate to stand at attention and await our next command. Out of the corner of my eye I caught a glimpse of the companions with whom I would share the next two years. They were everything I had read about in the comfort of boarding school. On all sides were young boys and older men from every conceivable background. A burly boson's mate passed around a big box and made the following announcement: "I want you recruits to put all of your personal possessions in this box. . . your knives, switch blades, sex books, and prophylactics." As I had nothing of that description to contribute, I sheepishly put in my only possessions, a Parker 51 pen and pencil. I definitely was not one of the gang.

We were all marched to our barracks, where we made ready for bed. My rear-guard skirmish with the Navy was under way. After getting into the bottom bunk, I waited for approximately an hour until the recruits were asleep, and then I made my move, hoping to gain the advantage of surprise. I quietly slipped out to my locker and donned a Frankenstein mask, which I had managed to conceal from the boson's mate, scaring the fellow in the bunk above me. He fell to the floor and twisted his ankle.

I am sorry to say that my beautiful mask was confiscated, and the next morning I was marched off to a psychiatrist. I had a pleasant talk with him and he made some notes, an evaluation.

Judging from the doctor's apparent good humor, I surmised that my visit was a success. Asking routine questions concerning my background, education, and so on, he appeared intrigued to hear that my family had hired a tutor for me. I explained to him that my tutor gave me fencing lessons, which I put to good use by challenging a friend to a duel, receiving a scar on my left cheek which, though prominent, had faded with time. It was beyond his comprehension that in twentieth-century America a young boy would fight a duel to defend his family's name. The doctor concluded with a quote from Graham Greene to the effect that an emotionally deprived child was a writer's gold mine. "Some time in the future," he addressed me, "you may feel inclined to write about it."

At the end of our talk, he instructed me to take his evaluation and give it to my company commander. I surreptitiously opened the envelope and read the contents. I was described as suffering from an F. Scott Fitzgerald complex; the evaluation included such adjectives as "bohemian" and "clubby."

With the visit to the psychiatrist behind me, I managed to remain on good terms with my immediate superiors. I was barely resigned to the rigors of training and naval indoctrination. The daily routine consisted of going to classes, marching, standing watch, preparing for inspections, and other such activities that were difficult to take seriously.

At the completion of my eight-week training, I graduated from boot camp with the dubious rating of seaman apprentice. Soon I was given orders to report to the USS *Canberra*, a guided-missile ship undergoing repairs in Norfolk, Virginia. My first impression of the ship was that of a monstrous wedding cake—huge gray slabs, pasted in layers, devolved from a cluttered superstructure to a dull monolithic plateau.

Weeks later, I found myself back in the psychiatrist's office, this time aboard ship. "Seaman Johnson, you're back," beamed the psychiatrist. "I thought we would see each other again. Your company commander and others are concerned about your mental state. What happened this time?"

"Well, sir, I'm not sure what exactly did transpire, but I'll do my best to explain. One of my first jobs aboard ship was to stand a four-hour duty watch. This entailed standing on deck way aft of the bridge near the fantail. Equipped with a microphone and headset, I was to keep an eye out for all foreign objects such as other ships, icebergs, whatever. After having taken a bearing, I was to report them to the bridge."

Leaning back in his swivel chair, appearing at ease in his surroundings, the psychiatrist looked at me with a knowing smile. I jokingly suggested that I should hire him to be my biographer à la Johnson (my namesake) and Boswell. A naval officer who happened to be present, hearing my suggestion, gave us both disparaging looks, smiled wanly, shook his head, and left the room. A few minutes later this officer returned and, on the pretext of taking care of unfinished business, remained within earshot.

Aware that I now had an audience, I commenced my story. "I remember the day was quite warm. While standing watch, I requested to speak to the captain of the ship. This was unprecedented procedure for an ordinary seaman like myself; after all, I was no admiral. My shipmates and I were instructed not to bother people higher in the chain of command. However, a higher duty called me that day. I wanted the captain to instruct me in my duties.

Our conversation went like this: 'Captain, Seaman Johnson—466–73–92—requests permission to discuss the nature and clarification of my duties with you.' The captain, somewhat taken aback, bluntly replied, 'Yes, yes, what is it, boy? I am a busy man; what is it?' I replied, 'I wish to perform my duties to the best of my abilities, with meticulous solicitude. Some of the fine points are somewhat unclear, and you, the captain, can help me unravel all their myriad complexities.' The captain, taking all of this in, paused for a second and then nervously replied in a guarded tone, 'Yes, yes, boy. Be brief; what is the problem?' I said, 'I'll get directly to the point. Is it really true that I am to report everything I see?' 'Yes, yes, boy, you've been instructed correctly. Report anything you see; what's the problem?'

"'Well, sir,' I said, 'for example, suppose I spot a whale, ten points off the starboard bow. Should I report it?' 'Yes, yes, by all means. If you sight a whale, report it to the bridge.' 'But sir,' I replied, and now the conversation was to take a deep and meaningful turn, 'suppose I don't see the whole whale but just part of the whale. It wouldn't be completely accurate to report that I saw something in its entirety when I didn't see all of it.'

"At this point, the captain, sounding a bit nervous, muttered something about not being sure what I was getting at, at which point I pressed home my advantage and started rambling incoherently about St. Thomas Aquinas, Duns Scotus, and medieval doctrines of inference and the relationship of the whole to its parts. My voice rose in pitch until it became frenzied. At this point the captain must have decided that I had had too much sun, so he gently tried to reassure me, telling me not to worry about a thing. Before I knew it, two sailors informed me that I was temporarily relieved from duty. Oh, I forgot to mention that, while discussing this thorny theoretical issue with the captain, I said, 'Suppose I don't see the whole whale, but perceive merely the whale's tail, that is to say, the tail of a whale. Should I report that I beheld only a whale's tail, or am I free to assume that the whole whale exists?'"

During the course of our conversation the doctor offered me a cup of coffee and pointed out that my hijinks—or inappropriate behavior, as he put it—was my way of asking for help. Reminiscing about my childhood, I confided how my father gave me laughing lessons as I stood at attention in front of family portraits, forbade me to mention Franklin Roosevelt's name, and so forth. At the close of our session the psychiatrist asked me whether I'd like to see him on a regular basis. I answered in the affirmative. Our sessions went fairly smoothly except for the few times when I found it difficult to talk. I would clam up, retreat from his probing questions, and stare at the floor. At one point, unable to say anything—but bursting inside—I started singing folk songs, low and sad, having to do with unrequited love, incest, and other tragic themes. I explained that these old songs, some of which go back to medieval times, are very basic, elemental, with not a wasted word or note. They get to the heart of the matter, the core of the human condition. Also, the tunes are wonderfully mysterious, full of magic, as if from another world. After singing or hearing them, I felt cleansed. The doctor would analyze the songs with reference to my bruised feelings, pointing out the significance not only of each song, but also of the order in which they were sung.

I looked forward to our weekly meetings. For the first time in my life someone was taking me seriously. Thanks to my regular contact with the ship's psychiatrist, I had for the first time the parental supervision I had always needed.

* * *

In addition to keeping watch, another one of our duties was what was referred to as "holy stoning." This task took place early in the morning. Three or four of us would line up abreast of each other with wooden sticks inserted into the holes of rectangular bits of sandstone. After the deck had been hosed down, we would scrub it with these crude implements, purging the wood of its oil slick and dirt. As it was awfully tedious, the only way I could cope with all of this unwarranted hard labor was to eliminate the source of the problem, the holy stone.

One evening, when no one was in view, I went to the boson's

locker, gathered up all the holy stones, and threw them over the side of the ship. This proved to be a major source of embarrassment for the boson's mate, when next morning everyone was at a loss at the disappearance of their scrubbing stones.

* * *

After several months of good behavior in which I refrained from committing any more naughty nauticals, my psychiatrist told me I was making good progress. By now dependent on him, however, I was afraid that if I became too sane I might be given a clean bill of health and lose the privilege of seeing him. I decided it was time to do something spectacular that would ensure the continuation of our sessions.

Issued a seventy-two-hour pass from Norfolk, I decided to go to Washington to visit friends. After long months of incarceration, a few days respite were a welcome change. I left on Friday and arrived *chez* friends in the evening. On Sunday my hosts, John and Phyllis Phillibert, and I went on a tour of the city, which included paying our respects to that venerable symbol of America's military might, the Pentagon. For this occasion, I was dressed in a conservative three-piece Brooks Brothers white linen suit, a blue button-down shirt from J. Press, a striped bow tie from the Andover Shop, and wing-tip shoes from Peal's. Through the sage use of makeup, I assumed the appearance of a middle-aged man of some importance, a senator or diplomat at large. Thus clad, I could have passed muster with even the stuffiest law firm. For added insurance, I borrowed an old Rogers Peet dress hat and wore it with the brim snapped down at the correct angle. I may add that my underwear was from Chip and my garters from Paul Stuart.

Our car was driven by John, who in keeping with the scenario wore the garb of chauffeur. We were dressed to kill. On reaching our destination, John got out of the car and opened the back door with great ceremony. Carrying my official-looking briefcase, I stepped onto the sidewalk. Scarcely had I done so when a moped pulled up in back of us, on which rode friends newly recruited for this occasion.

Disguised as gangsters with masks covering their faces, they pulled out guns and commenced firing in our direction.

Blanks make about as much noise as real bullets; consequently, they have the same disturbing effect on a crowd of people. I admirably acted out my end of the charade. Scarcely had the first shots been fired, when, by the accepted rules of cause and effect, I fell to the ground in the fashion of mortally wounded Hollywood gangsters and threw my briefcase in the direction of two distinguished gentlemen who were descending the stairs of the Pentagon. One of them turned out to be a four-star general, the other a senator.

"Quick," I gasped in a well-bred, subdued tone. "National security is at stake. Get this to Secretary Dulles." The approaching pair could hardly fail to see what was happening—an assassination right before their eyes. "Oh, my God, our man is hit," exclaimed the general in an urgent tone. The senator followed with, "Look, a briefcase. I'll get it."

I was gracefully stretched out on the sidewalk as a large crowd gathered to behold the specter of death. In retrospect my father would have been upset if he had witnessed this tragic event, but proud of me for dying in a socially acceptable fashion. Quietly, with no fuss, just expiring in an understated, well-bred way.

Police and ambulance sirens pierced the air. Several reporters arrived on the scene and took candid shots of me on the ground. I felt myself gently lifted onto a stretcher and carried toward an ambulance. One of my rescuers was checking my pulse. Lying on the stretcher, I felt a slight twinge of anxiety as a nearby female voice in the crowd cried out, "Oh, God, is he really dead?" The hot, muggy day, bringing perspiration to my brow, the rancid smell of my body odor, the taste of recently chewed gum, and the wailing of sirens, the idling of motorcycles, and other city sounds confirmed for me my continued existence on Earth. As if in need of further verification, I furtively opened my left eye just a slit, enough to see light from the outside.

I wondered what my psychiatrist would say when he heard about this. He was so understanding. I looked forward to seeing him again. Well aware that I was the object of everybody's scrutiny, I felt like the ridiculous and the sublime wrapped in one, but which was which?

Just as the stretcher was about to disappear into the waiting doors, I jumped up, Lazarus-like, and, with hands raised triumphantly over my head, celebrated my miraculous return to the land of the living. Gaining exposure as well as my equilibrium, I broke into song and regaled the stunned audience with my impromptu rendition of an old Irish folk ditty:

Some say the Devil's dead, the Devil's dead, the Devil's dead
Some say the Devil's dead, he's buried in Washington.

I was even so bold as to ask the crowd, my audience, to join in. Amidst cries of disbelief and wonder, a few people recovered from their shock and laughingly joined in on the second verse. "Some say he rose again, rose again, rose again; some say he rose again, he's alive in Washington." Scarcely had I finished when a policeman and a member of the Shore Patrol took a firm hold of me, and I was taken into custody. Happily, my friends got away.

The next day, after having been questioned, I was escorted back to the base in Norfolk. There was little doubt in anyone's mind that I was just a bit nuts. Once again, I was shipped off to my friendly psychiatrist for a visit. The good doctor greeted me with his cordial, enigmatic smile and asked me to explain the Washington incident. Toward the end of our chat, he pointed out the similarity among my various forms of disguise, notably the Frankenstein mask and that of my latest adventure as the diplomat. He suggested I lacked a sense of my own identity. More positively, he pointed out that with my pleasant singing voice and interest in things humanistic, I might consider channeling my feelings of aggression and anxiety into socially acceptable behavior such as some form of artistic expression. Pleased at hearing that, but feeling a trifle uncomfortable with any praise, no matter how slight, I broke into a silly song:

Dr. Freud, Dr. Freud,
How we wish you had been otherwise employed

When the circumstances help enhance the finances
We're all singing of Dr. Sigmund Freud

He smiled and commented, "That song is amusing, but you really have a hard time accepting anything positive about yourself . . . you find interesting ways to avoid coming to grips with your feelings." He then suggested that I might try out for talent night, an evening of entertainment the recruits provided for the entire base.

* * *

A month after my chat with the doctor, the company commander presented a talent night open to all recruits. A variety of material was presented on a humid August evening, including skits, ventriloquism, gymnastics, a juggling act, a puppet show, joke telling, a bluegrass band, and, for the highbrows, classical compositions played on the piano.

I was nervous at the prospect of performing on stage for such a large number of people. This was a much larger audience than those I had faced while acting in boarding school plays at Brooks and Salisbury. The entertainment was broadcast live throughout the base to Navy personnel who were not in attendance.

I anxiously awaited my turn to do my bit. "And now we have a special treat for you. Seaman Peter Johnson from B Company has promised to make it a memorable evening for us. Let's give him a big hand and make him welcome." Scattered applause filled the large amphitheater-like room. "Thank you very much for your kind words," I gratefully acknowledged the master of ceremonies. Wishing to please the doctor and in a perverse way myself, and to gain the goodwill of the crew, I decided that I'd sing a sea shanty, "The Drunken Sailor," that I had heard sung by Burl Ives some years earlier.

Noticing the thousands of people in the distance and hearing the low murmur of voices that emanated from a sea of sailors, officers, naval personnel, and their families, I was nervous being the center of attention, with all eyes and ears on me. I felt like I was the captain of a ship, having to give a command performance in the heat of battle to keep the good ship afloat. I'd sing a sea shanty with a chorus and get the audience involved with feedback, so we'd be in this together and I'd feel less alone and more a part of a community. Also, feeling a bit under the weather after having consumed too much beer the previous night while on liberty, I thought it fitting to sing "The Drunken Sailor" as a song of myself, which would add a touch of authority and bring to light a sailor's life on ship.

I addressed my faceless audience, saying, "I'm going to sing a sea shanty, but I need your help on this one. Singing shanties is a venerable Navy tradition and we're all part of it. Shanties were sung in the old days of square riggers and clipper ships, the days of sail, when American ships were found in every major port in the world. A shanty is a strong rhythmical work song sung by a leader, or the shanty man, to coincide with the effort and rhythm of the job at hand. I know some of you can relate to this. I'll sing 'The Drunken Sailor.'"

I paused and heard subdued laughter in the background. Knowing that I was on the right track, I continued, "'The Drunken Sailor' is a short-haul shanty, known as a runaway song, where the crew runs down the deck, gives a few short pulls on the rope, and sings the chorus. The song describes all the measures used to sober up the drunken sailor. It's quite simple and it will be fun. I'll be the shanty man that sings the verse and you can be the crew that joins in on the chorus. We'll have to sing this together to make the old ship go. Here's your part." I started singing:

Way, hay and up she rises
Way, hay and up she rises
Way, hay and up she rises
Early in the morning

"Now let's do it together," at which point they all enthusiastically joined in. Gratefully, I said, "You sound great. I'm glad to have you on my ship. I'll sing the first verse and then we'll sing the chorus again together." I commenced:

What do you do with a drunken sailor?
What do you do with a drunken sailor?
What do you do with a drunken sailor?
Early in the morning

Ending the song to generous applause after singing three or four verses, I added, almost apologetically, "This was a group effort, and thank you. I don't wish to hog the spotlight, but I'll sing several verses of another short-haul shanty, 'Haul on the Bowline.'" Soon we were singing.

Haul on the bowline
The bonny ship's a rollin'
Haul on the bowline
The bowline haul

After the singing I mentioned, "This is one of the oldest of the short-haul shanties; it goes back to Henry VIII. After 1800 the bowline was no longer important in working a ship, but it remained to serve in the hauling of other lines."

At the conclusion of my performance, I felt a sense of pride and relief, knowing that in a small way I had taken charge and interacted successfully with others. For the first time I was no longer a passive vessel for my parents' whims, taking orders, but was taking initiative and making things happen. It was a good feeling. My growing self-acceptance was positively reinforced when my commanding officer came up to me afterward and cheerfully exclaimed, "Congratulations. You did a great job singing that shanty and getting everyone involved. That was a great artistic contribution, especially as most people today know nothing about those songs. I know that you have a reputation for playing the clown, but you've shown that you've matured."

Later that evening several seamen and an officer confided that singing those shanties was great fun and asked me where one could hear them sung. I replied, "I'm sort of new to this, but there are records of sea songs, sung by Omar Blondahl, Paul Clayton, Ewan MacColl, and A. L. (Bert) Lloyd, and books on sea shanties with words, music, and a written introduction to the songs. One such book is by Joanna Colcord."

* * *

Another episode that foreshadowed my later life occurred on a weekend pass, when John Phillibert introduced me to two bohemian right-wing intellectuals, one of whom was John Kasper, who ran the Cadmus bookstore in Georgetown. They took me to meet Ezra Pound, then a decade into his commitment at St. Elizabeth's Hospital. I didn't yet know that Pound was a Fascist sympathizer, but I recall his being amused when I told him that my mother didn't like Hitler because he had a lower-middle-class Austrian accent. Pound commented that the privileged and the poor alike have their folklore—a theme that underlies my life's journey. He urged me to write and document the myths, rituals, culture, and way of life of the people I came from.

* * *

In the second year of my tour of duty, the *Canberra* went on a two-week cruise to Cuba; there we anchored off Guantanamo Bay, "Gitmo." The day after our arrival the port side of the ship had liberty to go ashore, where naval personnel went to pubs and houses of ill repute, with the more enlightened ones going for a walk, taking pictures, and taking a tour to see the historic sites or go to a museum. Early the next morning, when liberty was over, I recall seeing several of the sailors straggling up the gangplank, drunk to the gills, in various stages of sartorial disrepair, as they had lost their uniforms and were half naked in their skivvies. I saw some of them being escorted to the brig to sleep it off.

While we were in Cuba, President Batista, amidst fanfare, came aboard the *Canberra*. All of us present stood at attention and saluted him. Later that afternoon, after the president and his entourage left, some sailors took target practice on a group of sharks in the water below. Seeing the water turn red with their blood, I found the idea of shooting living creatures, predators or not, an unappetizing one.

The only time I felt the living presence of death was while standing my life buoy watch one cold late afternoon. Feeling the chill seeping through my pea jacket, the spray of wind, and the drizzle of rain, I heard the captain's voice on the loudspeaker: "All hands on deck—man overboard." A sailor from a neighboring division, while on watch, had lost his balance and fallen overboard. Despite our turning around to look for him, he was never found and was presumed to have drowned. Later that evening the chaplain had a memorial service for the drowned man. Listening to his voice and observing the grim and haggard faces of those present, I felt that I was in the company of death. I momentarily thought of my old nurse, Miss Searles, and my ride in the Coast Guard wagon on that violent night of the 1938 hurricane. Listening to the chaplain, I vowed that when I next stood watch I'd cheat death by being on my guard and taking care to avoid a similar fate, a watery grave.

Though not religious, never having given God either a second thought or the time of day despite years of compulsory attendance in chapel at boarding school and at camp, not to mention dutifully kneeling by my bed murmuring my prayers under the supervision of my governess, after the tragic loss of my shipmate, I asked God to rest the souls of that sailor and Miss Searles, my nurse, and gave thanks that I was still alive.

⇟ Chapter 25 ⇞

The Giggle Bin

A few years after my discharge from the Navy, living among fellow free spirits around Harvard Square, I was feeling confused and still searching for an identity. The Hayes Bickford restaurant, located at the corner of Massachusetts Avenue and Holyoke Street, had become a hangout for students, assorted beatniks, folk musicians and their entourages, and the police who watched over all of the above. One day I borrowed a friend's motorbike, brought it just inside the door of the Hayes-Bick, as it was called, and turned on the engine—truly a grand entrance. The running engine caused the dishes to shake. Sitting in a corner near the front window were friends of mine, including Chris Thompson, who welcomed me with a song, sung to the tune of "St. James Infirmary":

It was down in old Hayes Bickford
On the corner by the square
Where the usual bunch of hippies
Came to see if Pete Johnson was there

Flattered at being mentioned in the song and remembering that the Hayes Bickford manager would ask me and my friends to leave because we were drinking coffee without ordering food, I broke into a song myself:

This is not a meeting place
Quicken now your eating pace
Buy our eggs, buy our meat
Quickly vacate every seat

No sooner had I finished my ditty than two policemen showed up, escorted me to their car, and drove to the police station in Central Square. The chief of police arranged for me to see the resident police psychologist the following week. At the appointed time, I showed up at the police station with a live frog and mouse that a friend kept as pets. I put them on a nearby table, where the frog made frog noises (chugarum chugarum) and Miss Mouse just sat there and wiggled her ears for everyone's benefit. In my mind, I was singing, "Oh, Mister Frog went a' courting and he did ride; he went up to Miss Mouse's door, where he had been many times before."

Several police officers, privy to this nonsense, stared at me with their eyes bulging like teacups in saucers. One of them volunteered, in a thick Boston accent, "Peter Johnson, very nice family, but soft as a grape. He ain't operatin' with a full deck. Honest to gawd, he needs help."

The chief of police, realizing he was in over his head and eager to get rid of me and get back to normal business, made an appointment for me to see a social worker who lived across Fayette Street from Old Joe Clark, a folk music commune. Several days later, I showed up at the home office of the social worker, who, interestingly, turned out to be Mrs. Phillips, mother of Sam Phillips, a classmate of mine at the Brooks School. Mrs. Phillips and I had a nice chat. She made an appointment for me to return the following week.

As I was leaving her house, I noticed a lovely garden with a bed of red roses. God knows what got into me, but I started to pee on the roses. While performing my salutary ablutions, I sang a verse of a song about a rose: "Red is the rose and yonder garden grows. Red is the rose in the valley. . . "

Forgetting the rest of the song, I sang part of another: "Green grows the laurel and red blooms the rose. The dark birds will follow whenever she goes." I was just getting wound up when Mrs. Phillips came over to me, saying that this was my way of asking for help, so she was taking me to McLean Hospital. We then drove to my apartment, where I picked up some clothes, and she drove me to the hospital.

After I filled out all the required forms, I was taken to my dormitory, North Belknap. Later that afternoon, I noticed a young woman eating an ice cream cone. Some fellow came over to her, grabbed her cone, and crammed the whole thing into his mouth, where it got stuck. Fortunately, one of the orderlies standing nearby came over to help the fellow extricate the cone. Shortly after that, another inmate took off his clothes and ran around naked. Sadly, I didn't have my camera, as a picture is worth a thousand words.

Several days later, I participated in my first group therapy session. The psychiatrist suggested that we patients talk about ourselves so that we could get to know one another. I recall one fellow mentioning that his family didn't know what to do with him but didn't want him at home, so they put him in McLean for safe-keeping. When it was my turn to speak, I said there are some things that we can't say but can only sing, as I proceeded to do:

Here we go to the giggle bin
Here we go to the giggle bin
To be a little looney is no sin
Giggle bin

The words I made up, while the tune was taken from a song I heard Jean Ritchie sing. The psychiatrist, amused by my performance, proclaimed, "Peter, you missed your calling; you would be a great musical therapist."

My doctor at McLean seemed nice enough. In our one-on-one sessions, I told him about my childhood; my father's laughing lessons, which I think he thought funny; boarding school; the Navy; and everything else up to the present. I told him that playing pranks was a way of letting off steam, a way of surviving. I surmised, "I guess it's a little like creating a work of art. It's certainly healthier than having no escape valve and bopping someone over the head." Appearing to agree with me that I had had an unusual upbringing, he asked me to describe some of the offbeat things I had done over the years.

Relishing the prospect of hearing my own voice, I told him about a small-scale reprise of my caper in our nation's capital. "A few years ago, several friends and I decided it would be a kick to play a prank in Harvard Square at Christmastime. This was around 1958. As usual, I ended up being the sacrificial goat holding the bag. The incident began when my friends presented me with a Santa Claus costume; they all had rubber masks." At the mention of the word "costume," my therapist started scribbling on his pad. "The costume and the whiskers didn't fit all that well, but then they weren't custom-made at Savile Row. Anyway, I made my way to Harvard Square with my begging cups, standing outside the Harvard Coop, initially feeling a bit silly, and proceeded to collect bits of change that people threw in. I confess that I actually began to feel quite important as passersby began throwing in change. Several people put in dollar bills."

"You mentioned feeling important," the doctor noted. "That's important to you, isn't it?"

"Yes, I suppose it is. My family certainly didn't feel I was important. Anyway, I forgot to tell you that I was collecting money for little lost wayfarers who had no place to go."

"Lost wayfarers," he said. "Do you feel like you're a lost wayfarer?"

I nodded in the affirmative and continued. "About half an hour after I arrived in Harvard Square, my friends showed up, wearing their masks. My friends pulled out their pistols, which contained blanks. They came up to me and demanded that I give them all the money I had collected. Staying in character, I put up a gallant defense and told them they should be ashamed of themselves, as the money was going to the little lost wayfarers. Needless to say, my friends, disguised as robbers, didn't buy any of that charity stuff. They pointed their pistols at me, which made me a little nervous. One of them said, 'We need the money for booze, to get drunk.' By this time a small crowd had gathered and was standing at a respectful distance. My friends, satisfied with the size of their audience and not wishing to lose the crowd's interest, fired their pistols in the air. People were yelling, 'Don't be a hero; give them the money.' To tell the truth, I was not only nervous but was getting a bit scared as everything was getting out of hand. I even felt embarrassed being the center of attention."

"Attention, that's something you never got," noted the therapist. Again, I nodded. "This was street theatre at its best. People were willingly suspended in disbelief, but don't worry yourself; I'm alive to tell the tale. I wasn't about to let myself become a martyr and get shot by blanks. That would have been anticlimactic. Feigning moral indignation, I handed over my money. My friends, the robbers, then politely thanked me and walked away. I even replied, 'You're welcome.'"

I stole a peek at the doctor, still busily writing away, and realized I enjoyed keeping him in suspense. I continued my story. "This was not the end. Just the end of Act I. There's more to come. A good actor has to be prepared for the unforeseen; he's got to ad lib, wing it, and end up standing on his feet. You see, a policeman, not part of the script, came along. Hearing the commotion and seeing my friends make their getaway, he yelled at them to stop. They started running. The policeman then pulled out his revolver, a Smith and Wesson .38, and fired several warning shots over their heads, at which point they dropped to the ground, pulled out their .45 automatics—Army issue—and fired off a salvo of blanks at the policeman."

The doctor paused, looked at me quizzically, shook his head, and scribbled furiously on his pad.

"The whole thing happened so quickly," I continued. "The poor policeman, probably believing that their bullets were real, and not anticipating a gun battle in the middle of Harvard Square, yelled, 'Get down, everybody, get down.' With visions of being hauled to the police station for questioning, I quickly disappeared, went back to my apartment, and hid my Santa Claus uniform. About forty-five minutes later my friends showed up without, needless to say, their guns or masks. We went out, bought some beer, and gave all of the money, eighteen dollars or so, to a real Santa Claus who was collecting money for poor children."

The doctor, reviewing all I had told him, saw that my prank expressed unconscious resentment and hostility toward authority figures. He pointed out that as a little boy, fearful and resentful of my parents and unable to stand up to them, I had resorted to indirect ways of getting back at them and at all authority. In his words, I was engaging in a "rear-guard action, guerilla warfare."

"In some way," he speculated, "you are still that little boy. It's interesting to see how the success of your prank depended on a form of deception. Perhaps you're protecting or hiding something."

"Who knows why I do all these crazy things? Maybe it's as you say, letting off steam, sort of a sigh of relief. Perhaps it's my way of bringing order into my life, bringing body and soul back together by harmonizing all of those crazy contradictions, making sense out of things."

The doctor pointed out, "You have a keen intellectual grasp of your behavior, but the intellect, the conscious mind, is a defense against confronting your emotions." I understood him to be saying that the intellect provides a way of distancing oneself from a problem. He did have some interesting things to say about my mischievous and frolicsome ways, including seeing a pattern in the element of disguise. By assuming a persona, I could avoid taking responsibility for my actions; masking aggression was an indirect way of attacking authority figures.

"Tell me," he said, "do you have any like-minded friends, of a similar cast of mind, partners in crime, or is it just you?" Not wishing to disappoint him and enjoying my role as raconteur, I continued. "Well, now that you mention it, there's my good friend Freddy Lawrence." I explained that Freddy, cut from the same fabric, pleasantly outgoing, possessed a sense of humor ranging from high wit to low farce, which enabled people to see the light side of otherwise unpleasant situations. Both of us had gone to Bar

Harbor each summer and had suffered the rigors of discipline at Dexter School.

"Just the other day," I continued, speaking of Freddy, "he called and told me that the Playboy Club in Boston was interviewing women trying out to be bunnies. Freddy suggested that we go there disguised as reporters to interview some of the women. We did so, and I was amazed at the great variety of the fair sex. Spaced-out hippie girls, respectable-looking secretary types, divorcées, grandmothers, dreamy-eyed housewives—young, old, fat, thin, you name it. They were all there. Freddy did most of the talking. I just watched in astonishment. Maybe I was worried that I'd say the wrong thing and arouse suspicion. I got a big kick out of watching Freddy. He has the ability to empathize with those whom he's hoodwinking. What the heck. The women enjoyed it. He made them feel important, and we all had a good time."

With ten minutes left in our session, I quickly recounted another Freddy story to illustrate our brand of humor. "One time at a party, I introduced Freddy to this rather stuffy Englishman who started reminiscing about the good old days at Oxford. Freddy, playing right along, egged the fellow on, pretending that he too had gone to Oxford. Freddy, a master of accents, was very convincing. Putting on a posh upper-class accent, he had the fellow eating out of his hand. It was hilarious listening to those two go at it. You'd have to see and hear them to appreciate it. They were both smoking pipes and appeared oblivious to everything except the hallowed memories of their former existence as students to the manner born.

"About an hour later, Freddy's voice started to change. His accent had degenerated into that of a lower-class Cockney. Realizing that he had been had, the poor Englishman stepped back, looked at Freddy in horror, and told our hostess, 'This man's an imposter.' Well, I couldn't resist. Wanting to get in on the tail end of the action, I told the Englishman that it's rude to point fingers. 'It simply isn't done, very bad form,' I said in a stultifying tone. I also reminded him that gentlemen don't raise their voices. The poor man turned beet red. He was mortified."

The doctor, on a positive note, mentioned that my father's laughing lessons ironically had enabled me to reclaim my own humor. Hearing that, I realized how a good joke or funny situation puts me in touch with myself. I don't know how to explain it, but something that's funny has the effect of righting a wrong. People who are oppressed often tell jokes about their captors. It helps level the playing field. Physiologically, humor is understood to lower one's blood pressure and maintain one's homeostatic balance. The doctor, half humorously, asked me whether I intended to give people laughing lessons. "Sure," I replied. "I tell them lots of jokes."

At a later meeting, the therapist suggested that I might get involved in some communal activity at McLean. He suggested the theatre and mentioned John Hall, a director who helped patients put on plays. Whether from lack of interest or lack of self-confidence, I didn't follow his advice. Little did I know that several years down the road I'd be acting in plays at the Loeb Theater in Cambridge and even getting on TV. I told him, "I know this sounds pretentious and juvenile, but you know how I am with authority. In the first place, I might not agree with a playwright's concept of what's funny or sad. I don't like being told what to do by a director, or playing second fiddle to other actors—I'm not disciplined enough. I like street theatre or just being in funny situations where I call the shots. I can be the playwright, director, actor, critic, and choreographer, all in one. I can create, destroy, re-create, break the rules, and make new rules, all as I go along. I can pick and choose my audience and then, only then, am I truly alive."

My doctor, sounding intrigued, asked me to tell him about my last humorous, heroic adventure. I replied, "Not heroic, perhaps mock heroic. Someone had stolen a very precious art object—something like an amulet—from the Museum of Fine Arts in Boston. Freddy Lawrence and I decided to get constructively involved. Freddy and I drew maps of the Fenway, where, in our version of the robbery, those who stole the artifact had buried it. The map we created was wonderful looking; Freddy even spilt a little wine and candle wax on it to make it appear authentic. We waited for a few days until the weather was right—after all, appearances are important! On a rainy night when foghorns could be heard in the distance, Freddy and I got our shovels, picks, and a lantern and headed out for the Fenway. When we got there we found the area guarded by policemen in the aftermath of the robbery. That didn't stop us. You see, Freddy and I were presenting ourselves not as fortune hunters, but as archeologists dedicated to finding lost treasures and restoring them to their rightful owners.

"Pretending to be confused by the directions on the map, Freddy and I started arguing loudly as to where we should start digging. Well, the police who were guarding the premises came over and asked us whether we were looking for anything. We told them that we had a map showing where the lost treasure could be found. It was a beautiful map, but the directions didn't make much sense. They consisted of commands like 'go over to a stump near a brook, get blindfolded, count backward from five to one, make a 180° turn, take six steps forward, get down on your knees, stand on your head, point to the right, and then after a few more oddball things, you end up in the stream.' The funniest part was when one of the policemen tried to follow the directions and actually debated whether he should put on the blindfold.

"While the police were trying to sort this out, Freddy yelled loudly, 'I think the directions say that I've got to climb this tree.'" To demonstrate this for my therapist, I ran over to the corner of the room, knocking over a small table, and climbed on one of the empty chairs. "Now Freddy is sitting in one of the branches and starts peering out like he's looking for something," I explained. "The police ran over to the tree and told Freddy to stop making a fool of himself, but in reality all of us were making fools of ourselves. I ran and jumped into the stream, all the while yelling, 'I'll find it, I think it's in the water.'"

I went on to explain that the police, not amused by our little performance and feeling embarrassed for being played for fools, lectured Freddy and me sternly for wasting their valuable time. Freddy and I knew they would never arrest us as they had participated in our charade. "That's what good street theatre does; it gets everyone involved," I added.

"Incredible," said the doctor, "but if I may offer a suggestion, perhaps in the future you should learn how to control your material and not let the material get out of hand and control you. It's safer that way."

"No, no, no!" I exclaimed. "You're missing the point. In street theatre, or in any creative interaction between people, there are no rules that are rigidly followed; otherwise things would be too predictable and confining. Sometimes we have to go out on a limb and take chances, so the spirit can travel far and wide, soar like the lark in the morning and then return to its nest contented, knowing that it is the master of its destiny. That's a tall order. All of those crazy capers and zany pranks, Freddy and I don't plan those things beforehand. We're not following a script; we merely respond to a given situation, like the stolen artifact in the Fenway, and we interact with it, embrace the absurd, and give people an unforgettable experience."

"And what do you hope to get out of this for yourself?" he inquired.

"Nothing, really. Just having a good time," I remarked.

* * *

I spent a few months at McLean, but after attending nonproductive therapy sessions and several art workshops learning how to make wreaths and do calligraphy, I didn't want to become addicted to therapy. So, I ran away and never looked back. Nonetheless, I had several encounters at McLean that pointed toward my life to come. It was there that I met Lonnie Marquand, who lent me his father J. P. Marquand's book *The Late George Apley*, a novel of manners in the tradition of Howells, James, and Wharton. Reading it, I felt as if I were reentering my family's world, although the Apley family lived at a time when there still was an upper class that actively maintained the values and customs that my family mindlessly perpetuated.

While browsing in the hospital library I came across Cecil Sharp's book of English, Irish, and Scottish songs as sung in the southern Appalachian Mountains. I "borrowed" it, and I still have it and still sing the songs. At McLean, I sang some of those songs in therapy sessions when I found it too difficult to talk about deeply repressed feelings.

Finally, among my fellow patients was the poet Robert Lowell, who took me under his wing. By advising me to write about my experiences, he helped me turn the pain and confusion of my childhood into something positive and creative.

Peter's mother.

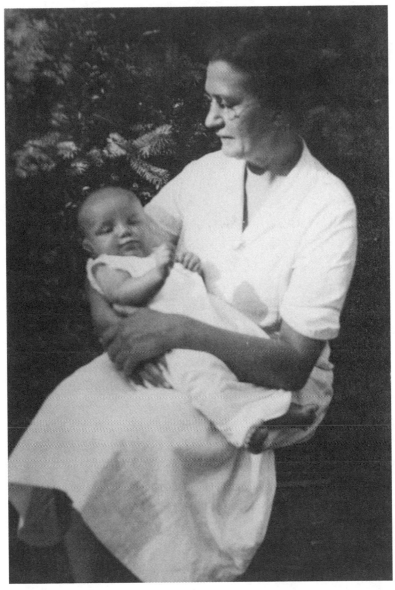

Myself as an infant with Miss Searles, my nanny. (Family collection.)

My mother, Lilias Johnson, at Ridgemere. (Family collection.)

Lt. Commander Pierrepont Johnson, Sr., in his US Navy uniform. (Family collection.)

My mother with a young me. (Photograph by Pierrepont Johnson, Sr.)

My mother with me, in sailor suit, in my tender years.
(Photograph by Pierrepont Johnson, Sr.)

My mother, in a frivolous mood, and me standing with our car,
"Cadwalader," in front of Ridgemere.

Baroness Olga Von Gillming, my maternal grandmother.
(Family collection.)

Pierrepont Johnson, Sr., in his navy whites, and his young son (me).
(Author's photo archive.)

Pierrepont Johnson, Sr., and the stunning Lilias Johnson, cocktail hour at
Ridgemere. (Author's photo archive.)

The Flying Cloud, my father's fifty-eight-foot yawl, moored near Eastcote, Maine. (Photograph by Pierrepont Johnson, Sr.)

Seaman Apprentice Peter Johnson 466-73-92 and his mother, 1957. (Photograph by Pierrepont Johnson, Sr.)

Painting of Ridgemere. (Family collection.)

Evelyn Pierrepont, the Duke of Kingston, my father's maternal ancestor.

Portrait of my mother's grandmother, Lilias White Sanford.
Painting by George Kingston.

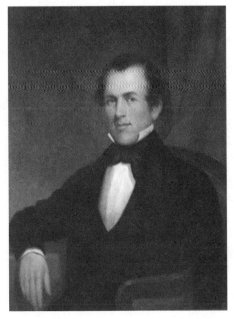

William Payne Sheffield, my mother's grandfather. Painting by George
Kingston.

PETER JOHNSON

SUIT SIZE 39L HEIGHT 6' SHIRT 15½ SLEEVE 34 WAIST 3‹
INSEAM 31½ SHOES 9½D HAIR BROWN EYES BLUE

My modeling card, with me dressed as a cowboy, working for the
Ford Modeling Agency, in Boston.

THE FORD MODEL SHOPPE   176 NEWBURY STREET BOSTON, MA 02116   617-266-6939

Poses from my days at the Ford Modeling Agency during the
turbulent '60s.

Evidence of my stint as the WBZ Turkey Man, a job which I got fired from for messing around with a farmer's bull. This photograph is by Bishop Frederic C. Lawrence, who also presided at Lorna's and my wedding.

Left to right: Michael Coughlin, Living Folk recording engineer; Howard Glasser, producer; and me.

One of Living Folk's many compilation albums, featuring fiddler Allan Block and other regular stars of the New England folk scene: John Schwab, Claudio Buchwald, Nancy McDowell, Dick Fegy, Lorraine Lee, Andy May.

LP cover for *Trouble in Mind*, a Barbara Carns album so poignant we decided to list the title twice!

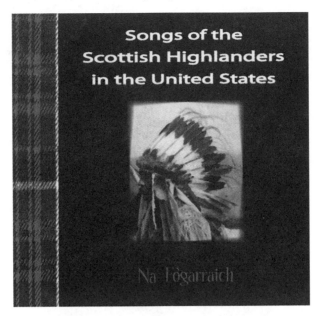

Songs of the Scottish Highlanders in the United States, produced by
Living Folk.

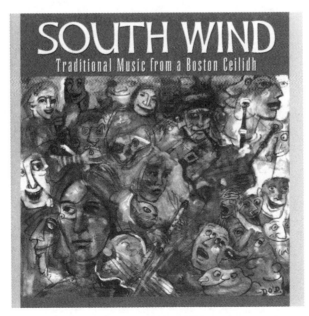

Album cover for *South Wind: Traditional Music from a Boston Ceilidh*,
produced by Living Folk. Cover art painting by David O'Dockerty.

Newport's Fair Town: Traditional Songs and Ballads from North America,
sung by yours truly, with friends, produced by Living Folk. Photograph by
Lorna Johnson at the Newport Folk Festival, at Fort Adams.

Thank You For The Music, the first CD (as opposed to LP) produced by
Living Folk. The recording was from a benefit concert I produced for the
Belmont Education Foundation.

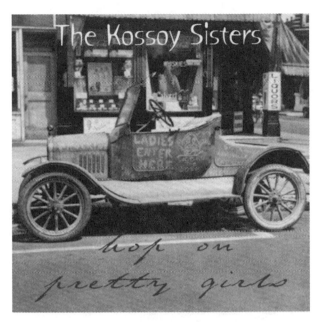

Cover for the Kossoy Sisters album *Hop on Pretty Girls*, produced by Living Folk.

CD case cover for *I Long to Hear You*, an album of instrumental American music, produced by Living Folk.

Margaret Barry, Queen of the Tinkers, singing "She Moves Through the Fair," at an outdoor fair in Ireland.

Norman Kennedy, a traditional singer, storyteller, and weaver originally from Aberdeen, Scotland.

Amy and Bill Lyons (with guitar), Jack Parmley, and Garcia.

My great chance to sing with Ramblin' Jack Elliott at a benefit for the Newport Folk and Jazz Foundation, at Rosecliff Mansion, Newport, RI. Rosscliff was the setting for the 1974 filming of *The Great Gatsby*. (Photograph by Lorna Johnson.)

Enjoying an opportunity to sing with Peggy Seeger at a benefit to raise money for the Eastern Service Workers Association (ESWA), Brighton, MA. (Photograph by Lorna Johnson.)

Hazel Dickens performing. (photo © Susan Wilson)

Jean Redpath, 1987. (photo © Susan Wilson)

Lisa Neustadt and Angel Band. (photo © Susan Wilson)

Lorraine Lee, 1989. (photo © Susan Wilson)

Betsy Siggins, 1999. (photo © Susan Wilson)

The Donlins, 1984. (photo © Susan Wilson)

Show flyer by artist Bob Doucet.

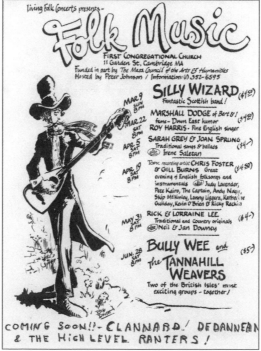

Show flyers.

Show flyers.

Show flyers.

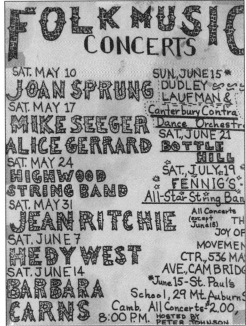

Show flyers. Top poster, logo artist, Gillian Charters

Show flyers.

Show flyers.

Our wedding at Peggy and Daniel Boone Schirmer's backyard, 1986.
(Photograph by Ava Kabouchy.)

Left to right: William Alfred, professor and playwright; Phebe Porras; Lilias
Johnson; Bishop Frederic Lawrence; Lorna Johnson; and Soledad Porras,
Lorna's mother; at the Johnsons' wedding in 1986.

Lorna's father, Marcelo Porras, in his dapper youth.

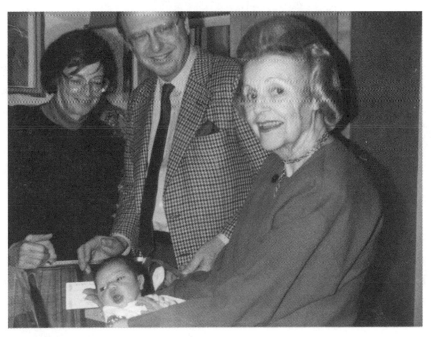

My mother with a five-day-old PJ. Lillie and Ned Johnson (a cousin) in the background. (Photograph by Lorna Johnson.)

An infant PJ, my mother, and me, at Ridgemere. (Photograph by Lorna Johnson.)

Lorna and my mother, Easter luncheon, 1998, the Ritz, Boston. (Photograph by Peter Johnson.)

PJ and me. (Photograph by Lorna Johnson.)

Lorna, PJ, and me at a clambake, Bailey's Beach, Newport.

Susan Keats, the Johnson archivist; Peggy and Daniel Boone Schirmer, PJ's godparents; and Carlos Rabito, at one of many parties. (Photograph by Lorna Johnson.)

Edgar Porras (Lorna's brother, in the background) with PJ and me at the Porras's home in Seattle. (Photograph by Lorna Johnson.)

A candid shot of me on the ferry to Whidbey Island, Puget Sound, WA, 1990s. (Photograph by Lorna Johnson.)

A more recent image of myself in front of the Ridgemere estate, Newport, RI. (Photograph by Lorna Johnson.)

My eightieth birthday, celebrating with Brian and Lindsey O'Donovan, producers and performers on *A Celtic Sojourn*; PJ; and Andy Hanley, the violinist at Lorna's and my wedding. (Photograph by Lorna Johnson.)

Halloween with the little monsters in front of my current home. (Photograph by Lorna Johnson.)

In repose in my bedroom, surrounded by memories and albums produced by Living Folk. (Photograph by Kate Crichton.)

Bailey's Beach Opening, May 25, 2019, my 84th birthday. Cannon by Paul Revere. (Photograph by Lorna Johnson.)

Cambridge Peace and Justice Award given to Lorna in 1998.

Chapter 26

To Brattleboro and Back

Not long after having left McLean, I became an invited "guest" at the Brattleboro Retreat in Brattleboro, Vermont. There I recall telling Dr. (or Mrs., as she was known) Boardman, my psychiatrist, how it was easier to run away from the different sides of myself than to face them, especially as doing the latter was painful. I described the different forms my escape took: playing pranks; fantasizing; poking fun at things, including myself; telling jokes and funny stories; and, on occasion, pretending to be someone else. Dr. Boardman replied, "It must be exhausting for you."

While at the Retreat, I had the good fortune to hear Margaret MacArthur, a folksinger who on occasion generously shared her songs, accompanied by her dulcimer, with the staff and residents. One of her songs, a version of "Jenny Jenkins," I learned partly for its catchy tune in a minor key, rollicking rhythm, and the last verse.

Oh will you wear the blue
O Rare-O, Rare-O,
Will you wear the blue, Jenny Jenkins
Oh I will wear the blue
It's the color that is true
So buy me a tally-Walley, I, sir.

I had long had a special fondness for the color blue, ever since girls told me they liked the color of my eyes. For me, the repetition of melody and rhyme in "Jenny Jenkins" reaffirmed an undying belief in the death and rebirth of the seasons, night and day, and living things coming into and out of existence.

After spending several months at the Retreat, I realized that my presence there was not doing anything for my well-being. Eventually, I was awarded ground and town privileges and was allowed to come and go as I pleased. After going to town one hot July morning, I hitchhiked several rides to the Putney School, where I looked up my old friend, Ian Laskaris, a teacher who was a former schoolmate from Brooks School. He told me that he was teaching dramatics and enjoying it.

Late in the afternoon, I decided to leave the Putney School and continue my trip. With no destination in mind, I was simply enjoying my outing. While walking along the side of the road, with not a care on my mind, I was picked up by the police, whom the Brattleboro Retreat had notified of my disappearance.

Thus caught, I vowed that next time I left I wouldn't proceed in such a footloose and fancy-free fashion, but rather would have a well thought out game plan. Again incarcerated and serving my time of penance with privileges taken away, I had to regain the trust of my keepers through heroic acts of omission, namely staying out of trouble.

Shortly after my aborted attempt to roam the countryside, my mother paid me a visit. All I remember of our conversation is her complimenting my appearance: "Oh, darling, aren't you cunning in your blue shirt?"

While at the Retreat, I was befriended by a gentleman perhaps fifteen years my senior who had worked as a train engineer. Prior to his discharge from the hospital, he told me that if I could make it to the train yards where he worked, he would see to it that I got on a train to Boston. Several months after his departure, I was once again given town privileges. Having received permission to go into town on the pretext of going shopping, with ten dollars in my pocket, I hitchhiked to the train yards and there met my friend. He got me a berth in a coal car bound for Boston. I arrived early in the evening, covered with soot and exhausted. Looking like a vagrant on the run, I was approached by a policeman who asked me for identification. Feigning moral outrage and producing a ten-dollar bill, I sternly asked him, "Look here, my good fellow. Can't you tell a king in beggar's clothing?" Shaking his head, he let me go, and I found my way back to my apartment in Cambridge.

I then changed into some old clothes and decided to celebrate my return to the land of the living by going to Bartley's Burger Cottage (still going strong half a century later). The owners, Mr. and Mrs. Bartley, appeared to have an amused tolerance of me, which was sufficient to recommend their restaurant. Sitting next to me was an acquaintance from pre-McLean days, Tim Buckley (not the singer-songwriter of that name), an undergraduate at Harvard. I told him about my experiences in the various giggle bins, to which he replied, referring to psychiatry, "Every age gets the religion it deserves." Hearing that cynical comment, I wondered what had I done to deserve my subjection to all those dreary therapy sessions.

* * *

My exposure to apartment living had begun in the late 1950s after I was discharged from the Navy and moved to Cambridge, where I took a one-room apartment on Bow Street, later moving to 65 Mt. Auburn Street, around the corner from Elsie's Restaurant. My parents, by then reconciled to my unsuitability for the role of master of Ridgemere, paid my rent and gave me a little money for food, public transportation, and other necessities. Self-exiled from their world, I nonetheless maintained a split identity expressed by my wardrobe, or wardrobes. Along with my hippie clothes—torn dungarees and sandals made in Greenwich Village—I kept a set of preppie, clubby clothes, complete with wingtip shoes, loafers, and stockings with garters, purchased at places like the Andover Shop and Brooks Brothers. I kept these contrasting outfits to please everyone, or perhaps no one, in that I sometimes wore a mishmash of both styles, making myself neither fish nor fowl, but a true outcast.

Not that this existential dilemma kept me from having fun.

Once when I was hosting a party with the roommates I lived with at the time, an attractive woman in her twenties knocked on our door and asked whether any of us were interested in her church literature. She was one of these Pentecostal-evangelical types, perhaps Baptist or Seventh Day Adventist. We invited her in, served her some wine, and before you knew it, she was down to her underwear playing strip poker with the lads. Instead of converting us poor heathens, she was converted to the Cambridge lifestyle.

Another domestic escapade involved three musicians recently arrived from Dublin—Declan Hunt, Johnny Beggan, and Seamus Walker—about whom I will have more tales in later chapters. While these lads were being interviewed on Jim Parry's radio show on WBCN, Seamus announced that since they couldn't get an extension on their visas to stay in this country, their only alternative was to find some American girls who would marry them. The lads put out an all-points bulletin, a grand plea for wives, promising their prospective spouses a good time. Declan addressed the entire female population of the Boston area, telling them that potential wives would be interviewed by Peter Johnson at his apartment at 65 Mt. Auburn Street.

After the radio appearance we all returned to my place, and before I could leave to escape the situation the doorbell rang. Every ten minutes or so it rang again, and we were besieged by women, young and old, who in a spirit of adventure, philanthropy, boredom, or curiosity offered themselves like the fattened calf to the call of matrimony. Finding myself surrounded, and realizing that there was a disproportionate number of girls to be interviewed, I sent out an SOS to several friends—Freddy Lawrence, Peter O'Malley, and Dick McHugh—to help judge the contenders. As the crowd thinned, I found myself engaged in pleasant conversation with an attractive woman in her early thirties. All of a sudden, completely out of context, she told me that I was a nice, attractive person and then asked whether I'd be interested in marrying her. I replied that I was extremely flattered and that I'd enjoy cultivating her friendship, but made clear that marriage, at least for the time being, was out of the question.

* * *

At some point, I moved into an apartment complex called Quaker Village. The owners, Mr. and Mrs. Ward, and the manager, Henry McMann, were pleasantly disposed toward their tenants and would even invite us in for late-afternoon tea. At Quaker Village, I not only readily made friends, but also made serious attempts to acquire some basic skills of survival, not the least of which was cooking.

Feeling ill-equipped to fend for myself, I rarely attempted to cook anything more complicated than a fried egg or hamburger. Instead, I invariably took my meals at local restaurants such as Elsie's, Bartley's, Tommy's Lunch, and the Hong Kong. One night several of my friends in Quaker Village—Anita Hider, Timmy Wilson, and Harry Rudlow—invited me over for dinner, and under their benign supervision I learned how to cook a fish. I remember putting a blue mackerel in tin foil, placing it in a pan, and then, at their suggestion, seasoning it with Dijon mustard, French herbs, and lemon. My friends showed me how to cut up the vegetables, carrots and asparagus, which were added to the fish. Setting the oven at about 350°, I nervously waited twenty minutes to see what would emerge. To my amazement and delight, the dinner turned out splendidly and was enjoyed by all. After dinner my friends served champagne and toasted me for a "first."

The nerve-wracking experience of preparing and cooking a meal was a rite of passage initiating me into the adult world. The next evening, having dinner alone and wishing to confirm that my success with the fish was no fluke, I cooked myself another mackerel. To my satisfaction it turned out quite well. This small feat felt more satisfying than earlier social accomplishments at boarding school, such as tying a bow tie or doing the Charleston, which had had more to do with pleasing others.

* * *

Several weeks after my escape from Brattleboro, the Retreat sent me my clothes. Still of two minds about who I was and what I wanted to do in life, I decided to broaden and deepen my perspective by taking courses on the GI Bill at Boston University's College of Liberal Arts. Courses in the history of Western philosophy, American literature, and cultural anthropology introduced me to writers and scholars ranging from Plato to Henry James and Edith Wharton to Margaret Mead, Ruth Benedict, and David Riesman. The readings and discussions gave me a foundation for engaging with the many cultural traditions to which I would be exposed in folk music, not to mention my parents' dying tradition and the chaotic yet invigorating cultural change of my own time.

That fall, I took a roommate, David Barry, an undergraduate from Harvard. David was gifted musically; he played the guitar and sang traditional American folk songs. At first he didn't know what to make of me or my apartment. I'd serve espresso coffee with Irish whiskey from a silver tea set that rested on an old stump of a tree, which I had rescued from the front yard. As if that weren't enough, I gathered baskets full of leaves from the yard and covered both floors of my apartment with them.

Some time later, when I was living on Grant Street, I had an opportunity to go to the theatre in New York, which I had long wanted to do, when the American Place Theatre put on *Hogan's Goat* by William Alfred, a professor in the English Department at Harvard, with Faye Dunaway in the lead role. This was a playwright's theatre, where the author was able to choose the director. Bill Alfred, who was a neighbor and friend of mine, gave me two tickets, so I drove to New York with a friend, Ilya Peet, for the opening night's performance. The play was about the political and family life of Irish immigrants, one of whom was going to be a candidate for mayor. After seeing the play and thinking about Irish immigrants in their role as outsiders, coupled with my awareness of the plight of Native Americans, I felt inspired to either write or act in a play about Native Americans, which I did a decade later when I acted in my friend John Brennan's play *Mashpee*, about the Mashpee Wampanoag Indians of Cape Cod.

Around that time, I was invited to attend a poetry reading by

Allen Ginsberg. Introduced to him by several mutual friends—Gay Sourian, Bruce Bennett, and Bob Fulton—I invited Allen and some friends in the audience to my apartment for a party. Among them was Freddy Lawrence, who brought Oakes Plimpton, brother of George Plimpton, one of the founders of the *Paris Review*. Chatting with Oakes, I found that he, unlike George, was rather easygoing. The guests also included Bill Alfred and Sheila Hoffman, estranged wife of Abbie Hoffman, who was an acquaintance of Allen's.

Also present was Edie Sedgwick, a friend of Andy Warhol's, who confided that once Andy urinated on one of his canvases, which sold for a lot of money. Freddy, hearing that, thought Warhol was merely showing his contempt for his groupies. Recalling that Renaissance critics and writers thought art should teach and please, I wondered skeptically what Warhol's art would teach and whether it was so pleasing.

Later that evening, the party picked up as a folk-singing friend, Billy Lyons, and his friend, Liam Clancy of the Clancy Brothers, made the rafters ring by singing sea shanties and getting others to join in on the chorus. I recall one such chorus:

> *Haul in the bowline*
> *The bonny ships a rollin'*
> *Haul in the bowline*
> *The bowline, Haul.*

⊰ Chapter 27 ⊱
The Newport Folk Festival

I n the early 1960s, Elaine Lorillard, a friend of my parents, knowing of my interest in folk music, suggested that I might enjoy going to the Newport Folk Festival, which she and George Wein had recently organized. Following my honorable discharge from the U.S. Navy and my move to Cambridge, I had often listened to live folk music in some of the coffeehouses in the area: Club 47, the Golden Vanity, Café Yana, Tulla's Coffee Grinder, Café Mozart, and the Sword and Stone. It was in the Boston area that I first met Tom Hall, Jingles, and Toby, who were folk musicians. Recalling Elaine's suggestion, I thought it would be fun to go to the festival, and my friends agreed. As Tom was playing elsewhere, Toby, Jingles, and I decided to go. Jingles, a large man with an abundance of dark red hair, borrowed a truck from a friend, and the three of us drove down to Newport.

As my parents were away, I thought there wouldn't be any problem with our staying at Ridgemere, my old home, which I hadn't seen in years. Driving down on a warm summer day, we sang most of the way, and before long we arrived at my parents' house. Toby and Jingles were momentarily taken aback by the sight of Ridgemere, so large and implacable in its mien. I knocked on the front door, which was promptly opened by a maid in uniform who barely recognized me. I asked her whether my friends and I could spend the night as we were going to the folk festival. In an apologetic tone, sounding almost sad, she explained, "I'm very sorry, but your parents gave explicit instructions that you are not allowed inside the home when they are not here." Not completely surprised, knowing my parents, I thanked her and asked whether we could use the facilities to get cleaned up, to which she agreed. She then invited us into the kitchen for a bite to eat, homemade Irish stew.

Finishing our meal, Toby, Jingles, and I got back in the truck and parked it at one end of the back driveway next to the house. We then made our way to the front lawn and pitched a pup tent in back of a centuries-old weeping willow tree that looked tired and rather sad. After getting ourselves squared away, we got back in the truck and drove to the festival, which was at Freebody Park, where I had learned to play tennis under the tutelage of Joe Leander. Upon our arrival, we saw many people sitting on the grass, including several friends from Cambridge. Joining them on the grass, all ears, I enjoyed hearing traditional old-time American songs sung by Doc Watson, Dock Boggs, and Almeda Riddle.

Following the concert, several of us hung around and sang some songs until we decided to call it a night and head for home. Back on the Ridgemere lawn, sitting under our tent, we told stories and sang some more, with Toby and Jingles accompanying us on banjo and guitar.

Sitting on a blanket outside the tent, I saw slices of yellow light filtering through the weeping willow tree as it sighed and wept its long sorrow. I started singing a ballad I had learned from Ian and Sylvia and Bob Gibson, "The Cruel Mother," which tells about a mother murdering her children.

> *There is a lady lived in York*
> *All-a lee and a loney*
> *She fell in love with her father's clerk*
> *Down by the greenwood sidey*
> *She leaned her back against a thorn*
> *All-a lee and a loney,*
> *And there three babes born*

Down by the greenwood sidey
She took out her own pen knife
All-a lee and a loney
And there she took their own sweet life
Down by the green wood sidey

She sees and recognizes the ghosts of her children, which leads to the last verse:

Babes, oh babes, it's heaven for you
All-a lee and a loney
Mother, oh mother, it's hell for you
Down by the green wood sidey – o

"Well sung. You love those sad songs in minor modes. I can see why," said Toby. "I've got a cheerful one—you all know it." He commenced:

It was pleasant and delightful on a bright summer's morn
Where the green field and meadow were covered in corn
Where the blackbirds and thrushes sang from every green tree
And the larks they sang melodies at the dawning of the day

Jingles and I joined in the chorus:

And the larks they sang melodious
And the larks they sang melodious
And the larks they sang melodious
At the dawning of the day

Near where we were singing and having a grand time, raising our voices to the heavens, lived Norman King, my family's gardener, in a small cottage that stood on one side of our back driveway, next to the stables and carriage house. Norman, hearing our singing and laughter and thinking we were trespassers, called the police. Soon Norman, accompanied by two policemen, made their presence known to us. Surprised at seeing me, Norman explained to the police that this was my home, which it wasn't. Before leaving, one of the policemen confided, "It's a shame you can't stay in your own house. I wish you luck." Norman then invited us to his cottage to use the facilities and have a bite to eat. He offered to let us sleep on the floor, but with his family asleep in the small dwelling, we thanked him, went back to our tent, and slept soundly beneath a starry sky. The next morning, Norman came over and invited us to come and have breakfast with him and his family. Sympathetic and mystified, they didn't understand why I wasn't allowed in my own house.

While driving back to Cambridge, Toby asked, "Isn't this like something out of the adventures of Tom Sawyer and Huck Finn?"

"That's a good question," I replied. "I know what you're thinking—our adventure of going to the festival, getting turned away from my parents' house, pitching a tent, making music, having the police come, and ending up at Norman's."

Jingles added, "Mark Twain's world in rural Hannibal is the opposite of Newport, with its large houses, servants, class distinctions, and privilege."

"Yes," I agreed, "Huck and Tom's carefree world. They played pirates, stole jam, and had a good time."

"Not so much Huck," corrected Jingles. "He was an outcast, running away from his father. Twain was a champion of democracy, hated injustice and oppression, and believed in the freedom of the individual."

"Peter, I can see why you might identify with Huck," Toby remarked. "He was an outcast running away from his father, and so were you, in your own way."

"You're right. I was on the outs literally and figuratively. One time as a teenager I returned home late from the movies and ended up sleeping on burlap bags in the stables. Another time, while visiting my grandmother at Eastcote, her summer house in Bar Harbor, I got back late from a local festival some friends and I went to (we told our parents we were going to the movies). Being locked out, I called grandma's chauffeur, Dwight Stevenson, who had a night job as a policeman. He put me up in the town jail, which was rather fun, but also sad."

I went on to tell Toby and Jingles how Dwight had made me feel at home in jail by cooking up some hamburgers with onions. He then introduced me to the middle-aged occupant of the cell adjoining mine. In need of a shave, wearing dungarees and a plaid shirt with suspenders, Jed greeted me in his down-home way: "How ya doin', Sonny? Glad to meet you. How'd you like to hear a ballad?" Surprised but delighted by the prospect of hearing a Maine fisherman sing a folk song, I blurted out my thanks.

Jed stepped out of his cell, spat his tobacco into a nearby spittoon, and said, "This here ballad I heard from my Uncle Seth when I was knee high to a grasshopper." Keeping a straight face, looking straight ahead without any sign of emotion, he sang a ballad about a sea battle between two ships with cannons. It reminded me of similar songs I had heard on Burl Ives's records: "The Golden Vanity," "Henry Martin," and "High Barbaree." His voice gravelly but on pitch, Jed gave a magical performance that touched the child in me. I clung to every word, every note, as memories of Nora singing in the kitchen flooded my brain.

"At six o'clock the next morning," I related, "Dwight woke us up and cooked us some eggs and bacon with muffins and coffee. Boy, was that good! He then drove me back to Eastcote, where I slipped in through the back door, cautioned one of Grandma's maids to keep mum, and made it up to bed with no one the wiser." Pausing, I concluded, "I think I'd have fit nicely in Mark Twain's world, especially with Huck, who was more the rebel than Tom."

"Right on," said Jingles. "Huck the outcast, Tom the all-American boy, and Jim the runaway slave are the three faces of this country."

"Huck and Tom didn't have to go to some fancy folk festival and pay money to hear what was part of their everyday life," added Toby. "They could make their own music. It was homemade, just like their instruments."

"True, they heard that music all of their life, but were just discovering it."

Toby concluded, "One good thing about the Newport Folk

Festival is that it makes people aware of the music, preserves it, keeps it alive and well, and helps the musicians as well. It's a bridge between those who make the music and those who listen to it."

This is another Newport story, I reflected. Sad, but also redeeming, because in the end I persevered. Norman and his family, the maid, the policeman, and my friends supported me, making me feel better about myself than I had. This little episode was a blessing in disguise.

⁂ Chapter 28 ⁂
Gemini

T he Hayes Bickford Restaurant was located at the corner of Massachusetts Avenue and Holyoke Street. Harvard Square's answer to anything Greenwich Village had to offer by way of zanies and eccentricity, it was a monument to whatever people wanted it to be. A meeting place for motorcycle gangs, a haven for intellectuals mulling their condition, a respite for working people on a coffee break, a crashing place for hippies seeking orientation, a Mecca for tourists who wanted to see the other half of life, and a theatre of the absurd as the attention-getting mannerisms and conversations of flamboyant artistic types never ceased to fascinate the onlooker. Both spectator and participant were fulfilled by the never-ending series of comic backroom dramas. This restaurant, infamous for the many interesting characters that assembled under its roof, was the mainstay and watering hole not only of the young, but also of the elderly, who at times seemed out of place, a curious dysfunction, lacking a frame of reference; nevertheless, they came, usually in the early hours of the morning—like one or two o'clock.

The Hayes Bickford was almost an eyesore to the outsider beholding it for the first time, a calculated offense to the eye, as there was nothing about the shape, color, or design of the building's exterior or interior that recommended it as an object of beauty. Observers may have felt deceived by their first impressions, as they saw an old tired body that covered a beautiful and expressive soul.

Ah, yes, the soul. The atmosphere of the Bickford was there for the taking by those inclined to do so. As I savored my coffee and feasted on the exotic goings-on, I discovered the essential function of this one-room restaurant in its atmosphere, created by people who, each in his or her own way, freely gave of themselves, creating sustenance for one and all.

Two of my favorite people, who frequented the restaurant almost daily, were twins—two elderly men, perhaps in their late sixties or early seventies. Had it not been for a sloppy-looking fedora jauntily perched on one of their heads, I could not have told them apart. They were short, about five-foot-six, wearing nondescript clothes, with tight-lipped, almost pugnacious expressions about their mouths. Their angular faces culminated in bellicose-looking jaws that thrust forward in seeming defiance of the outward world, to which they did not belong.

However, it was not their mode of dress or any physical characteristics that endeared the twins to my aroused imagination. It was more their mannerisms that were so remarkable. The twins, as much as any of the clientele, were creatures of habit. Their mode of entering and then leaving the restaurant was indeed interesting, if not bizarre. They would enter, wait in line to order their food, never acknowledging each other's presence, and find a place to sit down. Never once, as far as I can remember, did they sit at the same table. The brother wearing the hat sat as close to the window as possible, while the other sat closer to the counter, and never did the twins meet. Each ate his meal in isolation, never looking up, and when they were finished, perhaps through a veiled, half-hidden, intuitive signal, they got up in unison. The one sitting by the window, nearest the door, waited for his brother, and without a word or sign between them they left as they had entered, silent, incommunicado.

This scenario repeated itself day after day; not even once was the insufferable impasse between the brothers broken. Bursting with curiosity about them, I got to the point where I simply had to find out. I realized that whatever was going on or not going on between them was none of my business, but then who is to say what business is whose? My rationalizations surged as I conjured up images of all the great philosophers and scientists who made the mysteries of the universe their domain. After all, weren't these twins now part of my growing universe, which was in pressing need of an explanation? Fortified by these lofty thoughts, I realized that although I would never solve the enigmas of the universe, I could at least take an interest in what was going on around me, which in this case was just a mysterious pair of elderly twins.

Thus resolved to act, I waited until the brothers had finished their meals and, in their unmistakable fashion, had once again reenacted their primeval charade, in the manner of animals that instinctively do what they have always done. Repeating their programmed movements, they got up and left. This time I did likewise, determined to follow them. They crossed the street and, walking side by side, took a left down Massachusetts Avenue and crossed over to the subway. Their movement was almost mechanical when viewed in relation to each other, as if their every gesture, archetypical in its simplicity, was harmoniously synchronized yet mutually oblivious.

I followed at a respectful distance until we were forced into closer proximity as we boarded a subway. The subway being crowded at rush hour, I had to stand at one end of the car, positioning myself so as to keep an eagle eye on the two brothers standing together at the opposite end. I continued to observe them, waiting for one somehow to acknowledge the other. The subway passed Park Street and continued on, when all of a sudden the brothers adeptly navigated through the small crowd, exiting at the Savin Hill stop in Dorchester. I quickly followed suit, walking a safe distance behind, until they stopped at a bus stop, where almost immediately a bus appeared and they and I got on and found seats. The next ten minutes were a repetition of everything that went on before, with not one word passing between them. Finally, they got up and exited by the side door, and once more I discreetly followed them.

Having no idea where I was, I trailed the twins, who, like deaf mutes, continued on. They crossed the street, turned left, and walked for another two blocks. Taking a right turn at an intersecting street, they walked for about a block and a half and, still in perfect synchrony, crossed the street again. Scarcely had they resumed walking when one of the brothers—the one wearing the hat—suddenly entered a gateway and vanished behind the door of a house without a word of goodbye. His sibling, seemingly oblivious to his brother's departure, continued his travels alone, until a block later he quickly mounted a flight of steps and likewise disappeared into a house.

Not knowing where I was, I stood in awe of what I had witnessed. I had an eerie feeling that I was poised on the threshold of two worlds, one familiar, the other not. Desiring to return to the former, I quickly left that strange place and, getting directions from a passerby, headed for home.

To this day, no one to my knowledge has fathomed the mystery of the twins, and perhaps that's just as well. Probing the innermost recesses of human nature is perhaps like violating the sanctity of the universe's dark secrets. Some things should just be left alone.

Chapter 29

A Happy Halloween

As a child, I always considered Halloween a magical holiday. Wearing a mask was like transforming myself into another being with a totally different personality. I would feel temporarily immune to everyday cares. This sort of play-acting gave me a sense of self-importance, if only for a little while.

As I grew older, Halloween lost its fascination for me, and I came to lose touch with it. I became aware of it again as an adult living in Cambridge, when all the neighborhood children would come trick-or-treating. Until then I had remained oblivious to the rapprochement, the special relationship of adult and child coming together, that this holiday inspires once a year.

One year on Halloween my bell rang, and I was greeted by four or five kids, all in costume as witches. Feeling bad about not being able to offer them any goodies, I tried to make amends by inviting them upstairs and offering them what little cider there was. After serving them up some Pete Seeger records, I sang them a few Halloween folk songs about witches and ballads of the supernatural. Unfortunately, the cider ran out early, and the only thing left to drink was some very good blended Scotch and Irish whiskey. After I had generously treated myself to some of the whiskey, one of the children asked whether he could have a sip from my glass. Naturally I was quite reluctant to acquiesce to this request, as my guests were too young to hit the bottle. I told him that it was a bad idea, but he pleaded with me, explaining that on occasion his father and mother would allow him to taste a little under their watchful supervision. I'm not sure whether I completely believed him, but being a soft touch, I let him have a wee taste. I had mixed feelings about opening this Pandora's box, but when they all told me that this was the most fun they had had in a long time, I felt better about it.

Soon I felt that it was time for them to go home. I put away the whiskey, and reluctantly they left, thanking me for the good time. I then returned to my evening of reading and listening to records. Scarcely had I settled in my chair when my doorbell rang, and who should it be but the father of one of the little boys who had visited me. He seemed a bit perturbed that I had given one of those kids—his kid—some whiskey. What could I say?

Inviting him upstairs, I explained how bad I had felt about not having any goodies to offer the kids and reassured him that if it hadn't been Halloween, those kids wouldn't have received a drop of my prized whiskey. "Besides," I rejoined, "just think what would have happened had I not given them anything. They might have played a trick on me. Trick or treat and all that, you know."

By now pleasantly placated, he announced that he himself would have no objection to drinking some of my nefarious whiskey, a drop of the pure hard stuff, the very same malt of the earth that his son had sampled earlier in the evening. It was evident that the father had gotten nothing but a good report from his son on the quality of my whiskey. Wishing to be fully exonerated, I gave him two generous shots and made some coffee, as he had expressed interest in having Irish coffee.

He thoroughly enjoyed my offerings, and with each swallow he became more outgoing. He professed his love of Irish folk songs as we sang, "Whiskey, You're the Devil, You're Leading Me Astray," a song personifying the drink as love and affection, expressed through such lines as "The more I kissed her, the more I missed her" and "My first love is for whiskey." Our singing verged on the raucous, as we were informed by a complaining neighbor.

A few hours later, the father, realizing that it was time to leave, pulled himself together and thanked me. He confided that this was one of the best times he and his son had had in a while. I was relieved that after his departure his wife didn't also come over, demanding an explanation of why I had gotten her husband and her son drunk.

Chapter 30

On Stage at the Loeb Theatre

During the 1960s, some friends suggested that one way for me to get over childhood inhibitions would be to take a small speaking role in a play. I was terrified at the prospect of getting up on stage before a critically minded public. With no formal training, I nevertheless realized that I had several assets: I could speak the Queen's English; was a good mimic; could walk from one end of the room to the other without tripping over my feet; was reasonably attractive; could sing on key; and, most importantly, was determined to succeed.

Ironically, it was my father—notwithstanding his admonition that "one doesn't go on stage, Peter," because "actors are not looked upon kindly by polite society"—who helped bring out the actor in me. Just don't tell him! As a child, wishing to gain my father's approval, I had attempted to please him by imitating him, saying and doing the right thing at the right time in the right way. Sadly, though, a part of me realized that in acting out the role my father scripted for me, I was being untrue to myself. When I acted on the stage in Cambridge, I would not need to please anyone except the audience, the director, the cast, and—not least—myself.

To my surprise, dismay, and joy, after reading some lines of a play—the title of which escapes me—I was offered a medium-sized role. I turned it down, requesting a smaller part, as I feared that otherwise I might be in over my head. The play, written and directed by Elaine de Lott, a freshman at Radcliffe, ran for two nights at the Loeb Experimental Theatre, known as the Ex. Both nights were a success as the small audience enjoyed what they saw. To my amazement and satisfaction, several members of the audience, strangers as well as friends, came over to congratulate me.

In retrospect, I realized how important a part a director plays in the life of an actor. Elaine, realizing my nervousness, took me out for coffee and gave me an encouraging pep talk. Thanks to her and despite my father's dictum that a gentleman doesn't go on stage, I was able, as my father might also say, to "put my best foot forward." After that first acting experience, I attended lots of plays, observed actors both on and off stage, educated myself from the ground up, and witnessed the golden age of theatre in Cambridge. I made the acquaintance of some of the actors, directors, critics, and people associated with theatre. I kept my eyes and ears open and concentrated on the basics, such as familiarizing myself with stage right, stage left, upstage, downstage, center stage. I then focused on how to walk, sit down, stand, move gracefully, and project my voice. I also learned the importance of conviction, having one's role be believable to the audience. From time to time, I would attend seminars on some aspect of my craft.

Each opening night, I was slightly apprehensive at the prospect of appearing on stage before what I imagined was a critical audience. However, with the support and good will of the cast and the director, I learned to use my fear to my advantage, put my pre-game jitters behind me, and concentrate on the game at hand.

At first, I had difficulty working with directors, authority figures who called the shots. As such they reminded me of my parents, governesses, schoolmasters, and all the other people who had been in charge of me. Fortunately, I came to my senses and began to rely on and appreciate them greatly.

Two of my directors, Tim Mayer and Tom Babe, known as the Gold Dust Twins, frequently worked in tandem, sharing directorial responsibilities. Tim, theatrical and baroque in style, could charm one into doing anything, while Tom, low key, introspective, and naturalistic in his approach, could get the best out of anybody.

Another director I enjoyed working with was Laurence Senelick, classically oriented and literary in approach, who translated Feydeau and Chekov from French and Russian into English and produced some exciting plays. An important lesson I learned from him was to make the audience believe they are living through the experience dramatized on stage.

The acting, though for the most part on an amateur level, was excellent. Unlike students in professional drama school, who are given the best working conditions and equipment, we frequently worked under adverse conditions, which made us pull together. On our low-budget productions, actors had to bring some of their own props, help with publicity, repair their own costumes, help strike sets, and assist in many other ways. Sally Gates and Sharon King, costume designers at the Loeb, worked miracles out of what little they had.

Some of the people I worked with and admired were Jane Alexander, Stockard Channing, Pat Collinge, Lindsay Crouse, Dan Deitch, David Dunton, Patricia Elliot, Arthur Friedman, Dean Gitter, Peter Ivers, Steve Kaplan, Phil Kerr, Maeve Kinkead, Freddy Lawrence, Ann Lilly, John Lithgow, Mark Mirksky, Carl Nagin, Josh Ruebens, Dan Seltzer, Ken Shapiro, Lloyd Schwartz, Hal Scott, Ken Tate, and Joan Tolentino. On occasion, after rehearsals some of us would go to Cronin's restaurant to have a few drinks and rehash whatever had gone right or wrong, discuss theatre politics, or share amusing anecdotes culled from past performances. Over drinks, my friends Dan Deitch and Ken Shapiro provided constructive suggestions for improving my performances.

One person I came to know and admire was Joan Tolentino. Whereas some people were merely infatuated with the idea of the theatre, Joan, knowledgeable and dedicated, loved it, including its less glamorous aspects. In addition to acting, she was a jack of all trades as she managed, coached, worked on props, did publicity, painted sets, applied makeup, worked in the box office, and helped out wherever and whenever needed. One time, Joan broke her arm during one of the riot scenes in *Trojan Women*. Undaunted, she performed in a cast for the rest of the run of the play.

As an actor and spectator, I experienced many memorable events—some pleasing, some strange, and others scary. A highlight of my relatively brief stage career was appearing with Tommy Lee Jones in *Coriolanus* before a larger than usual audience. A scary moment occurred when I was in the audience watching a production of *Jesus*, a modern-day passion play. The text was the New Testament. During the performance, someone from the audience jumped on the stage, pulled out a knife, waved it wildly, proceeded to stab himself, and drew blood, which spilled on stage. This ghastly spectacle happened so suddenly that most of us in the audience were not sure whether this was part of the production. Some people even clapped. Eventually one of the actors grabbed the man, pulled him backstage, and called the police. It turned out that the fellow, who worked for the underground magazine *Avatar*, was on drugs.

I never gave the hazards of acting a second thought until one night, playing the role of a gangster in Brecht's *In the Jungle of Cities*, I experienced a minor but not insurmountable difficulty. It was a hot evening at the Agassiz Theatre and the cooling system was not working. Actors were popping salt pills and refreshing themselves with buckets of water. The script called for me to smoke a foul-smelling cigar, which, combined with the oppressive heat, nearly made me faint. During the last act several strands of my hair came in contact with the burning cigar. I ran my hands through my hair, damp from perspiration, and stopped the spreading embers.

≋ Chapter 31 ≋

The WBZ Turkey Man

For a while, I worked as a model for several local modeling agencies. For the most part it was rather dull. It was the same every day: going to visit ad agencies and showing them my portfolio; on very rare occasions, there would be a job for me, as when the Ford modeling agency arranged for me to model high-end clothes in an issue of *Life* magazine with Mae West on the cover. I spent most of my time pounding the pavement without much success. Through the Ford agency, I did get a walk-on part in the movie *The Boston Strangler*. I played a suspect sitting on a bus, wearing a pea coat and wool watch cap, and got to meet Tony Curtis. I also got a walk-on in *Charly*, another 1968 movie, with Claire Bloom playing the leading role.

Aside from these very brief, off-beat forms of employment, there was really nothing happening in my modeling career until the agency asked me whether I would be interested in working for radio station WBZ for a week. The job, I must say, was a bit unusual, as it entailed my putting on turkey feathers, leaving nothing of me in sight except for my poor, vulnerable sneakers. Each day, dressed as a turkey man, I would go to different towns, knock on people's doors, and explain to some startled faces that if they could guess who I was—the WBZ Turkey Man—they would receive one free turkey.

Dear Reader, don't be alarmed; I didn't really sally forth loaded with turkey carcasses, but merely gave the recipients a coupon they could cash in for a turkey at their local supermarket.

The prospect of masquerading as a turkey for a week was inviting. Eager for relief from the tedium of pounding the pavement and visiting ad agencies, I quickly took the job. The money was good, and there would be a few laughs. In some neighborhoods, I visited lower-income families, and although most of them owned televisions, many were unfamiliar with WBZ. Most people, opening their doors and finding themselves face-to-face with a real live Turkey Man, were startled to the point of not being able to think of a thing to say! I gave these families turkey coupons in any case; I was happy to make Thanksgiving Day a little brighter for them.

Every time somebody correctly guessed my identity (it didn't matter whether or not they did, for everyone I came in contact with received a turkey certificate as a matter of protocol), I called WBZ and gave them the name of the lucky recipient. No matter where I called from, a private house or a pay phone, our conversation would be broadcast live, informing listeners of my whereabouts and next destination.

Sometimes this did not work as smoothly as it might have. At one old lady's house, her cat formed a special attachment to me, or at least to my turkey feathers. It jumped on my headpiece and proceeded to throw a fit! There I was, trying to shake off a half-crazed cat while explaining myself to the astonished homeowner. At any rate, I managed to escape with nothing more than a few rumpled feathers.

For the rest of the week, I knocked on people's doors and put up with occasional skirmishes with some silly animal. I know it sounds strange, but slowly this fusion of turkey and man started to feel routine, so I invented a little creative diversion for my new self, spiritual self-preservation, in the form of calling WBZ and telling the disc jockey about my adventures with fictitious characters. I was testing their mettle, for you could see this Turkey Man charade was nothing but a promotional gimmick for WBZ.

A sample conversation: "Hello, this is the Turkey Man! I had the most amazing experience today. Oh, boy, it was a close one! I knocked on this door and a seemingly kind old man answered, and he didn't quite understand what was happening! He thought *I* was the turkey, so he grabbed his axe and chased me all the way around the block. I just got away by the skin of my feathers." (This was going live, on the air.)

The only repercussion of this conversation was that the next day I visited another town and came upon two nice old ladies. "Oh, you are the Turkey Man!" they exclaimed. "We heard about you yesterday, about that terrible man who chased you with his axe." They seemed genuinely concerned about my well-being; they even told me they had said prayers, a rosary for me. I gave them a couple of free turkey coupons, and we all went away happy.

Another conversation with the disc jockey went something like this: "Hello. Oh, boy, you won't believe this! But I had a most pleasant experience this afternoon. I knocked at a door, and guess who answered?" The disc jockey, by this time getting accustomed to the game, answered, "A little green man?" "Oh, no, no, no," I replied with enthusiasm. "It was a genuine turkey lady." I then commented on how lonely it was seeing nothing but human beings (unfeathered bipeds, by Aristotelian definition, as I told him) and then, to come upon a fellow turkey. . . Yes, I told him (again: this was going on the air) that the Turkey Lady and myself fancied each other's company and that we spent a short but pleasant time doing turkey trots and making turkey-talk. "Guess where the Turkey Lady and myself are going this Thanksgiving?" The disc jockey hadn't a clue. "We are going to Turkeyland, and guess what we're going to eat for Thanksgiving meal?" Well, the poor disc jockey was beginning to feel a bit put-on, a mite uncomfortable, so I quickly ended the conversation by telling him that our Thanksgiving feast would consist of a healthy portion of an insurance salesman's right arm.

Another conversation took a rather bizarre turn when my friend, Seymour Simpkins, a professor at Harvard, agreed to go along with my prank. At my instigation he called the top brass at WBZ and demanded to speak to the vice president or general manager. Upon making contact with Mr.—let's call him Schnooks—Seymour addressed him as follows:

"Mr. Schnooks, I don't know if this is your idea of a practical joke, but I am not amused. . . I live at 65 Mt. Auburn, on the third floor, and was shaving when I heard this dreadful clatter. To my horror, a Turkey Man came crashing through the window, breaking glass, and I thereupon cut myself badly with my razor. This Turkey Man mumbled something about WBZ. Anyway, I'd like some explanation!" Mr. Schnooks gasped, became somewhat hysterical, and promptly demanded to speak to me. He addressed me in tones of quiet rage. "Turkey Man, the mark of a good professional is not to overdo a good thing. Just what is the meaning of this? Have you taken leave of your senses?"

I replied to him with anger and pain in my voice. "Look here, you don't know the half of it. You think Seymour is bleeding; how about me?" I moaned.

"What happened to you? What is going on out there?" Mr. Schnooks sounded quite disturbed. "Mr. Schnooks, I never realized that this job was so fraught with peril. I am lucky to still be in one piece."

Mr. Schnooks, rapidly losing his composure, blurted out, "Are you all right? Are you both all right? What happened to you?" I, not wanting to build suspense any longer, related my counterfeit larks to him, as quickly as they occurred to me. I told him how, on nearing the building, I had been attacked by several mad dogs. This was simply too much for Mr. Schnooks. He insisted on sending an ambulance for Seymour and me. Both of us politely refused, insisting that we would be all right.

Alas, no longer did the WBZ brass trust me to go anywhere by myself. The next day, I was under the care of someone from WBZ personnel, who was to accompany me everywhere I went. I told my chaperone that I thought it would be a good promotional move to visit one of Harvard's classes. He was sufficiently impressed by the name "Harvard" that he agreed to accompany me to an introductory class in Scottish Gaelic, taught by my friend, Johnny Shaw. I wasn't sure exactly what I was going to do, so I improvised by jumping up on the table in full-feathered finery, singing a few verses in Irish

Gaelic, dancing a hornpipe, and concluding by muttering esoteric nonsense on the folklore of wild fowl.

At this point, the poor class didn't know how to react; the fellow from WBZ was quite beside himself; and Johnny Shaw was in stitches. Somewhat bedraggled at the end of my little performance, I exited with a flurry of feathers. The WBZ man was speechless for about thirty seconds; then he asked me to explain my behavior. I patiently explained, "Turkey behavior is quite unpredictable. Anything can happen." This unnerved him, and he made me promise not to do anything like that again, to mind my Ps and Qs in the future.

The rest of the day went quite smoothly, and that evening the fellow returned to the station and gave the brass at WBZ an account of the day's happenings. The next day, I was severely reprimanded for my unacceptable behavior and was given one more chance to carry out my Thanksgiving promotional mission. Latching onto this last chance with great fervor, I was prepared to make good and big on it.

The next morning, bright and early, I headed out to Dorchester to pick up my friend Jack Whyte, a pennywhistle player, poet, and good fellow, and we embarked for Natick. Jack was driving, reciting poetry, and playing a little pennywhistle. It was a bit nippy and so, to lighten the chill, Jack and I did the only thing we knew to warm up—we had a drink. We stopped off at the first bar we saw and got quite a few stares. One good ol' boy, stunned by my feathers, fell off his stool.

Finally, we arrived safely at Farmer McHugh's in Natick. Farmer McHugh and his wife were distant relatives of Jack's from Ireland. I had had so much to drink that I could barely flap my wings and keep one foot ahead of the other as I did my turkey trot. Nonetheless, Jack and I ambled our way to the farmhouse. Midway there, I was side-tracked by all the wildlife that populated one large field. Pigs, ducks, hens, horses, goats, and, lo and behold, a bull that appeared oblivious to all around him, at peace with the world, as he chewed the grass.

I don't know what got into me, but I climbed over the fence and started to run, or should I say stumble, toward the bull, making clucking noises and waving my turkey arms. To confuse the large beast in front of me, I mooed like a cow, then barked like a dog, and even tried to sound fierce like a lion or a bear. This will be an epic battle, I thought. The other animals, not knowing what to make of me, got out of the way, running in all directions. When that old bull finally got wind of me (and all I can *still* say is "THANK GOD!"), instead of charging me it turned around and knocked down poor Farmer McHugh's newly repaired fence. Mr. McHugh, brandishing his blackthorn walking stick, came running after the bull. The bull, his feelings sorely hurt, casting apprehensive glances in my direction, ambled over to a bog and just stood there, refusing to budge.

At that point, I was so tired and hung over that it was all I could do not to throw up all over my turkey feathers. Jack was lying on the ground convulsed with laughter. Then he got up, walked over to the bull, and started playing a few tunes—slow airs—on his pennywhistle, at which point Mrs. McHugh joined us, singing, "'Tis an awful sad ditty, I'll tell you right now; it's about an old woman who had one cow."

Finally, the bull was caught and all the straying animals were rounded up. "This calls for celebration," pronounced Farmer McHugh. On the spot he served us some homemade Irish whiskey, known as poteen. The rest of the evening was very pleasantly spent drinking Irish whiskey, telling stories, and singing songs. Of course, WBZ, hearing of my latest escapade, fired me—but I went out in style.

A short time after my stint as the Turkey Man ended, my Uncle Ted got wind of my escapade and said, "Pete, I heard about that turkey nonsense. Why don't you get a real job?" Taking his advice to heart, I got a job working for Hazen's Restaurant in Harvard Square. Dressed as a gorilla, I wore a large sign telling passersby, "You'll go ape over our food and prices."

Chapter 32

First Ceilidh at Passim

A s the 1970s began, having survived my brief acting career, I decided to give the theatre and myself a rest. Now in my mid-thirties, mostly withdrawing from social activities, parties, and coffeehouses, I spent time at home reading and renewing acquaintances with old friends. I was thankful that I had experienced the world of theatre actively as well as vicariously. It had made me some friends, given me a better understanding of people, instilled self-confidence, and prepared me for my next venture.

Fond as I was of folk music, it occurred to me that I might do something to help musicians express themselves creatively. They in turn would provide material for my own artistic expression. Thus resolved, I called some friends, Dave Stacy and Jack Whyte (my partner in that recent adventure with Farmer McHugh's bull), and we went to Passim coffeehouse at 47 Palmer Street in Cambridge, the site of the old Club 47, where I had heard some wonderful folk music. Paula Kelley, Betsy Siggins, and Joyce Chopra each had a hand in running Club 47. Jim Rooney, an esteemed musician in his own right who had played with Bill Keith, and Byron Linardos were in charge of management. Bill Henderson also lent a helping hand.

The new owners, Bob and Rae Anne Donlin, had resurrected the space and turned it into an amalgam of a gift shop, coffeehouse, and restaurant, but had yet to supply one missing ingredient: folk music. Bob and Rae Anne liked the idea of adding folk music at

Passim, especially as I reassured them that given musicians' need for a place to play and for people to listen, there would be plenty of people in attendance.

We scheduled Passim's first musical event, to be held over two evenings, which I would host. In my new role as promoter, I designed a poster, got it offset, and put copies on display at Sanders Theatre and in music stores such as Sandy's Music and Briggs & Briggs. I sent out announcements to friends, newspapers, radio stations, and schools. The event was announced at a Boston Folk Song Society concert.

I wanted the event to resemble a "ceilidh" (pronounced "kaylee"), a Scottish Gaelic word meaning a gathering or visit. A ceilidh in Scotland or a ceili in Ireland was a gathering in someone's house in the evening for recreation, which would take the form of singing, storytelling, and invariably dancing.

I invited musicians I knew and extended an open invitation to others as well. "The more, the merrier," I thought. Not knowing which musicians would show up—and in an effort to better acquaint myself with different genres of traditional music—I gave myself a crash course. I listened to records bearing labels such as Folk Legacy, Folkways, Stinson, Prestige, Riverside, Washington Topic Records, and Leader, and some Library of Congress recordings as well. I also read about various genres—blues, bluegrass, old time music, Cajun, gospel, and "sacred heart," which supplemented my scant but growing knowledge of traditional songs and ballads from Scotland, Ireland, England, and North America.

On the appointed evening, full of the jitters, I showed up half an hour early and was delighted to find a lot of people at the door waiting to get in. Some were musicians who carried an assortment of instruments: banjos, guitars, mandolins, fiddles, and a dulcimer. I was pleased to see a diverse audience—men and women, children, two babies, people of all ages. A few minutes past eight o'clock, Bob Donlin got up on stage, made a few announcements, and then introduced me as master of ceremonies.

Momentarily blinded by the glare of two spotlights that had

me in their sights, I welcomed the audience, apologizing to those faithful souls who for lack of chairs had to stand. "Some of the best music I've heard has been right here in this room when it was the old Club 47," I told them. "As a matter of fact, I recognize several of you from there, so you know what I'm talking about. I would like to thank Betsy Siggins, Paula Kelley, Bill and Jill Henderson, and all the other people who played a vital part in giving many splendid musicians a home and creating a community of folk music lovers. Let us help continue the tradition, maintain the high standards set by our predecessors, and have a good time. We'll make the rafters ring and the taverns roar. Because of time constraints I'm asking you to please limit your repertoire to two songs. If you're only up for singing one song, that's fine, too."

I then introduced Bobby Clancy, one of the famous Clancy Brothers. In a soft, lilting voice, Bobby reminisced about a particular day back home in Ireland. "The dawn was breaking when I went outside, so I sat on the bridge and, feeling a bit lonely, took out my harmonica and played a slow air. Soon I was joined by an old-timer who took out his whistle and played along with me. It wasn't long before more musicians appeared and did the same. Soon the bridge was full of people who were probably in the same boat as I was. Either they couldn't sleep or they didn't have a place to sleep. And so dawned another day of beautiful music and song."

Bobby's reminiscence and the sad sound of his harmonica brought back memories of the previous summer, when I had gone to Ireland and visited the Clancys and their families. We went to pubs, enjoyed gregarious company, walked in the fields, listened to stories, and felt completely relaxed.

I was awakened from my daydreams by applause for Bobby's playing. A priest spoke up in what sounded like a southern English accent. "Bobby," he requested, "give us the one about the three girls applying for residency in heaven."

"Oh, right you are, father," Bobby began. "One reason stories or jokes are sad or funny is that they contain an element of truth. In some ways they are educational. We recognize ourselves and others in them. Anyway, once upon a time there were three girls—Mary, Caitlin, and Theresa—who were seeking admittance to the heavenly city with all the angels, long departed loved ones, and God, the man Himself."

A female voice spoke up. "Himself? How do you know God isn't a woman?"

Bobby smiled. "My apologies. God may well be a woman who's dressed as a man."

There was subdued laughter, and someone sitting near me murmured, "Maybe he or she is a bit of both."

Bobby continued, "St. Peter asks the first girl, Mary, 'What kind of girl have you been on Earth?' Mary, appearing very shy in his presence, answers, 'Well, St. Peter, I've been a very good girl. I didn't smoke, drink, or take drugs. Did everything my parents asked me to, went to church every Sunday, and did some volunteer work.' 'Oh, good,' says St. Peter. 'You have more than earned your way to heaven. We are very proud to have you. Here's the golden key.' Then St. Peter says to the second girl, Caitlin, 'Tell me, my flower, what kind of girl have you been?' She answers, 'I'm not perfect. I'm just your average girl—not too good, not too bad.' 'That's alright,' says St. Peter. 'We can't all be perfect. Here, take the silver key and welcome to heaven.' St. Peter then turns to the last girl, Theresa, and asks, 'What kind of a girl have you been?' Theresa, assuming a provocative stance with her hands on her hips, says, 'I cannot tell a lie. I made many men happy. I drank champagne from slippers, got in barroom brawls. . . .' 'Whoa,' says St. Peter. 'I have to commend you for your honesty. Here, take the key to my apartment and I'll see you later.'"

The room erupted with laughter.

I introduced the next singer, Jack Langstaff, saying, "Jack, the recent founder of Revels, has brought out the musician in so many of us, including those who felt they hadn't a musical bone in their body until Jack proved otherwise. He helped them find the notes that had lain dormant, but now have been brought to life. Jack has resurrected the musical possibilities of our singing community."

Jack then started singing "Pleasant and Delightful."

It was pleasant and delightful on a midsummer's morn.
The green fields and meadows were covered in corn
The blackbirds and thrushes sang on every green spray
And the larks they sang melodious at the dawning of the day

On cue, the audience in one voice made the rafters ring on chorus.

And the larks they sang melodious
And the larks they sang melodious
And the larks they sang melodious
At the dawning of the day

Jack mentioned that he had learned that song from the singing of Lou Killen at Pinewoods, who got it from Sam Larner, a fisherman. Jack then introduced his second song, "Sir Patrick Spens."

"The age of the ballad and its historical circumstances are unknown," he explained. "It has been suggested that Patrick was going to marry a Danish princess in the late thirteenth century. Verses of this ballad have been found in Scotland, England, and this country as well. My former wife, Diane Hamilton, and her husband, Bill Meek, claim to have found an Irish version."

Jack's rich baritone expressed the stark beauty of the melody and its tragic theme. Afterward he fielded a question about ballads. "Scholars say," he began, "that ballads originated in the late Middle Ages. Their authorship is unknown, and they were passed down by word of mouth. In that way, they took on a life of their own and spread far and wide, sometimes going from one country to another with many variants emerging. A ballad is a narrative that tells a story impersonally, in the third person, and focuses on a single incident. The time is vague and the characters are depicted as types." Jack concluded, "I first heard 'Sir Patrick Spens' from the singing of Ewan MacColl, from Scotland, who now lives in England with his wife, Peggy Seeger."

The next performers were the Spark Gap Wonder Boys: Dick Fegy, Neil Rossi, David Doubilet, and George Nelson. A favorite of old-time music lovers, this group is reported to have been the first signed by Rounder Records. They opened their set with an old-time fiddle tune (Neil was a great fiddler), "The Great High Wind That Blew the Low Post Down."

After the next song, "Buffalo Gals," Neil explained, "Many of these dance tunes derive from English, Irish, and Scottish airs, which include jigs, reels, hornpipes, hoedowns, jumps, and quadrilles. In the old days in the country, the instruments on which they were performed might have been store-bought, mail-order, or homemade. Some of these old-time musicians, especially the older ones that have achieved amazing virtuosity, are for the most part self-taught and play only by ear, holding their fiddles in various positions of their choosing: on the lap, between the knees, or against the upper arm. Open strings are sometimes used as drones, producing a sound similar to that of a bagpipe, and continuous double stopping occasionally is facilitated by whittling the bridge to a flatter shape."

Guitarist Dick Fegy explained, "Though many of the tunes are in a major or Ionian mode, the Dorian, Aeolian, and Mixolydian occur with some frequency. Raising or lowering the fourth and seventh degrees of the scale shows a character of musical archaism."

Finishing their set with the song "Cluck Old Hen," George explained, "Songs about chickens have always been popular in old-time music. Perhaps this is because a fiddle can be made to sound like the squawking of a chicken. This song, like so many of its kind, is made of interchangeable verses. This version we learned from Frank Proffitt and Tommy Jarrell."

Marcia Palmater, the dean of Scottish music and host of the radio show *Downeast Ceilidh*, who was sitting up front next to her husband, David, said, "The old-time American songs and ballads like the ones you hear from Almeda Riddle, Jean Ritchie, and Sara Cleveland were the first music brought to America from England, Ireland, and Scotland. They were treasured keepsakes from home."

Sandy Sheehan, a banjo player as well as the owner of Sandy's Music, an institution in the folk music community, joined in. "I'm not an expert but it seems like it was the women more than the men who sang the old ballads. The menfolk were more interested in trying to get a squawk or two out of the fiddle."

"That's right," spoke up someone in the audience. "The women usually taught their daughters the ballads, and the men handed down their fiddles to their sons."

A woman in the audience piped up. "I know another verse. May I sing it?"

Looking pleasantly surprised, Neil responded, "By all means, we are always looking for more verses. Just sing it from where you are." The woman, Mary Faith Rhoads, commenced, "Cluck old hen, cluck I say, Ain't laid an egg since last payday. Cluck old hen, cluck and squall, Ain't laid an egg since way last fall."

I then invited onstage Robin Roberts Howard, whose face I had been in love with since I had first seen it on a record cover back in 1952 when I was a senior in high school. Listening to her sing, I committed to memory the poetic first verse:

Youthful in decay, Eileen O'Roon
Beauty will fade away, Eileen O'Roon
Castles are sacked in war, Eileen O'Roon
Chieftains are scattered far, Eileen O'Roon

Robin explained, "There was a poet in the eighteenth century who found work in a castle as a cobbler's assistant. One day he was instructed to make a pair of shoes for Eileen O'Roon, the most beautiful woman in all of Ireland. When she went to try on the shoes, he rolled up his sleeves and she saw the love mark on his arm, which instantly caused her to fall in love with him. They ran away together."

Someone asked Robin whether she sang the ballad "Edward."

"Alas, no," she replied. "It's a wonderful ballad but not one of mine. Perhaps one of these days I'll get around to learning it. Jean Ritchie sings a Kentucky version and Jeannie Robertson sings a Scottish version, and then there's Paddy Tunney who sings an Irish version. I wouldn't be surprised if Bert Lloyd sings an English version. He's a great scholar and knows many songs."

At that point Linda Morley, a friend and folklorist, said, "Forgive me for interrupting, but I thought I'd mention that 'Edward' is an international ballad with versions in several European countries. It appears in Percy's *Reliques* in 1765 and was sent to him by Sir David Dalrymple, who may have altered the lyrics and changed the hero's name to Edward. Another scholar, Motherwell, held that the ballad was an incomplete version of several longer ballads, perhaps 'The Two Sisters' or 'Lizzy Wan.' Dear me, I'm talking too much. Back to you, Robin."

"Not at all," said Robin graciously. "Thanks to you I know something more about 'Edward.' Anyway, I'll sing 'Lord Thomas and Fair Eleanor.'"

It was a tragic ballad, sad and grim to the core, full of death. Robin's way of singing this haunting tune in a minor key, with fateful words—stark, spare, unrelenting, hastening the action to its calamitous conclusion—made it all the more poignant.

Someone asked Robin, "Isn't that love mark reminiscent of Diarmuid and Grainne? She fell in love with Diarmuid, who also had a love spot."

"Yes," said Robin. "Once she laid eyes on him, she could not quench her love. She persuaded him, though he was unwilling to elope with her. At the time, she was betrothed to Finn McCool. Finn pursued them and caught and killed Diarmuid. After that, Grainne loathed the sight of Finn, but Finn wooed her with gentleness until she finally became his wife. Grainne, the glamorous, tragic, passionate Irish Woman."

Next on stage was Ellen Santis, an attractive woman appearing to be in her late twenties, accompanying herself with her guitar. She sang a lovely English ballad, "Blow the Candles Out," a song she praised for its directness and sincerity in the matter of love. I was reminded of the first time I had heard it sung back in the 1950s by Tom Glazer on the record *Olden Ballads*. The last two verses still stick in my mind.

Your father and your mother in yonder room do lie
A hugging one another, so why not you and I
A hugging one another without a fear or doubt
So roll me in your arms, love, and blow the candles out
And if you prove successful, love, pray name it after me
Keep it neat, kiss it sweet, and dab it on your knee
When my three years are over my time it will be out
And I will double my indebtedness by blowing the candles out

I reflected on how refreshingly frank that song was, with its easy acceptance of the pleasurable aspects of love, and without the doom and gloom of sin and salvation found in many of the old southern mountain songs. At the same time, there was gentleness and caring, an innocence, that made the man's love for the woman all the more poignant. Wishing to know more about the song, I later found it in one of my old copies of *Sing Out!* magazine, which mentioned that "it was collected in the United States by Nell Crumpley, a member of the American Square Dance Society, who learned it from her grandmother in the 1940s."

On Ellen's next song she was joined by her friend Lisa Neustadt, with Lisa singing the melody and Ellen the harmony to "Wayfaring Stranger." They explained that spirituals were sung by poor, illiterate dissenters who had come to find freedom to practice a religion in which everyone was equal in the eyes of God. The memory of that performance sticks in my mind more than forty years later, as a testament to the beauty of that song, with its soaring modal melody in a minor key, that once transported souls from early cares to heavenly grace.

Over those forty years, Ellen spread her wings and made a lasting contribution to folk music in the Boston area. She was involved in the Fox Hollow Festival, founded by Bob and Evelyn Beers; directed *Woody Guthrie's Bound for Glory*, a musical tribute to Woody, at the New England Folk Festival; hosted open-mike shows at the Emerson Umbrella and the Colonial Inn in Concord and the Nourish Restaurant in Lexington; and did outreach for the Folk Song

Society of Greater Boston. Ellen played with Jake Kensinger as a duo, Two for the Show, and on occasion they were joined by gifted musicians, including her daughter, Wendy Santis; Seth Connelly on guitar; Jackie Damsky on fiddle; and Hatrack Gallagher. When introducing performers, Ellen would say something interesting and supportive about them and their material, bringing performers and listeners together on common ground.

The next performers were Joanie Bronfman, accompanying herself on guitar, and Neal MacMillan, armed with his trusty set of Northumbrian pipes. Neal explained, "The Northumbrian pipes are bagpipes from the northeast of England that took on their current form around the early part of the nineteenth century. They have a soft tone, are played indoors, and are bellows blown. What's special about them is that the bottom end of the chanter is closed and the player opens one hole at a time, allowing the separation of one note from another. The pipes have eight finger holes and as many as seventeen keys, giving the instrument a range of two octaves. The tune I'm going to play is 'Barrington Hornpipe,' a familiar tune in the Northeast."

In closing, Neal mentioned, "If you'd like to hear Northumbrian pipes on a record, listen to Colin Ross and Billy Pigg." When asked about Irish pipes, Neal replied, "Willie Clancy, Séamus Ennis, and Leo Rowsome are some of the best."

Neal's performance brought back to memory what I had read– namely, that as folk instruments in Europe, the bagpipes served as an accompaniment for religious observances, weddings, funerals, dances, May games, and festivals. Their music was also thought to have a particular charm for animals and to be loved by the fairies. However, the bagpipe also was thought to be the devil's instrument and to have the power of speech. I also recalled that hornpipes were popular among sailors; for one thing, they occupied only a little space.

After Neal spoke, Joanie announced, "The song I'm going to sing is 'Wind and Rain.' It's powerful and succinct; it deals with the supernatural and has a lovely tune. It's a southern mountain version of 'The Two Sisters,' an English and Scottish ballad that tells of the drowning of a young girl by her older sister, who turned her hair into harp or fiddle strings."

I was reminded of other versions of that song, in which the murder is revealed by the instrument when it is played. This story reflects the ancient pagan belief that the soul of a murdered person is reincarnated as a musical instrument. Reflecting on this, I marveled how despite the efforts of the early church, the Reformation, the Counter Reformation, and the Enlightenment to eradicate pagan beliefs, those beliefs tenaciously survived as vestigial remnants in folk tales and ballads. The country people who sang those old songs, with their ancient beliefs, were considered to be, as one eighteenth-century collector put it, "children of darkness."

I introduced the next performers. "Rick and Lorraine Lee are no strangers to folk music lovers. They play a mixture of old-time music and some original compositions. Rick also plays a dynamite piano with a certain honky-tonk and ragtime flavor, and Lorraine teaches dulcimer at the Cambridge Center for Adult Education." (Lorraine later married Bennett Hammond, also a fine musician.)

Rick and Lorraine, accompanying themselves on dulcimer and banjo, sang two haunting southern mountain songs, "Locks and Bolts" and "Lady Isabel and the Elfin Knight." The mystical tones of melody wedded to the words had a hypnotic effect. Momentarily, I shut my eyes and thought away television, radio, and the movies; class-consciousness; and the modern confidence in progress, technology, nationalism, and secular modes of expressing hopes and fears. I imagined myself sitting on the wooden steps of a log cabin with pigs, goats, and chickens running in and out of the house and men, women, and children sitting on the front porch singing songs that had been in their family for generations.

At the end of their set, Lorraine said of the dulcimer, "It's a stringed instrument in the zither family, having a number of strings and either played with hammer or plucked. It's of Near Eastern origin. The instrument was carried to Europe through Spain by Arabs, who then passed it to Jews in Africa, to Eastern Europe through Turkey, and then to the Far East. In the mountains of the United States a three-stringed dulcimer is brushed with a turkey feather or goose quill or is plucked."

"Perhaps I should say something about the banjo," said Rick. "It was imported by black slaves from West Africa. Like other folk instruments, the banjo is a favorite of the Devil, a virtuoso player who will teach you to play it if you meet him at the crossroads at midnight and give him your soul. The banjo was played at dances and hoedowns and was taken over into the minstrel shows and spread throughout the country. The five-string banjo became popular and was adopted by the white mountaineers of the south. It developed a distinctive American music combining elements of black minstrel, old English dance, and ballads."

Kathleen Guilday was the next performer. Her modesty both on and off stage was exceeded only by her ability to make her harp sing. She explained that the harp is a plucked instrument, the only one in which the strings extend vertically from the soundboard instead of paralleling it. "In many countries the harp was the most highly honored of instruments for both religious and secular cere-monies. Harps were played in Sumeria around 3000 B.C. and have been found in Greek figurines and reliefs in Ancient Egypt. English bards chanted to the accompaniment of the plucked string. Those instruments appear on Gaulish coins."

Pointing to her own instrument, she continued, "This is an Irish harp. In Ireland, the legend is that a woman walking on the beach came across the skeleton of a whale, with the wind singing so sweetly through its bones that she was lulled to sleep. Her husband found her and, hearing the enchanting sound, made a harp to imitate it. In Ireland, Scotland, and Wales, the fairy folk were considered to be expert harpists. Their music, seldom audible to people's ears, was irresistible but ominous." Without further ado, she played a slow air.

Following Kathleen was David O'Docherty, a friend, a painter of considerable talent, a fine flute and pennywhistle player, and a dedicated collector of traditional Irish music. With his expansive frame, robust countenance, and generous nature, he reminded me of an earthy character out of Chaucer or Rabelais, or Friar Tuck, who proved more than once that he is as manly a man as any of Robin Hood's band.

The next performer, Barbara Carns, a pleasant-looking woman in her forties, had the appearance of someone sitting in her living room rather than being on stage, her husky low voice expressing the poetry of the blues, its tenderness, irony, bitterness, and humor. She explained that in her younger years in Georgia she had learned many of her songs, mostly blues, spirituals, and a few ballads. She said of her first song, "Jesus Met the Woman at the Well," "This song, I'm told, is related to the Middle English ballad 'The Maid and the Palmer,' in which Jesus is replaced by a palmer, who can give absolution." Barbara then sang the song in her rich voice, bringing warmth to the gathering.

"Singing the blues," Barbara commented, "is a way to say what would not be permitted in speech. Chain-gang bosses permit singing about bad working conditions or the misery of the prisons, so long as the picks and hammers keep swinging to the music. The words of the song don't matter except to those who sing them.

"I'll sing 'Pick a Bale of Cotton,' which was a favorite of Huddie Ledbetter, whom most of you know as Lead Belly. Its lively rhythm helped lighten the long days of work in the field. Some of the best blues were those sung by the country people, often blind or crippled, who wandered from one place to another. Eventually the music found its way to the town. I'll teach you the chorus and you can join in."

> O Lawdy, pick a bale of cotton
> O Lawdy, pick a bale a day

At the end of her song, someone commented, "Your guitar playing is almost like it's a second voice—a duo."

Barbara replied, "I'll take that as a compliment. Yes, they do complement each other."

The next performer, some twenty years my senior, was

Margaret Barry, whom at some point I promised to marry so that
she could get her green card and remain in the country. Known as
Maggi, she was referred to romantically as the Queen of the Tinkers.
With her trusty banjo with horsehairs as strings, she played in all
winds and weathers, at pubs, fairs, and on occasion grand concert
halls. She had once played for the Queen of England. Maggi and her
longtime companion Michael Gorman, a fiddler, composed a song
called "The Drunken Hens" in celebration of some chickens that had
consumed an abundance of fermenting corn. Rather than passing
out in a drunken stupor, they were jigging and jagging, squawking
and screeching, rolling all over the place.

A large woman dressed in black, with piercing dark eyes and
craggy features, a weather-beaten face like a map tracing the savage
beauty of the Irish coast, Maggi greeted us jovially and sang "She
Moved Through the Fair," a beautiful song translated from the Irish
by Padraic Colum. Her voice, full of humor and warmth and bending
notes, was a ray of sunshine that took us back to another time.

David O'Docherty said to me, "Maggi is one of the best singers
ever to come out of Ireland. When she sings, she takes fire. She's
more than just an entertainer. People are captivated by her; she
brings order out of chaos. Beethoven once remarked, 'I compose
not to entertain, but to change people's hearts.' That's what Maggi
does." Smiling, David added, "I once told her that I wanted to paint
her in the nude, and she would never let me forget it. She'd say,
'Davy, when are you going to paint me in the nude?'"

At the conclusion of Maggi's set, I introduced my sometime
roommate, an elderly gentleman from Sussex, England, who had
learned songs and stories from his family and neighbors. Cyril
Phillips, who had been a sheepherder all his life, was wearing his
smock, carrying his staff, and wearing a Sherlock Holmes hat with
an equidistant brim. When asked about his hat, he would explain,
"That's me deer stalker's hat. When the deer sees me, he don't know
whether I'm coming or going." Short and squat, Cyril reminded me
of someone out of *The Wind in the Willows* or *Old Mother West Wind*,
like Johnny Chuck ambling along a hedgerow. He was frequently

given to saying in his country accent, "Cuh blimey, strike me blooming blind!"

Sitting on a stool in center stage, Cyril sang "Oh, To Be a Farmer's Boy." Listening to Cyril brought a smile to my face, but also made me a little sad to think that people like him and Maggi were the last of a kind. Their way of life was disappearing, giving way to this modern mess, the seeds sown by the Industrial Revolution. Cyril, ironically counterpointing my dark thought with a bit of country humor, said, "Peter Johnson is a most unusual bloke. I've got him phrased up. This is an ode to Peter Johnson."

In Cambridge town I have an "amazing" friend
Who tells me at times he's around the bend
This fact to me seems right for sure
Once when he joined the American Fleet
By his "pranks" at night no sailor could sleep
Dressed as a turkey he toured the town
Hired by WBZ Radio worked his way around
But the next year on a very cold day
Boozing in pubs no turkey was given away
He went to a farm to scare a bull called Barley
The Irish farmer said, "Here, what's all this blarney?"
Pigs and ducks they just went everywhere
And farmer McHugh stood tearing his hair
Now when the radio men gave him the sack
He said, "Well it was all done for the crack"
Dressed in Cambridge as a gorilla too
Folk took one look and simply flew
They gave him a part in a movie you know
About Lawrence Mill strike he said I'll have a go
Naked when he was in a tub of water he sat
When making this movie in somebody's flat
He was running around in his birthday suit
While girls looked on at this crazy coot
At what pranks next will this feller play

Now any girls that feels the cold at night
Contact this "folklorist" he'll hold them tight
He has a soft bed where they'll feel snug
Or as warm as any "old bug" in a rug
Thanks for my camp now I will travel along
Across the country just singing a song

Amid the applause and laughter following Cyril's poem I over-heard remarks from nearby tables. "Did Peter really do all those things? He's quite eccentric. Never a dull moment with old Peter." That was music to my neo-adolescent ears.

On that note, we brought a thrilling evening—our first ceilidh at Passim—to a joyous conclusion.

§ Chapter 33 ‡

Second Night at Passim

With no dearth of musicians eager to perform, we had a full card for a second ceilidh at Passim. First up were John Roberts and Tony Barrand, recently arrived from England. In a short time, they had become a hit with folk music lovers. They sang a variety of songs: supernatural, historical, tragic, romantic, and border ballads; sea shanties; songs of courting and complaint; and seasonal songs associated with ancient rites promoting fertility and celebrating the renewal of the year.

Dressed for the occasion in white trousers, frilled shirts, and top hats with features, John and Tony said a few words about their ritual songs and their meaning and then sang "Tam Lin," a supernatural ballad that tells how Tam Lin, a mortal, is captured by the faeries, only to be rescued by his lover Janet, who holds him fast while he is being transformed into terrifying shapes.

The next song, a jig, was "The Shepherd's Hay." John sang, "I can whistle, I can sing, I can do most anything. I can dance the Shepherd's Hay." He explained that in the old days people would make boundaries in their fields, weaving the hay together to form a hedgerow, and that the in-and-out movement of the dancers simulated this weaving. The dancers wore plumed hats and breeches and had their faces blackened. The dancing was a collective reaction to life's critical cycles, celebrating the preservation of the individual and the community.

I thought of John and Tony not so much as entertainers, but as ancient druids or shamans, and that's why they were such good entertainers. They taught in a pleasing way. Reflecting on their performance, I understood how these occult pagan beliefs and practices helped maintain a balance between people and their environment, reinforce group solidarity, reduce stress, and integrate the community.

The next performers were Margaret MacArthur and her family, who would soon record an album, *On the Mountains High,* for Living Folk Records. I recalled first meeting Margaret nearly a decade earlier when I was a "guest" at the Brattleboro Retreat in Vermont. Margaret would come to the hospital to entertain the staff and patients with her lovely songs and ballads, many of which she collected.

Professor Linda Morley, a friend and folklorist, introduced Margaret. She mentioned that some of Margaret's songs came from the Helen Hartness Flanders Ballad Collection or from Edith Sturgis's book, *Songs from the Hills of Vermont*. Margaret's first song was the "Cambric Shirt," a Vermont version of "The Elfin Knight (Child 2)" or "Scarborough Fair," a ballad on the theme of the test of love, in which the suitor demands impossible tasks from his true love, who answers by naming equally impossible tasks for him to perform.

Linda, sitting in the audience, mentioned that when Margaret was young she benefited from various musical influences as she and her family traveled across the country. Margaret explained that when she was living in Arizona while her father was in the forestry service, she heard country songs sung by Mexican women. From there she moved to the Ozarks, where she was exposed to a whole other tradition. In her words, "Everyone sang. All the kids at school, my friends, and their families—they all sang."

After Margaret came Dwayne Thorpe, who sang about the shattered dreams, suffering, and death (from starvation, disease, exhaustion, or accident, let alone homicide) that resulted from the raging greed that drove the Gold Rush of 1849 in California. Asked how he had learned this song, he replied, "I first heard it sung by Eric von Schmidt in New York." Hearing Eric's name, I felt a twinge of guilt as Eric, a fine artist and blues singer, some years earlier had sublet me his apartment on Boylston Street in Cambridge. Shortly after moving in, I threw a large party with many musicians, who played and sang until the wee hours of the morning. The next day the landlord, having received a number of complaints from my neighbors about the noisy party, terminated my lease. Needless to say, Eric was not overjoyed at my irresponsible behavior; nor was I.

I then introduced Joe Heaney, one of Ireland's finest traditional singers in the Sean Nos style (old style) and a superb teller of tales. Joe said, "When I was a lad at school in Connemara, I was not allowed to speak one word of Irish. If I was caught saying anything in Irish, the school would tell my family and they would have to cut a notch on a piece of wood and give me a beating. I'm glad to say that my parents not once ever did beat me. They put a notch on the stick and we spoke Irish at home." Rather than sing in Irish as we expected, he sang "Red Is the Rose," set to the tune of "Loch Lomond," with everyone joining in on the chorus.

Next to sing was Bridget Fitzgerald, an attractive woman in her twenties, who was very generous with her time and talent and was, to my mind, one of the finest singers of songs in Irish. Bridget, who came from Connemara, not far from Joe, began, "I learned my songs from members of my family—my mother, uncle, and godfather. Joe said that when he was a boy, he was not allowed to speak any Irish, but when I was a girl, I was paid by the government to speak Irish. How times have changed!"

"Hey, Bridget," spoke up someone from the audience, "tell us about your name. Doesn't it go back to Celtic mythology?" "Yes, as a matter of fact it does. Originally it was an ancient goddess of fire and associated with fertility, cattle and crops, poetry and wisdom. She appears in Gaulish and British inscriptions. Her husband, Bres, was king of the Formonians. In the sixth century she became St. Bridgit.

"You heard Joe Heaney. He's a wonderful singer and storyteller," said Bridget. "I've learned several songs in Irish from him." Bridget then sang in Irish, in the traditional Sean Nos style, "Brid Og Ni Mhaille," a song of unrequited love.

Bridget's singing took me back to my childhood, when I'd be sitting in the kitchen listening to Nora, my family's cook, who had come from Connemara, County Galway, sing in Irish. Although I could not understand the words she sang, the music and the sound of her voice dispelled my feelings of loneliness and sadness. Though no longer that child, I felt the power of Bridget's singing and in an odd way felt comforted.

After Jack Whyte played a slow air on his pennywhistle followed by several reels, I introduced David Stacy, from Saffron on Walden in England, one of many musicians who would crash on my living room floor or, space permitting, the couch. David, none the worse for wear, appeared a bit tipsy as he had spent a good part of the afternoon in the Plough and Stars, a local pub and hangout for musicians. He presented a colorful spectacle with his long blond hair that covered part of his purple jerkin. Stridently and with a touch of Cockney cockiness, he addressed the crowd, "Allo! Allo! How are we today? A bit of the all right, I hope." That sense of working-class pride, with its touch of resentment, contributed to his flamboyant personality. David explained that he learned some of his songs while traveling through southern England and parts of Ireland. He commenced:

Sure in the merry month of May
I strolled through my grandfather's farm
Oh, there I spied a pretty maid
And to her I gently said
May I wind up your little ball of yarn

David concluded, "The poor girl in question got pregnant and issued the traditional warning, 'Keep your hands on that little ball of yarn.'"

I announced the next performers, Tony and Irene Saletan, an attractive couple appearing to be in their mid-thirties. Irene and her twin sister, Ellen, had known Woody Guthrie when they were growing up in New York, and she and Tony had recently put out an album on Folk Legacy records. While Tony was tuning his banjo and

Irene her autoharp, I mused about how different they were musically, but how good they sounded together. While Tony's repertoire consisted largely of international songs, humorous ditties, and spirituals, Irene was steeped in the Southern Mountain tradition that had become more widely appreciated thanks to Alan Lomax, Moses Asch of Folkways, and Jean Ritchie. Tony and Irene sang "The Old Granite State," a funny temperance song sung in a spirited way like a march. Hearing that song had a reverse effect, making me thirsty for a drink.

Tony then said, "The slaves who were brought over from West Africa brought with them their songs, which later became Americanized, transformed into hollers and spirituals, which in turn led to the birth of the blues and then jazz." Irene explained that a holler was an improvised song sung by slaves at work, usually at a solitary task, in reaction to work, the weather, a mule, or one's own feelings. Tony and Irene then sang "Bright Morning Star," with everyone joining in from the beginning.

Bright morning star a rising
Bright morning star a rising
Bright morning star a rising
Day is a breaking in my soul
We'll go to the valley praying
We'll go to the valley praying
We'll go to the valley praying
Day is a breaking in my soul

Tony concluded, "Spirituals are folk hymns of dissenters, the disenfranchised in America. The word 'spiritual' distinguished the righteous from the profane. They became popular around 1800 in the Great Revival at camp meetings, with wandering saddlebag preachers and sacred harp conventions. The earliest spirituals were slow and dreary. Later they became more lively as they borrowed tunes from old ballads. The white spirituals were about freedom for the faithful from religious persecution and social rejection, while black spirituals were about freedom from slavery."

Introducing the next performers, Seamus Connolly, Larry Reynolds, and Paddy Cronin, who were teaming up to play a few tunes, I offered a eulogy. "Irish people, if I may make a generalization, are good conversationalists. They have the gift of gab. Now Seamus, he's another story. His fiddle does the talking and speaks volumes. He won the national fiddling championship when he was twelve years of age and has won it ten times, which is a record." Knowing very little about fiddling, I nonetheless asserted, "His phrasing is excellent and he has total control of his instrument."

Seamus explained that the national championship held in the summer in Ireland is hosted at different places such as Sligo, Kilkenny, Mayo, and Galway. "I'll let you in on a little secret," he continued. "I started learning to play when I was a young boy. At some point, I was making a mistake in my fingering. My fiddle was tuned in fourths when it should have been in fifths. I also didn't know that you had to use your little pinky, but after that was corrected, I was okay."

I then said a few words about Larry. "If you don't know Larry, go down to the Village Coach House in Brookline, where he runs a session. If you're a musician, he'll welcome you and make sure you get a chance to play. Larry is very generous in supporting other musicians. And, with John Curran, he hosts *The Sound of Erin*, where you can hear the best of traditional Irish music." Seamus, Larry, and Paddy then played two hard-driving, foot-stomping reels. When someone asked for a recommendation of the best collection of Irish tunes, Paddy explained that many tunes, jigs, reels, slip jigs, hornpipes, marches, and set dances can be found in *O'Neill's Music of Ireland*. He added that Francis O'Neill, born in Ireland, became chief superintendent of the police in Chicago and hired many musicians as police officers.

Hearing that, I had a funny thought. No wonder the Mafia got away with murder in Chicago; the police were too busy making music. Nero fiddles and Rome burns. Seamus pointed out that there were difficulties in transcribing some of the tunes, due in part to faulty notation and sloppy printing. Moreover, a musician would play the same tune differently each time. Listening to those knowledgeable musicians, it occurred to me that the collector, without a good and experienced ear, might put down on paper not what they heard but what they thought they heard.

Following Seamus, Larry, and Paddy, were the Hudson Valley Boys, a bluegrass group consisting of Richard Brown on mandolin; Dan Marcus, banjo; Dave Dillon, guitar; John Ross, fiddle; and Joe DiViney on bass. Dave said a few words about their first song, "Highway of Regret," written by Ralph Stanley. It was the story of a fellow jilted by his girlfriend for another man. It was a fast-paced song with all the instruments harmoniously in sync. The performance was counterpointed by the sounds of the audience stomping their feet and someone playing the spoons.

Someone asked Richard about the difference between old-time string-band music and bluegrass. Richard explained, "One of the differences is that in bluegrass the harmonies among the voices and instruments are tight, carefully worked out arrangements, whereas in old-time music the players have more leeway. In old-time music the banjo player tends to use a clawhammer or frailing style, while in bluegrass the player might use three-finger picking styles. Also, in old-time music many of the songs are traditional, passed on from generation to generation, whereas in bluegrass many of the songs are newly written. There is no hard-and-fast rule as there is a lot of overlap between the two styles."

Sandy Sheehan volunteered, "Bill Monroe gave bluegrass a new start in the thirties. When he was growing up, he was exposed to church-choir harmonies and to the blues, and this helped lay the foundation for his bluegrass style." The Hudson Valley Boys finished with an old favorite, "Old Joe Clark," an old-time song played in a bluegrass style.

I looked at my long list of musicians and asked, "Is Bruce McCormick here?" Earlier in the evening he had announced that he was going to sing an old ditty. A voice from the back of the room replied, "Oh, yes, that's me. At your service." Apprehensive but amused, I noticed a strange-looking apparition shuffling down the

aisle. Appearing to be in his sixties or seventies, Bruce was dressed
in a Scottish kilt, sneakers, mismatched socks, a plaid shirt with
patches, and a pith helmet that resided precariously on top of his
head. Ascending the stage, Bruce shook my hands with both of his
and greeted me with a theatrical gesture of salutation. "Thank you,
thank you," he loudly exclaimed. "My song is 'Mack the Knife,' a
rare old Boston folk song."

When he got to the line "The shark has no teeth," he opened
his mouth wide and held that pose long enough for people to see a
wide cavernous expanse of gums and practically no teeth. Afterward
he thanked everyone, made a theatrical bow, and, to the sound of
laughter and applause, ambled down the aisle. He reminded me of
someone from that delightfully wacky movie, *King of Hearts*.

Then Bruce turned and asked whether he could make an
announcement. Before I could answer, he informed us that he
knew all the places in Boston and Cambridge where one could get
a free meal every day of the week. "So if you want a free meal," he
instructed, "come and speak to me."

In search of sanity, I found Maggi Peirce, a known quantity
and favorite performer of many of us. She would right the keel
and set things straight. Maggi, formerly of Belfast, Ireland, founded
(with Barbara Carns) the Tryworks Coffeehouse in a church in New
Bedford, which for thirty-five years gave people of all ages a place
to sing and play and a sense of community (Maggi hosted a fifti-
eth-anniversary celebration in 2017). Maggi sang the lovely "Star of
the County Down," which has been beautifully recorded by Scott
Alarik.

Listening to those high notes soaring and then returning, I
thought of those good times spent at Tryworks singing and listening
and meeting like-minded people. I remembered how several months
prior, while on stage with Jack Whyte at Tryworks, I had succumbed
to his rendition of a long-winded tale, followed by the hypnotic effect
of his pennywhistle playing, by falling asleep, only to be awakened
by Maggi, Jack, and members of the audience informing me that it
was my turn to sing. Offering a poetic but truthful explanation for

my momentary demise, I said, "I'm sorry about falling asleep, but it couldn't be helped. You see in ancient Ireland there were three types of music—first there's sleep music (suantraí), then there's lively music (geantraí), and finally sorrowful music (goltraí). I think Jack played a form of sleep music."

Jack, coming to my rescue, said, "That was partly my fault, playing a lullaby."

"Oh, thanks, Jack. Just think, if you had played a lively jig I'd be cutting a caper on stage, and if you played a lament I'd be weeping crocodile tears."

Reminiscing about Maggi as she sang on the Passim stage, I admired how earlier in life she left her home in Northern Ireland, came to America, and settled in New Bedford. She married, raised a family, and brought people—especially young people—together through the power of love and music. (Maggi tells her story in her memoir, *A Belfast Girl*, published in 2013.)

Maggi enabled me to see folk music in a new-old light. Many of my friends who sang folk songs were unattached people doing their own thing, for whom folk singing was avant-garde, esoteric, and romantic. Maggi, on the other hand, communicated the age-old notion that folk songs are not some mystical, romantic fiction super-imposed on life, but rather a natural expression of what we are, a part of life. Through her music, happy marriage, children, friends, and community, Maggi honored her commitments and responsibilities as an ambassador of good will, fun, and stability.

As Maggi finished her set, she told me, "I was very careful not to sing anything that would put you to sleep. We wouldn't want a repeat performance. I must say this is a wonderful gathering of people. Congratulations!"

I next introduced Bill Lyons. After singing a Nova Scotia version of "The Flying Cloud," which painted a vivid picture of piracy on the Atlantic during the early nineteenth century, Bill was asked whether he ever sang at the Golden Vanity coffeehouse in Boston.

"Oh, yes," sighed Bill. "I'm afraid I did. I was hired by Fred Basler to sing there, and guess what? I never got paid, so I took matters into my own hands. I went down to the Golden Vanity at one o'clock in the morning, after it was closed. I put some epoxy resin in the locks. Several months later I asked a friend, 'What's cooking at the Golden Vanity?' He replied, 'Not much, but they put in two new doors.'"

A group of singers then took the stage together: Peter Marston, Daisy Nell, John Millar, and Fudd Benson, along with Dreadnought— consisting of Neil Downey, Steve Wilson, and George Thompson. With them were Neil's wife, Jan, and Barry Finn. While listening to Peter, I recollected with amusement how the previous summer he had sung at his barn with some musicians (including Gordon Bok), some of whom had too much to drink. After wandering out onto his neighbor's lawn and passing out, I was awakened by a goat licking my face. I distressed the poor creature by licking back.

Steve, George, and Barry explained that a sea shanty is "a rhythmical work song sung by sailors performing certain tasks, with a solo passage sung by the leader or shanty man and a refrain roared out by a chorus of all hands in rhythm with the concerted effort of the task at hand. These songs whipped a sullen, drunken crew into action. The American shanties, drawing their inspiration from pioneer songs, lumbering songs, and black work songs, were heard in the China tea ports, in the Alaska fur anchorages, on the Liverpool packet runs, and howling around the horn to California gold rush songs."

"Hey, Peter, you've been awfully quiet," someone said. "You got us all together, so you can't escape without giving us a song. Come on, Pete, get up here and give us a shanty."

"Oh, okay, fair play," I said, projecting nonchalance while concealing my enthusiasm and nervousness. "I'll sing 'Santy Anna.' You'll pick up as we go along."

We're sailing down the river from Liverpool
Heave away, Santy Anna
Heave her up and away we go
All on the plains of Mexico

Finishing the song, I commented, "'Santy Anna' is a capstan's shanty, which goes back to the Mexican War. A capstan is a drum revolving on an upright spindle for moving heavy weights. In hoisting or lowering the anchor, the line was wound around the barrel of the capstan and the men walked steadily around it, pushing the capstan's bars before them. The capstan's bar is a lever that turns the capstan by hand. Stan Hugill, in *Shanties and Sailor Songs*, suggests that the air may have come from Breton sailors' prayers to their patron St. Anne. Here's a poem about shanties. It was written by Harry Kemp."

These are the songs we sing with crowded feet
Heaving up the anchor chain
Or walking down the deck in the wind and sleet
And in the drizzle and rain
These are the songs we sing beneath the sun
Or under the stars of night
And they help us through with the work to be done
When the moon climbs into sight
These are the songs that tell our inmost hopes
While we pull and haul amain
The bo'sun booming as we lean with the ropes
And we bring in the refrain

Next on the stage was John Shaw, a graduate student in Celtic studies at Harvard, a fine singer, storyteller, and collector. Introducing his material, he said, "Most of the Gaels who arrived in Cape Breton from the western highlands of Scotland during the first half of the nineteenth century had little or no knowledge of English. With only a little in the way of material possessions, they had a wealth of stories, legends, songs, and tunes. Some of the hero tales can be traced back to their Irish sources and traditions from the Middle Ages and the Vikings as well. The songs were sung and the tales told in the ceilidh house, where people of all ages got together in the evenings, usually in winter, to pass the time in conversation and informal entertainment. Such storytelling maintained the Gaelic intellectual life that continued even after the aristocracy stopped supporting performers. It's a culture that has rarely received any support from formal institutions; on the contrary, a child used to face physical punishment for speaking Gaelic in school."

Listening to John put me in mind of my visits to the Canadian-American Club in Watertown, where Cape Bretoners would socialize and listen to Bill Lamey and Angus Chisholm play fiddle tunes and the North Shore Singers, mostly elderly men and women, sing in Scottish Gaelic.

John continued, "As I've spoken longer than I intended, I'll tell you one short story that I collected. In Gaelic it's called 'An Fear a Fhyair Paid hr Bhroy an Asgaith,' which in English means the man from North River who got a pair of shoes for free. The story translates as follows.

"There was a man from North River who was going to Baddeck. Now there were no stores over here in those days, so people would always go to Baddeck to buy clothes. So one day the man told his wife that he was going to buy a pair of shoes. His wife told him that he should wash his feet before making the trip. He wasn't very partial to washing his feet; however, he gave one of them a quick once over without making a good job of it. Eventually he arrived at Baddeck and went to the store for some shoes. When he found a salesman, he took off his boot and the sock came off with it.

"The salesman exclaimed, 'Your foot is filthy.'

"'No, it isn't,' replied the man. 'I washed it last night.'

"'Well,' said the salesman to the man, 'if you can find another foot in Baddeck as dirty as yours, I'll give you the shoes for free.'

"The man replied, 'I think I can do that.'

"So, he pulled off his other boot and sock and showed the foot that he hadn't washed at all. And so he got a new pair of shoes for free."

The next performer, Murray Forbes, was a friend I had met shortly after my discharge from the Navy. A Renaissance man accomplished in many fields, notably photography, painting, singing, and writing, he could converse on any subject with ease and with the authority of a savant. Murray sang the ancient Scottish ballad, "The Battle of Harlaw."

Next up were the Friends of Quadrivium: Constance Cook, Michael Punzak, John Fleagle, Marlene Montgomery, June Howe, June Matthews, Margot Chamberlain, and Lisle Kulbach. Constance invited everyone to join in repeatedly singing a Shaker hymn, "Come Life, Shaker Life," which was only one verse long: "Come life, Shaker life, Come life eternal, Shake shake out of me all that is carnal. I'll take nimble steps, I'll be David, I'll show Michael twice how he behaved." The words and music can be found in Alan Lomax's book, *The Folk Songs of North America*. Hearing that lovely melody in a minor key, I felt at peace.

Constance invited us all to join in another Shaker hymn, "Simple Gifts."

> *'Tis a gift to be simple, 'tis a gift to be free*
> *'Tis the gift to come down where you ought to be*
> *And when we find ourselves in the place just right*
> *It will be in the valley of love and delight*
> *When true simplicity is gained*
> *To bow and to bend we shan't be ashamed*
> *To turn, turn will be our delight*
> *Till by turning, turning we come round right*

I looked around for the next performer, Desmond O'Grady, who at the time was a member of the Celtic Department at Harvard University and a published Irish poet who called himself The Wandering Celt. Desmond, having had too much to drink, was not up to reading from his translation of the Tain. I felt guilty, as I was partly to blame. Earlier that evening there had been a gathering of the Celtic Department in Quincy House, hosted by Charles Dunn, master of Quincy House and chair of the department. When no one was looking, I poured some rum into the fruit punch, transforming some reserved Yankee personalities into fun-loving Celts. People who normally were reticent became outgoing, and those who were outgoing became more so. In Desmond's case, the punch made him sleepy. Perhaps I am rationalizing, but it seems only fitting that if people are going to study the Celts and appreciate their culture, they should get in the spirit of things and behave like Celts, at least temporarily. What better way to become divinely inspired than by drinking Ambrosia, the nectar of the gods?

The last group of musicians, collectively known as the Battering Ram, was comprised of Declan Hunt, Seamus Walker, Johnny Beggan, and the fiddler Clive Collins. They had recently made a record on the Rounder label. I was glad, though surprised, to see Clive, who had passed out the previous night in my bathtub. Ah, the drink! As I was living in the basement of 65 Mt. Auburn Street, my bathroom was exposed to the public, specifically to those tenants who came down to use the laundry room. Two ladies who lived in the building had come down to the basement to wash some clothes. Smelling alcohol emanating from my bathroom, they discovered Clive passed out in my bathtub. Horror-stricken, they retreated to the first floor and told Mr. Price, the superintendent, "There's a dead man in Peter Johnson's apartment."

To Mr. Price, who was not skeptical by nature, this was old hat, a repetition of countless other such episodes. He put the ladies at ease, blithely replying, "Oh, don't worry. It's just those drunken Irish musicians. They wouldn't harm a flea."

Truth be told, Clive was not Irish; he was an Englishman from Birmingham, a city that was home to a lot of Irish. Snapping out of my reverie and looking at the lads tuning their instruments, I recalled the previous night's singing party, during which some of the lads rode up and down the elevator, singing, "Come out you Black and Tan and fight like a man." I thought, God, I live a charmed life. It's a wonder I haven't been thrown out.

Musically speaking, the lads were in great shape, singing on key and not slurring—let alone forgetting—their words. Declan, in true Declan style, opened with a joke. "Did you hear about the Irish tinkers who try to get into heaven? Standing outside the Pearly Gates, they meet St. Peter, who takes one look at them and says, 'You're a scruffy-looking lot. Maybe you should put on some clean

clothes and then come back. But wait a minute; we're very democratic here. We don't judge a man by his clothes. Let me go and
check with God; I'll be back in five minutes.' St. Peter checks with
God, and five minutes later he comes back. He looks around and
exclaims, 'The tinkers, they're gone. And the Pearly Gates, they're
missing, too!'"

Amidst the laughter and catcalls Declan said, "Just to show I'm
not a racist, I'm going to sing an English song, 'Bedlam Boys.' It's
about mad people. I'm sure some of us can relate to that. Feel free to
join in the chorus." He sang:

> *Still I sing bonny boys*
> *Bonny mad boys*
> *Bedlam Boys are bonny*
> *They all go bare*
> *Live by the air*
> *And want no drink no money*

The audience, captivated by the racy tune in a minor key, the
music wedded to the words, mythical and magical, joined in paying
heartfelt homage to bedlam. Singing along, I thought of sea captains
on tall-masted square-riggers, their crew of rowdy men and serving
maids in taverns roaring with rollicking tunes. Mesmerized by the
moment, captivated by the mood, I momentarily fell into a dream,
losing track of the first verse, but awoke in time for the second.

> *Then I took up a cauldron*
> *Where boiled ten thousand harlots*
> *'Twas full of flame, yet I drank the same*
> *With a toast to all such varlets*

By now the room was in a frenzy of sound, as the orgy of
voices found release in the chorus. It was like an ancient tribal ritual,
whereby the sounds of glasses and spoons, counterpointed by the
cacophony of voices, was taking us on a journey from the profane
to the sacred.

My horn is made of thunder
I stole it out of Heaven
Still I sing Bonny boys
Bonny mad boys
Bedlam boys are bonny
They all go bare
Live by the air
And want no drink no money.
My staff hath murdered giants
My bag a long knife carries
To cut mince pies from children's thighs
With which I feast the fairies

It was exhilarating, yet comforting, to listen to "Bedlam Boys," with the familiar reassuring sounds of rhyming words, each echoing the other, with notes defying gravity, flying off the page, but, true to their homing instincts, returning to the tonic. I began to understand that life could be experienced not just as a linear progression, a purposeless sequence of happenings, but rather as patterned repetition, whereby summer always followed winter and sunset looked forward to sunrise. Exhausted from the long evening, I felt that this was a turning point in my life as I channeled my neo-adolescent rebellion against authority and transformed it into something worthwhile that gave pleasure to others as well as myself.

As the concert ended, some in the audience came over to thank me, saying how much they had enjoyed the evening and looked forward to the next ceilidh. Someone started singing, and others heading out the door joined in.

O the summer time is coming
And the leaves are sweetly blooming
And the wild mountain thyme
All around the blooming heather
Will you go, lassie, go

As people left, singing in the streets, I was left with memories and echoes of magical moments murmuring their contentment. Little did I realize that as a result of our ceilidhs, Passim would soon have live entertainment nightly and would become, to this day, one of the best folk clubs in the country.

Chapter 34

Living Folk Records and Concerts

Nineteen seventy-one was a good year for folk music in the Boston area, as it continued the revival and the spirit of the 1960s. Jack Langstaff, a classically trained singer who loved folk songs, with the help of Raine Miller, a costume designer, founded Revels in Cambridge, where performers and the audience came together to celebrate the cycle of the seasons through dance, story, and song.

By that time, I had broadened my exposure to folk music by taking a trip to England, Ireland, and Scotland, where I spent time in pubs, meeting people, and learning their folkways. In England, I visited the Cecil Sharp house and met Bert Lloyd, a singer and scholar of English folk songs. In Ireland, I visited the Irish Folklore Commission and met Donal and Sean O'Sullivan. Finally, I crossed over to Scotland and met Hamish Henderson, cofounder of the University of Edinburgh's School of Scottish Studies.

With that background, and with the help of Caleb Loring and my Uncle Ted, I started Living Folk Records and Concerts, a nonprofit educational foundation dedicated to presenting, preserving, and perpetuating traditional folk music in all its forms.

After the rousing success of the first concerts I produced at Passim coffeehouse, Bob and Rae Anne Donlin, the owners, asked whether I'd be willing to run regular singing sessions there. My friend Howard Glasser, an artist who taught at the University of

Rhode Island and the University of Massachusetts, had introduced me to the Scottish Gaelic word "ceilidh," and I thought it was fitting to use this term for these sessions. For years, I ran ceilidhs at Passim twice a month. Musicians and friends from far and near came to have a good time, make the rafters ring, and fall in love with a song or tune and take it home.

I also ran ceilidhs at Maggi Peirce's Tryworks coffeehouse in a church in New Bedford. Maggi, a fine folk singer from the north of Ireland, and her friend Barbara Carns, a wonderful blues singer from Georgia, encouraged young people to come to Tryworks and share their music. As the reputation of Tryworks grew, musicians and listeners came to enjoy the ambience and Maggi's hospitality. Frequently at the end of one of Maggi's concerts, Barbara would generously open her door to those who wanted to continue the good times. Those were the days!

In addition, I ran singing sessions in Cambridge (the Center for Adult Education; the International Student Center on Garden Street; the Radcliffe Graduate Center; The Plough and Stars Pub and Restaurant, run by Peter O'Malley, who was also the co-founder of *Ploughshares* literary magazine; Odd Fellows Hall, later renamed the Joy of Movement Center; the Cantab Lounge in Central Square; the Friends Meeting House in Longfellow Park; St. Paul's School; and First Congregational Church), in Boston (The Black Rose pub, run by Michael Sherlock and Dick McHugh), in Brookline (the Village Coach House, run by Henry Varian, who was a good singer from Ireland), and in Natick (the New England Folk Festival [NEFFA], held in Natick High School). I organized song swaps at Izzy Young's Folklore Center in Greenwich Village, New York; Caffe Lena, owned by Lena Spencer in Saratoga Springs, New York; Buzzy Warburton's Black Pearl in Newport, Rhode Island; the New Haven Folk Song Society; and Lowell House at Harvard University, in conjunction with Professor Charles Dunn, a fine bagpipe player and chair of the Harvard Celtic Department, which cosponsored some of the appearances of Scottish and Irish musicians. Many events were recorded on reel-to-reel tapes for archiving.

Living Folk introduced local audiences to performers from the United Kingdom, Ireland, and Australia such as Silly Wizard, the Watersons, Martin Carthy, Dave Swarbrick, the Boys of the Lough, the High Level Ranters, De Dannan, the Battlefield Band, Clannad, Norman Kennedy, Simon Nicol, and Jean Redpath. Among the American performers were Almeda Riddle, Hazel Dickens, Marshall Dodge, Jean Ritchie, Patrick Sky, Gordon Bok, Michael Cooney, Ola Belle Reed, Sara Cleveland, Rick and Lorraine Lee, the Red Clay Ramblers, Joe Val and the New England Bluegrass Boys, Bruce "Utah" Phillips, and Rosalie Sorrels. With the help of Marcia Young (later Palmater), who had a long-running program, *Downeast Ceilidh*, on the MIT radio station, I staged performances by Canadian musicians such as Barry O'Neill, Tom Kearney, and Enoch Kent. Marcia's knowledge of Cape Breton music and culture enabled audiences to be captivated by the sad, lovely melodies and pulse-quickening rhythms of those ancient songs.

Traditionally, folk musicians typically were not paid, except in some form of communal barter. People sang and played because they loved it. Some of that spirit survived among the musicians I hosted, but most of them still had to earn a living. I did what I could for them, putting up visiting performers in my apartment and paying them what we took in after expenses.

* * *

Living Folk also produced records. Producing records was in some ways easier than putting on concerts, as I didn't have to do publicity, call radio stations and newspapers, and put up posters. For the most part it was a matter of setting up a recording date with the performer and recording engineer and finding people to design a record jacket and write the liner notes.

Most of the musicians who came to record performed either solo or as duos, trios, or occasionally as a quartet. I liked making compilation records that featured a variety of performers and musical styles coming together in a common flow of feeling.

I named my first record *Pleasant and Delightful*, after an English folk song, initially collected by Cecil Sharp, that was sung by the Copper family in England, Louis Killen, and the duo of John Roberts and Tony Barrand. The songs and ballads on the two-volume album were from England, Ireland, Scotland, Canada, and the United States. Janet Kelley designed the artwork and also sang on the record.

One of the performers on the record was Murray Forbes, whose strong baritone voice lent itself to the big ballads. On the record Murray sang "The Battle of Harlaw," a Child ballad, which Murray called a family ballad. It is an account of a battle in 1411 between Highlanders and Lowlanders, the winner of which would rule Scotland and speak either Gaelic or some Lowland form of Middle English. Unfortunately, John Coles, who wrote the liner notes to Murray's song and who also sang on the record, minimized the role Murray's ancestor Lord Forbes had played in the battle.

When the record was completed, I paid a visit to Murray's studio on Bromfield Street in Boston. I gave him a copy of the record, assuming he'd be pleased. Au contraire—a scowl materialized on his face. Crying out, "How dare you!" he picked up a decanter that had been in his family for generations and threw it at me. Fortunately, I ducked and saw it crash through his window and narrowly miss an elderly couple taking their promenade on the street below. Then and there I realized that folk music was not for the faint of heart!

Taking a few swigs and swallows from the whiskey bottle, Murray took his walking cane that had once belonged to his grandfather, pointed it at the wall, drew an imaginary map of the Highlands of Scotland, and proceeded to describe the ebb and flow of a battle between Vikings and Highlanders, identifying the chiefs from both sides—Germanic and Celtic. It goes without saying that, at least in Murray's account, the valiant Scots carried the day and drove the heathen Vikings away.

Other records produced by Living Folk include *I Long to Hear You*, a compilation of traditional songs and ballads from England, Ireland, Scotland, Canada, and the United States; and *A Man and a Maid*, featuring four traditional English singers—David Jones, Frankie Armstrong, Cliff Haslam, and Clive Collins— accompanied by Louis

Killen on the concertina. Solo albums include *Alive, Well, and Fiddling,* with Allan Block and friends; *On the Mountain High,* with Margaret MacArthur and Family; and *Trouble in Mind,* with Barbara Carns and friends. Although my activities with Living Folk tailed off starting in the mid-1980s, after the turn of the century I produced *Thank You for the Music: A Collection of Memories from Belmont Folk Concert;* the Kossoy Sisters' *Hop On Pretty Girls; South Wind: Traditional Music from a Boston Ceilidh;* and *Newport's Fair Town: Traditional Songs and Ballads from North America.*

* * *

At first I did everything myself; I certainly couldn't afford to hire any help. Eventually a loosely knit staff took shape, consisting of volunteers who worked on an informal "whoever's free at the moment" basis. Professor Linda Morley wrote reviews of my concerts and records, while another folklorist, Millie Rahn, got us several grants. Audrey Drummond kept everything organized (as far as possible) and running on even keel. Robin Blecher took care of publicity, with a boost from Bob Doucette's colorful posters. Kari Estrin and Richard Korn also helped out. It was not just their physical help, but also their moral support that kept us going. Then, of course, there was Freddy Lawrence, who hosted singing parties for the musicians and audience after some of the concerts. Freddy's parties played an important part in the Boston-Cambridge folk-music revival.

Living Folk also worked closely with the most important folk music organization in the area, the Folk Song Society of Greater Boston, some of whose members sang at my concerts and ceilidhs. I'm grateful to the Society for announcing my concerts in their newsletter. The Society, which has roughly four hundred members, puts on a monthly concert, and some of their members host small concerts in their homes. They have also organized summer weekends of folk music on Cape Cod, with workshops and a staff of dedicated musicians. The Society continues to send out a monthly newsletter that publicizes folk music events in the Greater Boston area. Sadly, several of the members I have known over the years have died: Rob Joel, Florence Brunnings, Lisa Neustadt, Tom Gibney, Irma Selling, and Saul and Alice Aronow.

* * *

Naturally, our efforts at Living Folk elicited a good deal of appreciation from performers and audiences. Nor did my work go without notice closer to home. At one point my initial backers, my Uncle Ted and Caleb Loring, took me to lunch to celebrate my progress. "It's good to see you, as always," said Uncle Ted in his rousing voice. "I'll be straight with you. Your mother and father meant well, but they didn't know how to bring up children. I know it's been tough sledding for you, but you can do anything you set your mind to. I've heard nothing but good reports on you and your music. Keep up the good work—you're performing an important service for the community."

Whatever appreciation came my way, however, was of little moment compared with the appreciation I came to feel for the music and the people who perform it—without affectation, but with naturalness and grace. Rather than call attention to their virtuosity, they subordinate themselves in service to the song. Aside from giving listening pleasure, these old songs provide a historical record and give insight into beliefs and practices not otherwise documented. They also reveal aspects of language, both verbal and musical, such as the old modal tunes that go back as far as Gregorian chant.

From listening to different versions of the same song and, for example, hearing John Roberts and Tony Barrand explain how ballads change in the process of oral transmission, I came to appreciate the richness of their diversity. Folk songs, unless kept inert on a dusty shelf, are always on the go, traveling fluidly through time and space as they change their outward appearance and blend with their environment while preserving the essential emotional core, the heart of the story. It is said that folk songs are at once young and old. Old in that a ballad may have had its origin in the late Middle Ages; young in that with each telling and retelling, the song, communally recreated, gives birth to new variants. Like any form of folklore, a song that is accepted by the community finds fertile ground, blossoms, and spreads its wings far and wide, crossing linguistic and cultural barriers, although it may die out where it falls on deaf ears. I came to realize that a song changes as the listener mishears it or forgets a word or a note and makes up something in its place. Also, a person may deliberately change a word or a note for personal, cultural, or ideological reasons, to fit their own aesthetics or to conform to the expectations of others.

What makes these stories and legends so memorable is something basic and elemental: they connect the present with the past, creating continuity with history and sometimes guidance for the future. As my good friend, psychologist Don Kalick, put it, "There's something almost sacred about them, yet they're down to earth. As youngsters we learn stories from our parents and friends that give us a sense of where we come from. These stories are direct and simple and have narrative tension. We will always need stories to tell us about our lives."

≋ Chapter 35 ≋

Venues and Adventures

O rganizing concerts was a way of keeping the music I loved alive and well. Concerts gave musicians a chance to perform and made the audience aware of the music. My other role of producing records was a way of preserving traditional folk music for posterity, including for people who would perform it themselves. In so doing I saw myself as a conduit, a "culture broker" between musicians and their audience.

I had many adventures while putting on concerts in Cambridge and environs and around New England. In 1971, I produced my first concert, featuring Aly Bain, a fiddler from the Shetland Islands, and Mike Whellans, a singer from the mainland of Scotland, at the First Lutheran Church in Cambridge. The entrance fee was $1.50, with the entire proceeds going to the musicians. (Given the rise in the cost of living, if I were running the concert now, forty-five years later, I'd charge $15.00.) During the intermission, while free coffee, tea, and cookies were being served, I kept my eyes and ears open and overheard many interesting conversations.

After the concert, Freddy Lawrence, my closest friend in Cambridge, invited Mike and Aly and the audience of about fifty people to his house on Raymond Street to continue the good times. Concert halls were fine and necessary in the scheme of things, but I preferred to hear and make music in someone's home, where the performer and audience could interact in a more intimate way.

At some point during the party, with music and conversation emanating from every room in the house, Freddy went upstairs to check on his young daughters, Amelia and India. Entering his bedroom to get to his daughters' room, he saw his wife, Wendy, in bed with Aly, who upon laying eyes on Freddy jumped out of bed, naked as a blue jay, and dramatically exclaimed, "Would you slay a naked man?" Afterward Freddy said that the incident reminded him of something out of a Scottish ballad.

* * *

Another of my concerts that raised a few eyebrows and got tongues wagging was given by Margaret Barry, "Queen of the Tinkers," who had once performed for the Queen of England and had also performed at my first Passim concert. My friend Robin Roberts, a splendid singer, collector, and actress, had discovered Maggi Barry, who accompanied herself on a banjo that had horsehair for strings.

I had called Maggi, who at the time was staying with Dan Millner in New York, and asked her if she would be interested in giving a concert in Cambridge. Maggi said she'd like that, but insisted that she wanted to do the concert without her partner Moira, the dancing fiddler. Maggi said emphatically, "Moira is a disgrace to the music. The last time we were on stage together, I almost gave her a belt."

It staggered my imagination to think of two musicians coming to blows at a concert I produced. Maggi and I agreed on the terms and set a date for the concert, about two months in the future.

Several days before the concert, I drove my old, battered Hillman Minx to New York. By good luck and planning, I managed to sneak into Maggi's building and into her room, where she was sitting on her bed. She had a craggy, weather-beaten face, a lantern jaw, and smiling brown eyes. Smoking a cigarette and drinking a bottle of Guinness, she offered me a drop of the pure.

Finishing our drinks, we made our way down the fire escape with our bags and her banjo. We made it safe and sound to my apartment in the basement of 65 Mt. Auburn Street, Cambridge. Later that evening, Maggi called Dan, who said that several people across the street from his apartment had seen Maggi and me going down the fire escape and—thinking we were burglars (or, as Maggi pronounced it, "booglers")—called the police. Dan said that Moira was furious at being left behind, and he never heard the end of it.

The following evening, in front of a capacity audience, Maggi gave a wonderful concert at the Joy of Movement Center in the Odd Fellows Hall in Central Square in Cambridge. Despite the fact that liquor was not allowed on the premises, I made an exception for Maggi, who had a case of Guinness next to her. You name it—jigs, reels, hornpipes, marches, slow airs—she played it, and, of course, she sang "She Moved Through the Fair," one of Ireland's most beautiful songs.

* * *

I'll never forget the concert given by the wonderful Scottish singer Elizabeth "Lizzie" Stewart. Before the concert I had to pick her up at South Station in Boston. My friend Periwinkle kindly offered to take me to pick her up. Another friend, Cyril Phillips, came along to keep us company.

Periwinkle, Cyril, and I met Lizzie at South Station, helped her with her bags, and headed back to Cambridge. In retrospect, I can see that I got off on the wrong foot as Lizzie appeared to be shy, especially since she had never set foot out of her village. Attempting to make her feel at home, I put my arm around her shoulder in what I thought was a brotherly fashion and proceeded to sing a Scottish ballad that I assumed she'd know, namely, "Maids, When You're Young Never Wed an Old Man." With my arm around Lizzie, I started to sing; at the time I was in good voice. I first heard "Never Wed an Old Man" sung by her older relatives, Jeannie Robertson and Lucy Stewart. I finished the last verse:

When he was asleep out of bed
Into the arms of a handsome young man
He's got no faloorum; he's got no ding-doorum
Maids, when you're young never wed an old man

At this point, betraying anxiety, Lizzie looked at me and said in a deadpan voice, "Please remove your hands from my shoulder. You're NOT Peter Johnson. You're an imposter." Flabbergasted, I was at a loss for words. She added, "I want to get out of the car now and call a policeman."

Periwinkle and Cyril, coming to my defense, vowed that I was who I said I was, but to no avail. Acceding to her wishes, we parked on Massachusetts Avenue in Central Square, where we saw a policeman chatting with someone standing near the theater. Soon the policeman, Lizzie, Cyril, Peri, and I were engaged in animated conversation. The policeman noticed Peri's war bonnet in the back of the car and heard Lizzie with her Scottish brogue and Cyril with his Sussex accent. Not wanting to feel left out, I spoke in what I thought was an Irish accent. The poor cop didn't know what to make of us. Shaking his head with an expression that said, "How did I ever get into this?" he said, "Miss Stewart doesn't have to go with you if she doesn't want to. Is there anyone she knows who can identify you?" Much relieved, I blurted, "That's a good suggestion, officer. Why didn't I think of that?" The poor policeman, caught in the middle of this street theater, shook his head and rolled his eyes.

I went to a pay phone and called Linda Morley, a folklorist, and Marcia Palmater, host of the *Downeast Ceilidh* radio show. Soon they showed up, looking as bewildered as the policeman. Lizzie, greatly relieved, thanked them for coming. She apologized to me for the misunderstanding and I, in turn, expressed contrition for my insensitivity. The policeman said, "All's well that ends well. I should write a book!" He kindly wished Lizzie good luck with her upcoming concert.

Later that evening Lizzie gave a wonderful concert, with about sixty people enjoying every minute of it. That evening I fell in love with several songs she sang: "The Dewey Dens of Yarrow"; "The Twa Corbies"; and an English song called "Lay the Bent to the Bonny Broom," which she had heard from Isla Cameron.

* * *

The year following Lizzie's concert, I arranged a concert for my part-time roommates Declan Hunt, Johnny Beggan, Seamus Walker, and Clive Collins—collectively known as the Battering Ram. Earlier that year, thanks to Professor Kenny Goldstein, I managed to get them booked at the Philadelphia Folk Festival, where they were enthusiastically received. They had just finished making a record for Rounder Records, and unbeknownst to them, the person who wrote the liner notes to their songs and tunes, and perhaps romanticized the Irish Republican Army (IRA), included how to build and set off a bomb in the notes. The lads, upon discovering this, were not happy.

Declan, who was a frequent guest in my basement apartment at 65 Mt. Auburn Street, was a colorful character with a wry sense of humor. Several months previously, he had run for Lord High Mayor of Newburyport—in reality there's no such office; only in Dublin is there a Lord High Mayor. One of Declan's campaign promises was that he would solve the traffic problem by passing a law that said, "On even-numbered days of the week, cars with an odd last number on the license plate would drive *down* the street, and on odd-numbered days cars with an even last number on the license plate would drive *up* the street."

On one occasion Dick McHugh, the manager of the Black Rose Restaurant in Boston; Peter O'Malley, owner of the Plough & Stars Pub; and I organized a benefit concert at the Village Coach House, owned by Henry Varian, a top-notch musician. Some of the musicians who came to lend their support were Tony and Irene Saletan, the Spark Gap Wonder Boys, Rick and Lorraine Lee, Ricky Rackin, Elliot Ribner, and some Irish musicians I didn't know. Unfortunately, Declan never showed up as he was in hiding because the FBI was looking for him. It was something to do with passing bad checks and fooling bank clerks by wearing a disguise.

I was worried that Battering Ram might not show up for the concert I had arranged as, a while back, my friend Robin Roberts had invited the lads to sing at a concert in Carnegie Hall with Pete Seeger; Peter, Paul, and Mary; Theodore Bikel; and the Clancy Brothers. As the lads had been paid in advance, they got drunk on the night of the concert, went busking in Central Park, and never showed up to perform.

On the night of my concert, Freddy Lawrence, known in exalted circles as Fez Da Feen, and I showed up at the First Congregational Church at 11 Garden Street to set up the chairs and make sure everything was in order. To our dismay, we were informed that due to a miscommunication the church had been booked by another group. With no time to spare, Freddy and I made some signs saying that the concert had been moved to the Mt. Auburn Cemetery and that as compensation for this inconvenience, admission would be half price, seventy-five cents instead of the usual dollar and fifty cents. I called Declan and let him know about the change of plans. Despite the reduction in the price of admission, the musicians would still come out ahead as I didn't have to deduct the rental to the church.

Fortunately the group, stone sober, showed up at the cemetery on time and gave a wonderful concert. The Battering Ram, despite missing out at Carnegie Hall, was slowly gaining a good reputation as performers.

The evening was like a folk festival, featuring an all-star cast of musicians as many of the Battering Ram's musician friends showed up. Appearing were Sally Applegate, Maggi Barry, Bobby Clancy, Mixie Clarke, Sally Coyne, Paddy Cronin, Bridget Fitzgerald, Kathleen Gilday, Jack Geary, Steven Kelley, Seamus Kennedy, Kathleen Lyons, Johnny Mullins, Sean Tyrol, Henry Varian, Patsy Whelan, Grainne Yeats, and several more. About sixty people showed up, and although some got there late due to the mix-up, a good time was had by all.

I was weary from the strain and stress of promoting the concert, which included calling radio stations, designing and putting up posters, sending out newsletters to people on my mailing list and the Folk Song Society of Greater Boston, contacting the newspapers and the lads on Robert J. Lurtsema's radio show *Morning Pro Musica*. I was also a bit hung over from Guinness, so during the concert I got up and wandered several hundred feet away and lay down next to a gravestone whose skull and crossbones leered at me. I looked up and saw a family of gray clouds trailing each other; stars, orbs of gold, lighting up the sky; a pale full moon watching everything below and recalling a song that I learned in Maine at summer camp, I silently sang, "I see the moon; the moon sees me, down through the leaves of the old oak tree. Please let the light that shines on me, shine on the one I love."

Suddenly all was quiet. The music had stopped. A few seconds later I heard a lovely voice: Bridget Fitzgerald was singing a song in Gaelic that (just as Bridget's songs had done at Passim) reminded me of the beautifully mysterious songs sung by Nora, my friend and my family's cook at Ridgemere. I then recalled Mr. Waterston, my English teacher at Brooks School, who had taught me to appreciate English ballads not just by reading them, but also by listening to records. I recalled him playing "The Three Ravens" sung by Richard Dyer-Bennet, "Little Mattie Groves" sung by John Jacob Niles, "Pretty Saro" sung by Jean Ritchie, "At the Foot of Yonder's Mountain" sung by Susan Reed, and "Santy Anno" sung by Burl Ives.

Listening to ballads was reassuring because of their lovely modal melodies, mysterious stories, and regular rhyme schemes, which seemed to echo and augment the natural repetition by which black night could be counted on to give way to rosy-fingered dawn and cold grim winter, full of death, would yield to life-giving spring.

Half-asleep, I heard the hard-driving tune "The Great High Wind That Blew the Low Post Down" with Alan Stowell playing the fiddle backed by Kurt Anderson, which was followed by Alan singing a silly song "The Farmer's Curst Wife," which tells of a farmer's wife who is so bad that she gets sent to hell and upon her arrival "Nine little devils come rattling their chains. She picked up a cudgel and beat out their brains. Sing heigh ho rattle ding day." Hearing the silly song put me in mind of the Jack tales collected by Richard Chase and thought of the Devil as a comical, likeable figure who could be outwitted by anyone with half a brain. I wondered, "Who was the Devil earlier in his life?" Perhaps a pagan fertility sprite? Ironically it was God not the Devil who was the scary figure in our early religious literature with such frightening sermons as "The Day of Doom" and "Sinners in the Hands of an Angry God."

Lost in thought, I fell into a slumber for about half an hour, until I was awakened by my friends Freddy Lawrence and Penn Gardner, who had come looking for me. We returned to the concert just in time to hear a teenage boy and girl sing a rollicking nonsense song, "The Rattlin' Bog," with everyone joining in on the chorus. Soon it was time to call it a night and let the dead rest in peace.

* * *

One of the most interesting musical events I planned was a weekend benefit for a Baptist church in a small country village outside of Amherst, Massachusetts. Some friends volunteered to come and provide the music: Peter Colby (from Old Joe Clark), Tom Hall, Jingles, Peter Lentz, Bill Lyons, Jack Parmley, Winston Pettis, Ricky Rackin', Elliot Ribner, and Toby.

On our way to our destination, we stopped at a small village fair where people were selling homegrown vegetables and cider. Singing on a small stage was a group that included young children, their parents, grandparents, and a few friends. One of the songs they sang was "Bright Morning Star." As most of our group knew the spiritual, we heartily joined in.

> *We'll go to the valley praying*
> *We'll go to the valley praying*
> *Day is a'breaking*
> *In our soul*

Afterward a man appearing to be in his seventies told us that after sundown he and his family, all ages, would sit on the front porch and sing old songs that they had learned as children from their parents and neighbors. "Trouble is," he said, "a lot of the young folk today have lost interest in the old songs because of those dang juke boxes that play any old thing."

Also at the fair was a family selling rugs and lovely quilts. A middle-aged woman who had made some of the quilts, taking me into her confidence, explained, "When we sell what we make to our neighbors, we make the quilts the traditional way. Some people can't afford to buy them, so we trade them for something we can use, but when we sell them to outsiders we make the quilts a little differently." The idea was that if they sold to outsiders what they sold to neighbors, then somehow those outsiders could take possession of their souls and identity.

Hearing that reminded me of my readings in folklore and anthropology in which I had learned that tribal people didn't like having their picture taken or using their real names for fear of jeopardizing their very being. This is what Sir James George Frazer in *The Golden Bough* calls sympathetic and contagious magic.

As we were leaving the festival, some of the people we had met said they would come to the benefit. We headed to the church where the concert was to be held. The rising spire of the church faced a meadow in which there were a farmhouse, a barn, horses, cows, a tractor, an old-time carriage, pitchforks, bales of hay, and several people mending the fence. It reminded me of America before the Industrial Revolution. It was like something out of a John Constable or Benjamin West painting, where God had blessed the land. For a moment I was hypnotized by this compelling old world.

Shortly before the concert, the minister, wearing a black suit, came out to greet us; with him were several of the village elders in their Sunday best. The women wore bonnets and the men wore overalls with plaid shirts and stern expressions, reminding me of Grant Wood's painting, *American Gothic*.

During the first set of the benefit concert we sang "Amazing Grace," "David's Lamentation," several sacred harp hymns, gospels, and the spirituals "Joshua Fit the Battle of Jericho" and "A Poor Wayfaring Stranger," with the audience joining in. Adding variety to the program, we sang the Revolutionary War songs "Butternut Hill" and "Katy Cruel," and a Civil War ballad, "The Battle of Shiloh Hill." The first forty-five minutes went well. The audience was largely church members, who got into the spirit of things by joining in the singing.

At the intermission, the minister asked Bill Lyons if he had a regular job besides singing. Bill, in his taciturn way, replied, "God has given me my humble vocation for which I am most grateful. I work in a prophylactic factory and test condoms." Bill then made the sign of the cross and said, "I'm doing God's work." Pointing to me, he said, "This here is Peter; he's my helper." Momentarily caught off guard but not at a loss for words, I crossed myself twice and said, "God be praised. I love my job so much I sometimes work overtime for free." The minister and all those in hearing distance looked at Bill and me with horror and revulsion, their mouths agape and their eyes bulging like teacups. Surprisingly, the rest of the concert went well and at the end we received a rousing ovation.

* * *

For the most part, my concerts went smoothly, but occasionally, thank God, there were exceptions that made the evening more entertaining. It so happened that the year I turned forty, the date of my birthday, May 25, coincided with an evening on which I put on a concert. Performing that night was a five-piece woman's band known as the New Harmony Sisterhood Band, all excellent musicians. Their repertoire consisted of a few traditional folk songs, but for the most part they performed feminist material. Some of their songs were anti-chauvinist, with lyrics like "I'm going to kick my man out of town." The feminists in the audience responded most enthusiastically to the musical castigations of men and all their foibles. Meanwhile, the men in the audience, who were outnumbered by the large contingent of women, took it good-naturedly.

After the New Harmony set and an intermission, David Jones, a neighbor and singer from England, sang "Sally Free and Easy." The cavalier sentiments of the song were effective in retaliation as the lyrics incurred the ire of numerous women in the audience. David was greeted by hisses and boos from the women and cheers from the men. Following his song, a rather large woman with short-cropped hair, wearing a brown leather jacket and boots, loudly exclaimed in a deep voice, "I've got no use for these seventeenth-century wah-wah ditties." So saying, she proceeded to leave the room as noisily as possible. She made quite a racket: stomp, stomp, stomp.

Scarcely had she departed when my good friends John and Jill Shaw entered the room bearing a cake and sang "Happy Birthday" to me. At the time John, a gifted fiddler and singer of Cape Breton songs in Gaelic, was teaching a course in Scottish Gaelic at Harvard. His lovely wife, Jill, had just come over from England. Suddenly a stunned cry of outrage issued from a large segment of the women in the audience—and no wonder! For there in front of the room my friends were holding a scrumptious-looking cake which on closer inspection bore a striking resemblance to a large, perfectly proportioned female breast with a cherry inserted on the top doing its best to simulate a nipple.

My birthday evening with all of its goings-on was not exactly conducive to promoting good will and harmony between the sexes, but memories of it etched in bold relief on my tranquil mind provided a pleasant chiaroscuro, a stellar recollection of a most remarkable and unusual birthday.

Chapter 36

The Actors Studio, The Lion's Head Pub, and the White Horse Tavern

Robin Roberts Howard, with her scant resources, has done as much as anyone to support traditional folk music through her singing, collecting, writing liner notes for record albums, and befriending other musicians. She has done so with little thought of personal gain, save only for enjoyment of the camaraderie of other musicians and music lovers. In Ireland, she sang in many venues and worked with Sean and Donal O'Sullivan of the Irish Folklore Commission, Alan Lomax, and Seamus Innes. She discovered and promoted the careers of Joe Heaney, Maggi Barry, Elizabeth Cronin, and the Clancy Brothers. In Scotland, she worked with Hamish Henderson, head of the School of Scottish Studies, and there discovered Jeanne Robertson and Lucy and Bill Stewart. In England, she worked with Peter Kennedy of the BBC and performed with Ewan MacColl and Peggy Seeger, Bert Lloyd, Isla Cameron, and Shirley Collins. In America, she appeared on Oscar Brand's radio show, sang at the Philadelphia Folk Festival and at Carnegie Hall, toured with Happy and Artie Traum and with Jack Langstaff (with whom she had a daughter, Caitlin), and had the lead in Revels-off-Broadway.

Robin also was an accomplished actress who performed off Broadway and helped Brian Heron start the Irish Arts Center in

New York. She was a member of the Actors Studio in New York, which I visited in the early 1970s. While watching Robin and other actors rehearsing, I could scarcely believe I was there, a place that was home to many famous actors, where they stimulated their imaginations, developed their skills in an experimental and creative environment, and created characters in the context of specific situations.

Robin, who had joined sometime in the late 1950s or early 1960s, explained that the Studio gave her "a place to work when [she wasn't] working." She mentioned that one of the most prominent members, Paul Newman, was "a dear; he was generous financially and very helpful in keeping the Studio going, and [was] a gracious man. As the Studio is run on a tight budget, the actors are asked once a year to make a contribution to keep us afloat." Robin was very glad to count Paul Newman as a friend.

I also asked Robin about Marlon Brando. She said that she knew him, but not very well. She confided, "I run into him on occasion at the studio or at parties, and we both have the same teacher, Stella Adler. Recently he called me up and we had a nice chat."

The Studio was in the vicinity of the Hell's Kitchen neighborhood. As we chatted with friends of Robin's about the neighborhood's colorful past, one woman said, "I remember reading that Davy Crockett said something to the effect of 'In my part of the country, when you meet an Irishman you find first a gentleman, but they are too mean to swab Hell's Kitchen.' That's not the exact quote, but you get my drift." Unable to control my enthusiasm, I exclaimed, "Too mean for Hell's Kitchen—that reminds me of a song." I sang the last verse:

Oh they say the women are worse than the men,
O Daddy Be Gay
Oh they say the women are worse than the men,
When they get sent to Hell
They got chucked out again
Daddy be gay and eat Candy.

Scarcely had I started singing when Robin joined in with me, to the accompaniment of people clapping.

* * *

Later, I asked Robin about her early experiences with acting. Robin confided, "When I was at Nyack High School, I was offered a chance to go to Hollywood, but I turned it down as I didn't want to become part of Sam Goldwyn's entourage. Also, my parents wanted me to go to Sarah Lawrence." I asked her what had attracted her to the theatre. She replied, "When I was young, I was very shy, but when I was on stage I could be anyone I wanted. I could live in a world of the imagination."

I inquired about whether anyone had taken her under their wing when she first joined the Actors Studio. "Heavens, no," she replied. "Anyone who joins the Actors Studio is a professional and is not going to be treated with kid gloves. However, I must say that when I joined, people were most helpful and friendly and I felt right at home. In order to be accepted one had to perform three scenes; however, I had only to do one, from 'Hills Like White Elephants' by Hemingway."

I wondered what scene I would choose, maybe something out of *Lucky Jim* by Kingsley Amis. The characters are laughably artificial in their behavior, full of clichés and affectation. They reminded me of old Newport society. *Lucky Jim* is funny and satirical but, giving it a second thought, there was another book I was fond of—*Under the Greenwood Tree* by Thomas Hardy. The story is set in Dorset around the beginning of the Industrial Revolution. It's like a genre painting that depicts the lives of village people—apple picking, country dancing—where the description of nature and customs helps define the character and shape the story.

Robin replied that she had also loved that book, with all its music and country life. Our conversation then turned to my experiences with acting. Someone asked when I had first become interested in acting. I replied that I had started when I was very young. "It was a matter of my psychic survival," I explained. "I started acting by emulating my parents to please them. Some of it was unconscious. I kept my eyes and ears open, observed my parents from top to bottom, noticed what they were wearing, their gestures and expressions, tone of voice, how they interacted with others, and tried to get inside their minds and see what made them tick. I was a lonely child who desperately wanted to please them, which I attempted to do by making myself a clone of their upper-class selves. On rare occasions I'd gain a token nod of approval, but at the same time I felt like a traitor to myself by pretending to be what they wanted me to be. At that age, I was too young to rebel by trying to establish my own identity. Back in the 1940s and '50s there was a pale semblance of an upper-class world, but it was dying, all form but no content. It was like a chicken with its head cut off that still flopped around, a reflex action, but in fact it was dead. The old guard still had their money and possessions, but they were no longer leaders of our country, so they retreated into the past, living vicariously in the myths of their ancestors. Frustrated and impotent, they sought cold comfort in their country clubs far removed from the rest of the world, drank themselves silly, and took out their hostility on their children."

"A world of emotional poverty, surrounded by riches," interrupted someone.

"Insane," said one of Robin's friends. "No wonder the old guard went the way of all flesh. That sort of thing is a sign of deep insecurity."

"Exactly," responded Robin. "When the old gods are no longer believed, they become burlesque figures and caricatures."

"Yes," I agreed, "but I still feel haunted by them, ancestral spirits, which I'd like to banish to their netherworld. I think of my parents as powerful pagan priests, shamans who performed paradigmatic gestures, exemplary models to be followed with no room for error. I had to do everything by the book, bow correctly, laugh correctly."

After we had chatted a while longer, Robin and I said our goodbyes and headed for the Lion's Head Pub in Greenwich Village with several friends, including two members of the Clancy Brothers, Paddy and Liam. We indulged ourselves in drops of the pure, singing, telling funny stories, and gossiping. Robin and her friends sang some songs, and when it was my turn I sang:

> Come all you fair and tender maids
> That flourish in your prime, prime,
> Beware, beware, make your garden fair
> And cover it over with thyme, thyme,
> Cover it all over with thyme
> And when your time is past and gone,
> He'll care no more for you, you,
> Beware, beware, make your garden fair,
> And cover it over with rue, rue,
> Cover it all over with rue

Scarcely had I finished when Robin looked at me with concern and surprise and asked, "Where did you learn that song?" I explained that I had learned it some years ago from the singing of Theodore Bikel and that it was also in one of his songbooks.

"I should have known," responded Robin tartly. "I sang it at a party in London, and there was Theodore recording everything that anyone sang. He didn't even ask my permission if he could use it."

"Oh, that was just borrowing," said one of the Clancys with a sardonic grin.

"Pernicious borrowing is more like it," I added. "Bob Dylan did that. He took a tune from a traditional American song, 'Nottamun Town,' which was collected and sung by Jean Ritchie. He set it to his own words, called it 'Masters of War,' and didn't get permission from Jean to use it. She sued him and won."

Robin's friend added, "Bob Dylan wasn't his real name. He was really Bob Zimmerman, but I guess Dylan makes a better stage name. It has an all-American flavor."

"Other people have done that," said Robin. "Ewan MacColl, who as you know is Scottish, was originally Jimmy Miller."

"That's right," I added, "and Paul Clayton was originally Paul

Worthington. Hell's bells, if I were going to become a professional folksinger, I'd change my name, too. Pierrepont is not very folksy sounding. I'd reinvent myself, to appear genuinely authentic and be just plain Pete, like someone out of Li'l Abner, with dungarees that had patches and toes sticking out of my boots, and I'd hail from Hogswill, North Carolina, as I'd speak and sing in an old-time twang. I'd spin a few yarns for folklorists, make up stuff, and they'd take it all down and publish it in the *Journal of American Folklore*. These tall tales, a pack of lies, would appear as god's truth in the archives of the Library of Congress or the Smithsonian. Perhaps I'd become much sought after by folk-song societies, which are starving for authenticity. If I couldn't make it as a Southern hillbilly, perhaps I could become an authentic down-home Maine fisherman, sound like someone out of 'Bert and I' [Robert Bryan and Marshall Dodge], sing Child ballads in a rustic accent, and tell people that I learned them from my great-uncle Ebenezer, who in turn learned them from his grandpappy."

At some point we headed to another watering hole, the White Horse Tavern, to meet some other friends. Sitting at a long wooden table facing the bar, someone remarked, "Remember the words of Bert Lloyd: 'Folk music is a comforting friend to the poor.' I wonder what would happen if ever Ireland got rich. How would that affect the music? Would everyone go highbrow?"

"No, don't worry," reassured a friend. "There'll always be the music in one form or another. Customs change and so does the music. If Ireland got rich, there'd be universal literacy, and more people would learn songs from records and books. There would be cultural organizations that would teach folk dancing and fiddling, and the music would be brought to more people's attention. It's easy for people who are well off to romanticize poverty. Those who are poor certainly don't. Sometimes noblemen would shed tears at the sight of poverty and misery among the poor, but how many of them would do something to ease their suffering?"

Somehow this exchange led into a discussion of the complicated relationship between vocal and instrumental music and the predominance of instrumental music as entertainment in traditional societies. The ethnomusicologist Bruno Nettl suggested that instrumental music does not imitate singing and that there is more stylistic variety in instrumental music, perhaps on account of the limitations of the human voice as compared to the freedom and complexity allowed by the instruments.

"Yes," agreed David O'Docherty, recently arrived from Dublin and then living in Boston, "there certainly is a great variety in the many forms of folk dancing found in England, Ireland, Scotland, and America—jigs, reels, hornpipes, sword dances, quadrilles, highland flings, hoedowns, and square dances."

I remarked, "The folklorist in me impels me to mention that in pagan pre-church times, obscene dances were frequently done in connection with the cult of the gods and the spirits of fertility."

"Oh Christ, Pete," remonstrated David, "you've got sex on the brain."

"Not at all. Look at staid old Victorian England," I replied, "where several of those exotic dances can be found. The dance mentioned by Thomas Hardy in the opening chapter of *Tess of the D'Urbervilles* seems to belong to that class."

Suddenly and spontaneously our table, led by Paddy and Liam and David, burst into song.

> *Oh it's all for me grog*
> *Me Jolly, Jolly grog*
> *All gone for beer and tobacco*
> *I spent all me tin*
> *On the lasses drinking gin*
> *And across the western ocean I must wander*

My head reeling with music, humor, and the drink, I fell asleep in my chair and woke up early the next afternoon on Robin's couch with pleasant recollections of my visit to the Actors Studio, the Lion's Head Pub, and the White Horse Tavern.

Chapter 37

The Seeger Family

I first met Peggy Seeger when she was an undergraduate at Radcliffe living in an old campus building, Peach House, around 1953 or 1954. Before I met her, I knew little about her except that her well-known brother Pete was a member of The Weavers, America's best-known and best-loved folk group. Listening to her sing, accompanying herself on the banjo, I enjoyed her unaffected delivery. At some point after that, I bought one of her records, *Songs of Courting and Complaint*, from the Folklore Center in Greenwich Village, run by Izzy Young. From that record I learned several songs that I still sing, namely "The Young Man Who Wouldn't Hoe Corn," "The Butcher Boy," and "Whistle, Daughter, Whistle." Some time after that, in the 1960s, I lent several of my records—*Songs of Courting and Complaint*, one by Jean Ritchie and another by Shep Ginandes—to Joan Baez, who learned and performed several of the songs on those records and later recorded them herself. She recorded "Butcher Boy" as "Railroad Boy," a more romantic image.

The next time I heard Peggy, she was singing with her husband Ewan MacColl, a leading figure in the British Isles folk revival. Some forty-odd years later, I heard Peggy sing at the 150th anniversary celebration of Francis James Child, the world's foremost authority on English and Scottish ballads. The Harvard Folklore and Celtic departments organized the celebration. Peggy accompanied herself on a variety of instruments. Her voice was just as I remembered it from when I first met her, and it brought back pleasant memories of those early days when life was fresh, young, and full of promise. After Peggy's set, there was an informal ceilidh with members of the Celtic and Folklore departments, students and faculty, contributing songs.

* * *

In the early 1970s, while living in the basement of 65 Mt. Auburn Street in Cambridge, I was paid a visit by a portly gentleman, Cyril Phillips, dressed in sheepherder's clothes, wearing a Sherlock Holmes hat, and carrying an old suitcase and an accordion. Sticking his head through the door, he explained, "Joe Hickerson at the Library of Congress said I should pay you a visit." Cyril, like the man who came to dinner and stayed for two weeks, became a permanent fixture, sleeping on my couch for the better part of a year.

Several months after Cyril's arrival, he received an invitation from Pete Seeger to visit him at his home in Beacon, New York. Delighted at the idea of going on a trip to meet Pete Seeger, I persuaded some friends with a car to take us there. Arriving in the late afternoon with the sun setting in the west, we were met by Pete and his lovely wife, Toshi, with dinner waiting for us. Unfortunately, I didn't get to know Pete as well as I would have liked, as he was fully engrossed in conversation with Cyril, who was regaling him with stories about living on his family's farm in Sussex.

That evening, the musicians who had driven to Beacon with me—Seamus Walker, Johnny Beggan, and Declan Hunt, collectively (along with Clive Collins) known as the Battering Ram—having consumed great quantities of "drops of the pure" (whiskey), decided to walk it off, where they passed out in a neighbor's barn. Shaking his head in bewilderment when he heard about this, and concerned about the well-being of my friends, Pete was mystified by all this unprecedented adventure.

The following year, I arranged a concert for Pete's brother, Mike, and his wife, Alice Gerrard. Mike, who played a variety of instruments—autoharp, banjo, fiddle, dulcimer, guitar, mouth harp, and dobro—was (with Tom Paley and John Cohen) a member of the New Lost City Ramblers, an old-time string band that contributed to an awareness and appreciation of that kind of music. After the concert, we went to Old Joe Clark on Fayette Street in Cambridge, a cooperative where musicians lived and played. Other musicians who were there included Dick Fegy and Neil Rossi from the Spark Gap Wonder Boys, Clay Jackson from the Mother Bay State Entertainers, Bob Siggins from the Charles River Valley Boys, and Joe Val of the New England Bluegrass Boys. While enjoying the music I met other old-time musicians and organized concerts for them as well, including the Red Clay Ramblers; the Highwoods String Band; Tracy and Eloise Schwarz; and Allan Block, Alan Stowell, and Peter Hoover.

Once the music at Old Joe got going, it never let up until the wee hours of the morning. During the merry making a neighbor across the street complained about the loud music and called the police, who asked the musicians to play more quietly.

* * *

In the early 1970s, I had the privilege of auditing a summer course at Harvard given by Professor Charles Seeger, a musicologist and father of Pete, Peggy, and Mike. Early in life, he had become a conductor with the Cologne Opera in Europe and later was the head of the music department at the University of Cologne; a teacher at the Julliard School of Music and the New School for Social Research; and a collaborator with John and Alan Lomax, starting the Archive of American Folk Song (now the Archive of Folk Culture) for the Library of Congress. He was also the assistant director of the Federal Music Project of the Works Project Administration (WPA). A friend of mine, Ann Morrison Spinney, who taught at the Irish studies program at Boston College, reminded me that Charles Seeger also invented a machine that compares singing styles of different traditional cultures. In addition, according to Professor Jerrold Hirsch, from whom I had audited a course in folklore, Charles Seeger was a link between the New Deal and applied folklore, which redefined the study of the subject and its role in a democratic society.

In Professor Seeger's course, I read one of Bruno Nettl's books on ethnomusicology. Nettl maintained that there were four types of music in the world: tribal, folk, popular, and classical, the latter being the beaux-ideal of Western civilization. I also learned about Alan Lomax's theory that a country's style of singing is related to its social structure.

Professor Seeger mentioned that untrained musicians hear only what they think they hear, as hearing is culturally determined. What he said was helpful to me whenever I attempt to learn a melody from a record.

Professor Seeger wrote that folk music was not a productive weapon in the class struggle because it was ineffective and defeatist. I wonder about that. The Nazis and Communists used folk music and folklore to further their political agendas; likewise, smaller nations in the nineteenth century used their newfound folklore to overthrow their monarchies and establish republics. Folklorists from those countries performed Brothers Grimm-like services for their people, discovering a wealth of folklore among the peasants and using it as a way of establishing their national identity as they rebelled against the eighteenth-century enlightenment view that the superior classical culture of Greece and Rome was to be emulated by all others.

* * *

The only member of the Seeger family whom I never met was Ruth Crawford Seeger. However, I got to know her indirectly through her marvelous collection of folk songs in her children's books, which were helpful when I was looking for new songs to sing with children at their school.

In the 1930s, Ruth Seeger studied in Berlin to become a composer. In the context of her socialist concerns and beliefs, she composed in the atonal style, which was radically different from anything that had gone before. Apropos of that, I remember once listening to compositions in the strange and disturbing style of

Schoenberg and Hindemith, along with several of Ruth Seeger's compositions, and not enjoying them. Those strange discordant melodies based on a twelve-tone chromatic system were alien to my ears, as there was no resolution in the songs, no reassuring return to the familiar tonic notes at the end. Instead, the listener was left hanging, lost in limbo land, in a confusing cacophony of notes that appeared to have no reason for being.

In contrast, one of the things that attracted me to folk songs was that at the conclusion of each verse, no matter how tragic the story, I felt grounded, as the notes soared high and wide, filling every nook and cranny of the room, and then returned to the place from which the song had begun its musical journey, reassuring me that one can go home again.

* * *

I once saw a documentary film about Pete Seeger at the First Church in Belmont, a Unitarian Universalist church. The movie showed Pete building his own house with the help of family and friends, cutting wood, planting crops, and feeding the animals. Next it showed him with his group, The Weavers, playing at Carnegie Hall in New York for people of all ages. Rather than sit in quiet appreciation, the audience enthusiastically joined in the choruses, bringing everyone together in a common flow of feeling. The documentary also showed Pete singing with school children. By the look on their faces and the sound of their voices, everyone, including the teacher, was having a great time.

Another scene in the film showed Pete's wife, Toshi, and their children performing chores around the house and in the yard, thereby enabling Pete to be Pete as he traveled around the country meeting other musicians, collecting songs, and presenting them to the public. Toward the end of the film, Pete was shown playing with a traditional mountain singer, Bascom Lamar Lunsford, whose record *Smoky Mountain Ballads* I bought in the 1960s and from whom I learned several songs.

In his pioneering effort to collect America's hidden treasures and bring them to the attention of an appreciative public, collectors, scholars, and musicians, Pete entered previously undiscovered parts of rural America, wrote books on regional collections (giving the tune and text of songs and their history), and made records of old-time singers. With the advent of his folk music revival, folk-song societies emerged around the country to hold monthly concerts and hootenannies at college campuses. As a result, folklorists gained more autonomy in the universities and America discovered the wealth of its heritage and history in song.

Some of the musicians who became known to the public as a result of such pioneering efforts were Clarence Ashley, Joan Baez, Dock Boggs, Paul Clayton, Elizabeth Cotton, Sara Cleveland, Barbara Dane, Hazel Dickens, Ramblin' Jack Elliott, Lightnin' Hopkins, Cisco Houston, Mississippi John Hurt, Blind Lemon Jefferson, Robert Johnson, "Aunt" Molly Jackson, Lead Belly, "Uncle" Dave Macon, Almeda Riddle, Edna and Jean Ritchie, Frank Warner and his sons (Garrett and Jeff), Doc Watson, Hedy West, and Josh White—to name just a few. Oh, I mustn't forget—there's Allan Block, Omar Blondahl, Fletcher Collins, the De Corimer family, Texas Gladden, Sara Grey, Joe Hickerson, Sandy Ives, English Logan, Bascom Lamar Lunsford, Margaret MacArthur, Sandy Paton, Caroline Paton, Faith Petric, Obray Ramsey, Susan Reed, Robin Roberts, Jim Rooney, Molly Scott, Hobart Smith, Ralph Lee Smith, Ellen Stekert, Heather Wood, and so many more. I treasure their music. Thank you, Seeger family, for enriching my life by making me aware and appreciative of the music that since the dawning of the day has nurtured men, women, and children and hopefully will continue to do so.

Chapter 38

A Christening

I had just returned from a late evening bout of singing and drinking at the Plough and Stars, a local Irish-American bar in Cambridge, and was just about to call it quits for the evening when my bell rang. It seemed a bit late for company, but then I was used to that sort of thing. Ever since I had started living in Harvard Square, musicians, artists, and all kinds of offbeat people who kept their own crazy hours dropped in to visit at any old time, defying the conventions of social visitation portrayed by Henry James and Edith Wharton. With resignation, I went to the door to greet my late caller, and there, to my surprise, was a friend whom I hadn't seen for several years. It was none other than Bobby Clancy, a folksinger from Ireland who was here on a tour of singing and partying. He greeted me jovially, saying, "Hello, Peter, good to see you. Come on, let's go out and have a sing-song." Two o'clock in the morning seemed an odd hour for this sort of thing, but then I suppose the divine muse does not respect the mundane boundaries of time and space. I acquiesced, and we made our way to the heart of Harvard Square, proceeding with some difficulty, but arriving all in one piece.

It so happens that I had in my possession a bodhran—a Celtic drum which at Bobby's behest I brought along. So there we were, the three of us, at two-thirty in the morning—Bobby, myself, and the bodhran. Despite the drowsifying influence of alcohol that Bobby had consumed in great quantities earlier in the evening, he seemed more inspired than ever, and forthwith he sang a very beautiful love song in Gaelic, followed by some lilting, all to his own accompaniment on the bodhran. I, being a little out of condition, valiantly croaked out a few old ballads, inspiring Bobby to more of the same.

At some point in all this drunken merriment, Bobby announced that he was going to bestow the ultimate favor on my bodhran—namely, to christen it. "How nice," I thought to myself; I had never seen a bodhran blessed before. Being a traditionalist, I beamed enthusiastically, relishing the thought of the invisible metaphysical transformation that would lift the spirit of the drum out of the realm of the ordinary. With a sense of impending awe, I contemplated the prospect of my drum being joined to all those drums that for centuries had received a blessing, establishing its link in the time-honored chain of all sanctified bodhrans, beating, as a collective heart, the rhythms of a nation. With reverent solemnity, I passed the drum to Bobby.

Before I knew what was happening, there stood Bobby Clancy, to my amazement and horror, thunderously tinkling into my drum. I pinched myself several times to make sure this was really happening. Had my whiskey-plagued imagination gotten the better of me?

After what seemed an interminable time, his unholy water having administered its smelly sanctification, Bobby looked up at me and said, "Peter, if you don't piss on this bodhran with me, you're a bleedin' Protestant."

I was a Protestant—not a good one, but one nevertheless. Without suffering undue worry as to my religious status, I bade Bobby good night and gave him the bodhran as a present. Subsequently, every time we crossed paths, he would cheerfully inform me that his bodhran was slowly improving as a result of his benediction.

Chapter 39

Eisteddfod

According to the *Dictionary of Folklore, Mythology, and Legend*, the eisteddfod historically was a periodic assembly of Welsh bards to conduct examinations and competitions in poetry, prose, composition, and music, with qualified candidates admitted to the highly esteemed and trained Bardic profession. Begun probably sometime before the twelfth century, recognized in the time of Queen Elizabeth I as an institution of authority, the eisteddfod lost its prestige during the seventeenth and part of the eighteenth century and lapsed until its revival in 1792. Since then it has become once more a national institution to celebrate Welsh folklore and traditions.

A modern American version of the eisteddfod, a folk festival founded by Howard Glasser, was first held in 1972 at Southeastern Massachusetts University (SMU), which later became University of Massachusetts–Dartmouth. In the 1960s, Howard had run ceilidhs at the University of Pittsburgh, where he was on the faculty teaching art. In 1970 he moved to Rhode Island, where he taught at the University of Rhode Island (URI); there he ran ceilidhs on a monthly basis.

Howard came to love traditional music during his high school years, when he had heard it on the radio and on recordings. Wishing to experience the music in its natural setting, he went to Scotland in the 1960s. Armed with a tape recorder, he met

Hamish Henderson, then head of the School of Scottish Studies, and there discovered some of the great Scottish singers, notably Jeannie Robertson, Jimmy McBeath, Lucy and Belle Stewart, and Lizzie Higgins. While collecting in Scotland in 1960, he became good friends with Arthur Argo, Jim Cross, and Ray Fisher, with whom he exchanged recordings. Interestingly, Arthur was the great-grandson of Gavin Greig, a well-known collector of songs from the Northeast. After his stint at URI, Howard moved to SMU, where he set up his first eisteddfod, a three-day weekend festival featuring mostly traditional and revival singers from England, Ireland, Scotland, Canada, and the United States, with an appreciative and knowledgeable audience that came from New England, New York, Pennsylvania, and Washington, DC.

The character of the festival reflected Howard's easygoing and generous nature, a guiding presence throughout. During the day there were workshops in which musicians shared their expertise in some aspect of their music with those who were interested. The festival being relatively small, the musicians were not separate from the audience; they were part of the community, not outsiders coming to perform. The eisteddfod reminded me of the Fox Hollow Folk Festival in upstate New York, run by Bob and Evelyne Beers. The Fox Hollow Festival was held in a clearing in the woods where people sat on wooden benches with the trees over their heads and pine needles and cones under their feet. Musicians and audience were on the same plane, with easy access to each other.

At the eisteddfod, many of the musicians and those who heard them were acquainted with each other, which contributed to a relaxed and friendly atmosphere. Howard felt strongly that the traditions belonged to everyone and that nonprofessional singers and musicians needed encouragement to develop their skill and talent. It was a peaceful occasion, with no riots or disturbances, and people had a place to stay at the campground, rather than crashing on beaches, parks, or private property as at the old Newport Folk Festival.

A few of the many singers and musicians who performed in

concert at the eisteddfod over the years were Margaret Bennett, Archie Fisher, Cilla Fisher, Sara Grey, Norman Kennedy, Enoch Kent, Gordeanna McCulloh, Geordie McIntyre, Alison McMorland, Jean Redpath, Willie Scott, Alex and Belle Stewart, Elizabeth Stewart, Sheila Stewart, and Artie Trezise, all from Scotland. From Ireland there were Maggi Barry, Bridget Fitzgerald, Joe Heaney, Janet Kelley, Mick Moloney, and Maggi Pierce. Singers from England were Tony Barrand, Peter Bellamy, Bob Davenport, Roy Harris, David Jones, Louis Killen, John Roberts, Heather Wood, and Royston Wood. Finally, from America there were John "Fudd" Benson, Martin Grosswendt, Richard Hughes, Peter Hoover, Rick and Lorraine Lee, Margaret MacArthur, Tony and Irene Saletan, and Walter Scott.

Howard asked me to run a ceilidh at his first eisteddfod, an invitation I enthusiastically accepted, especially as some of my friends would be taking part. Many of those who appeared were members of the Folk Song Society of Greater Boston, an organization dedicated to the preservation and perpetuation of traditional music in all its forms. Some of the performers at my eisteddfod ceilidhs over the years were Rick Avery, Tony Barrand, Battering Ram, Peter Bellamy, Joanie Bronfman, Paul Cole, Bob Davenport, Jan and Neil Downey, Tom Gibney, Roy Harris, David Jones, Rob Joel, Louis Killen, Neal MacMillan, David O'Docherty, Cyril Phillips, Ricky Rackin, Elliot Ribner, John Roberts, Jacki Spectre, Royston Wood, and Heather Wood.

* * *

At his first eisteddfod, Howard established an award recognizing an outstanding individual who supported the ideals of the folk community. The first award went to Dr. Kenneth S. Goldstein. The second year it went to Joe Hickerson of the Library of Congress. At the third eisteddfod, Howard got my attention when he announced from the stage, "The recipient of the 1974 Eisteddfod Award is Peter Johnson for his important contribution to folk music, promoting concerts, ceilidhs, and records of high quality, true to traditional values." I was, of course, delighted, but was also aware that I had a lot to live up to and would have to work doubly hard to make his words continue to ring true. The award has continued with an impressive list of recipients, such as Estelle Klein, Alan Jabbour, and Israel "Izzy" Young. I am pleased and honored to be included.

* * *

In 1996, having retired from teaching with a Distinguished Service to the University Award, Howard stopped running the eisteddfod. For several years following his retirement there was a fallow period, until in 2003 he turned over the reins to Jerry Epstein and Heather Wood, who ran it at Polytechnic University in Brooklyn. It was then moved to the Renaissance Charter School in Queens, NY, then to a lodge in the Catskills with the delightful name of Friar Tuck, and later to a Hudson Valley resort. Jerry, a fine singer, well versed in musicology, performed over the years with Jack Langstaff, the founder of Revels. Heather, who came from England, was at one time a member of The Young Tradition, which, along with the Watersons, was one of England's finest traditional music groups. I recall Heather as having a delightfully spontaneous nature. Once while walking down the hall at the eisteddfod, she suddenly broke into song. Standing nearby, Joanie Bronfman, Neal MacMillan, and I joined in on the chorus. In the early 1970s, Jerry and Jack Langstaff performed for Living Folk in Cambridge at the Odd Fellows Hall. Some thirty-five years later Heather, with David Jones and the late Tom Gibney, collectively known as Poor Old Horse, did a concert for Living Folk in Watertown.

Howard Glasser made many contributions to the folk music community beyond organizing the eisteddfods. Howard was formally recognized for his contributions with the creation of the Howard T. Glasser Archives of Folk Music and Letter Arts at The Claire T. Carney Library at the University of Massachusetts–Dartmouth. Now included within the collection are the archive of the New Bedford Tryworks coffeehouse, recordings from Clyde Tyndale of the Woods Hole Folk Song Society, and recordings of my own ceilidhs and concerts. This library archive is a major area resource.

* * *

Many years after I ran my first ceilidhs at Howard's eisteddfod, I moderated a workshop he gave in collecting at the Hudson Valley Resort and Spa in Kerhonkson, nestled in the lap of the Catskills, a range of the Appalachian Mountains west of the Hudson River. Along with Howard, the host, the workshop featured a panel consisting of Robin Roberts, Robin Morton, and Caroline Paton, who were musicians as well as collectors. At the beginning of the workshop Howard briefly mentioned working in Scotland in the 1960s with Hamish Henderson, head of the School of Scottish Studies, collecting songs and ballads from several of Scotland's finest singers.

Introducing the panel, I spoke of the important part Robin Roberts, through her collecting, singing, and writing, had played in the Irish folk music revival. Among her many contributions, she had written an introduction to a book on Séamus Ennis, written by Jimmy O'Brien Moran. Caroline Paton, along with her late husband, Sandy, were long dedicated to the preservation, perpetuation, and enjoyment of traditional music. They founded the Folk-Legacy label, based in Sharon, Connecticut. Recording folk music from England, Ireland, Scotland, Canada, and the United States, Folk-Legacy became one of the most respected and successful folk record companies. Its records were well produced and well recorded, with simple but attractive covers, informative liner notes, and effective distribution. Sandy and Caroline also sang at camps, schools, institutions, folk-song societies, and festivals throughout the country and abroad. At the request of their friends, they produced a record of themselves on their own label.

The third panel member, Robin Morton, from the north of Ireland, was one of the founding members of the Boys of the Lough, consisting of Robin, Cathal McConnell, also from Ireland, Dick Gaughan, from Scotland, and Aly Bain, a superb fiddler from the Shetlands. Robin had collected songs, ballads, and tunes from Ulster, the home of Ireland's legendary hero, Cú Chulainn; produced records for his company, Temple Records; and compiled and edited the books *Folk Songs Sung in Ulster* and *Come Day, Go Day, God Send Sunday*.

Later that day, after the panel discussion, Robin Morton's wife, Alison Kinnaird, one of Scotland's finest traditional harpists, gave a workshop on both the gut- and wire-strung harps, about which she has written several books. In my own research, I learned that the earliest harps were bow-shaped and were played by Sumerians around 3000 B.C. Some were depicted on Greek vases and in relics of ancient Egypt. Gaulish bards were said to have chanted to the accompaniment of the plucked strings to dispel evil spirits. Irish harpists at different times in history were outlawed as spreaders of sedition. During Cromwell's time, they were personae non grata. During the Jacobite period, however, harpists were held in high esteem by the Stuarts.

At the conclusion of the workshop, some of us gathered informally and continued our discussion. Mark Katz, an active member of the Folk Song Society of Greater Boston who had attended many Living Folk concerts, remarked on the difference between early folklorists and those of today. Nowadays they are more hands on and not given to wordy speculation and far-fetched theories. I volunteered that Richard Dorson and D. K. Wilgus had pointed out that some nineteenth-century scholars had concocted fanciful theories about the origin and meaning of folk songs and tales, but in recent times folklorists, taking their cue from anthropologists, were more interested in how folklore functions in a society. Some folklorists today are known as culture brokers, in that they act as a liaison between the people they are studying and the general public.

Later that evening, after spending an enjoyable day hearing good music, going to workshops, and seeing friends I hadn't seen in years, I went to sleep early to be well rested for the long drive home. Lying in bed, I wondered what would become of the old songs I'd loved for years. Young people aren't singing them any more. Many of the songs have survived in books or records, but will those "last leaves" atrophy, expire from old age, and wither on the vine, or will they get a second life and once more become a pasture of plenty?

≋ Chapter 40 ≋

Texas Tall Tales

I n the early 1970s, I took on a roommate who exhibited strong
macrobiotic tendencies. Like it or not, I found myself privy to
his thoughts on the matter, usually in the form of lectures at
mealtime. Every time Jimmy Murphy served up a meal, it would
emerge on the table in its pristine simplicity, accompanied by a
lecture concerning the pros and cons of macrobiotic delicacies versus
other foods. "Eat this—this is ying," or "Don't eat that—that's yang,"
Jimmy would hold forth in a reverential tone. Against all my indif-
ference and inertia, he was determined to make a convert out of me.

Jimmy was born and raised in Cut and Shoot, Texas, real Bible
Belt country. This may explain the evangelical fervor with which he
spread the Gospel of Natural Foods—his substitute for religion, or
perhaps I should say his new religion. When I knew him, he had
long forsaken the Baptist doctrine of his childhood. That void had
been filled by the promise of a better life offered by the messianic
scripture of macrobiotics.

When Jimmy invited friends over for meals, he invariably
preached a sermon quoting such authorities as George Ohsawa and
Michio Kushi. As is typical with conversion campaigns, he would
follow through with his guests by inquiring, in the manner of a
minister tending his flock, how they were doing and what they were
eating. In time, a few people were converted; many more were not.

After a time, I learned to appreciate some of Jimmy's culinary concoctions. At first the food tasted a little bland, but on request he added some seasoning, which worked wonders. At the end of a meal Jimmy would light up a cigarette. He smoked about a pack a day and consumed generous helpings of whiskey. When asked about how smoking and drinking fit into his macrobiotic principles, he replied that miso soup counteracted the ill effects of nicotine and alcohol. The more Jimmy talked about this stuff, the more it reminded me of how good old boys got around Bible Belt fundamentalists' prohibitions.

Standing about six feet tall, lean and lanky with a weather-beaten face, sandy hair, and an angular, protruding jaw, a modern version of Ichabod Crane, all arms and legs radiating in all directions from a skinny torso, Jimmy was what I thought a Texan should look like. Besides macrobiotics, his *idée fixe*, Jimmy was fond of singing cowboy songs and telling Texas folk tales, which I enjoyed. One time, we were entertaining friends for dinner, including Andy Hanley (a fiddler who was to play at my wedding and my eightieth birthday celebration) and his brother Martin. We sat around the kitchen table chewing the fat, telling jokes, rehashing old gossip, and singing. Jimmy was asked to sing. Putting out his cigarette and taking a final swig of his Black and Tan, he sang in a gravelly voice a variant of "The Old Chisholm Trail":

> *It's cloudy in the West and looking like rain*
> *And my darn old slicker in the wagon train*
> *Feet in the stirrups and seat in the saddle*
> *I hung and rattled with them long-haired cattle*
> *Oh, I ride with my slicker and I ride all day*
> *And I pack along my bottle for to pass the time away*
> *With my feet in the saddle and my hands on the horn*
> *I'm the best damn cowboy that ever got born*
> *No chaps, no slicker, and she pours down rain*
> *And I swear to my boss that I'll never herd again*
> *I'll head back south and marry a squaw*
> *And live my life on the sandy Washita*

Following an appreciative round of applause, Jimmy said, "There's millions of verses, but I can't remember any more. I've a funny thought, that singing lots of verses that go on and on, wasting valuable time, would be a great form of filibuster to kill a ludicrous bill in the Senate."

"Good man yourself, Jimmy," said Martin Hanley. "It's interesting how these old songs capture the flavor of a cowboy's life, herding and all that. It's like these songs are to the land what sea shanties are to the sea."

"That's for sure," replied Jimmy. "A lot of cowboy songs tell the story of hardships suffered on the long cattle drive from San Antonio to the grasslands of Montana and the Dakotas, and then the celebration at the end of the journey. Cowboy songs are the work and recreational songs of the American cowhand. They're made up of bits and pieces of older ballads, 'come all ye's' music hall songs, and the songs of the southern mountains, which is where many cowboys came from. They've got a bit of everything in them, the whole kit and kaboodle. There's a touch of Spanish influence from over the southwestern border, not to mention a trace of Indian war whoops in the refrains."

Later in the evening, after all of us got pleasantly soused on various rum and whiskey concoctions, Andy asked Jimmy to tell one of his Texas tall tales. Jimmy proceeded to tell one of the more heavily embellished versions of the variously reported story of his hometown's origins. "Let me tell you how Cut and Shoot got its name," he began. "More than a hundred years ago, I reckon it was [actually more like sixty]. There was a small settlement of farms, a small country community with only one church. Now there was one small problem, at least as far as I've been told. There were two church groups, Baptists and Methodists, and I needn't tell you they didn't take kindly to each other. It was hate at first sight. According to my grand-uncle, and he remembers way back, the majority of the community, who were Methodists, decided to exclude the Baptist minister from the church because, according to the Methodists, he was preaching a false doctrine. Well, that old Baptist minister just wouldn't take no for an answer. He was hopping mad, cussin' a blue streak. He swore and vowed that come hell or high water he would cut and shoot his way back into the church. Sure as shooting, so to speak, that's what he did. That started a feud that lasted for years and claimed the lives of some twenty or thirty people. People were shootin' each other right and left in the middle of the street. Baptists and Methodists were doing a number on each other in broad daylight, all in the name of God. It was a Holy War, no holds barred, and at that time there was no law enforcement to stop it. It was every man for himself. Anyway, that's how Cut and Shoot got its name. The minister cut and shot his way into the church."

"Cut and Shoot," exclaimed Andy. "How apropos. I guess the name fits. Say, Jimmy, what was that story again about the guy with the funny name? You said it was a true story."

"Well, I reckon I know who you mean," said Jimmy. "I heard this from my great-grandpappy, who swore that it was true because he knew the people. This fellow Turlelury and his uncle went deer hunting in the middle of winter, and they had to walk about three miles into the woods. It was the dead of winter and colder than a witch's tit. They brought along a little comfort, you know, a drop of the pure, the good stuff, whiskey, jes to keep them warm. Well, they was almost there when the old man, feeling a bit tired, had to sit down and rest, and so for about twenty minutes his nephew Turlelury looked around for some deer signs. When he came back he found the old man leaning against the tree with his head slumped over. Turlelury thought that perhaps the old man had too much to drink or else was jes plain tuckered out. He tried to wake the old man, saying, 'Come on, it's time to git a going.' Wal, that old man didn't bat an eyelash, didn't move a muscle, so his nephew tapped him on the shoulder, and the huddled form of the old man jes plumb fell over and lay on the snow. Wal, poor old Turlelury didn't know what went wrong; he jes reckoned that the old man had passed out from fatigue and drink. Turlelury picked him up and loaded him on his back like he was carrying a deer and headed out fur his truck a couple of miles away. After a long trek through the woods, he finally reached his truck and tried to put the old man down, but couldn't, 'cause he was stuck to him; he couldn't get him off his back. At the time, Turlelury didn't realize that the old man had died. Rigor mortis had set in, with the result that the old man's arms and legs became attached to Turlelury."

"Good God," interjected Andy. "Incredible."

Jimmy pressed on. "Let me tell you, Turlelury was beside himself. He was going mad. Around the bend. He didn't know what was happening or what to do. He tried to shake off his uncle by brushing against a tree. This didn't work as the body still clung fast. Turlelury was getting desperate. He tried everything—jumping up and down, rolling on the ground, and yelling at his uncle—all to no avail. Finally, with a huge effort, he managed to disengage himself from the dead body. He threw his uncle over his shoulders, put him in the back seat of the old pickup truck, and drove at breakneck speed to the nearest hospital. That old truck zig-zagged back and forth as he raced over those narrow winding roads, running dogs and chickens off the road. His horn was blaring furiously until he arrived at the hospital, where he was immediately redirected to the nearest funeral parlor."

"I'll bet that poor guy hasn't been the same since," I commented. "How can you put to rest the memory of something like that? Speaking of funeral parlors, I had a friend, Dunia Carey, who was born in a funeral parlor. She told me that when she was young, she saw the body of a handsome young man laid out on a slab of stone. She fell in love with that boy, and ever since then she'd fall in love with men who resembled him. That's a modern Gothic tale for you. Edgar Allan Poe or Faulkner would have a field day with that."

"Christ, this is all so morbid, Jimmy," objected Andy. "Tell us something cheery."

"Oh, sure, I'll tell you something funny, and it's true. My uncle Bob Harris, when he was a kid living in East Texas back in the twenties, was fond of playing tricks and pranks on friends and neighbors. He had a great sense of humor. He recalled how one evening he caught an old turkey buzzard in a jaw trap. While witnessing the incarceration of the bird, his devil-may-care imagination came to life as he envisioned all sorts of pranksterish possibilities, which quickly resolved themselves into a course of action. Spying a long piece of string, he attached it to some old rags tied into a ball, which he soaked with kerosene. Uncle Bob then released the turkey buzzard from his trap, but not before tying it to the ball of rags, which he then set afire. Uncle Bob paused for a few seconds, as if collecting his memory, and then described the strange-looking apparition that sought the sanctity of the evening sky as it slowly and majestically spiraled upward in full view, with the glow of the fire illuminating the countryside below.

"Uncle Bob then speculated on the psychological effect this strange sight had on the local folk in this God-fearing Bible Belt. 'The inhabitants of these parts,' Bob explained, 'lived with a heap of sin and guilt on their shoulders. So when they became privy to this nocturnal nightmare, featuring the dark silhouetted form of a buzzard accompanied by a great glow of fire, the bird and the ball of fire moving in perfect harmony with each other, circling higher and higher, I reckoned those folks must have freaked out. Imagine if some of them were stone drunk!'"

Jimmy continued. "Those folks down below were quite taken aback, so much so that they thought this was a sign from God that the world was coming to an end. As a result, they mended their evil ways and, as a last desperate measure of repentance, emptied all of their whiskey bottles and threw them on the ground along with their snuff.

"Uncle Bob then concluded, 'and that was the talk of Montgomery County for miles around and years to come.'"

"Jimmy," queried Don Kalick, a friend and neighbor and professor of psychology at U-Mass, "isn't that a pretty rough neck of the woods where you came from? Isn't that what they call the Badlands of Texas?"

"Yup, I reckon it was. Folks took the law into their own hands. There was no sheriff, no police. Hell's bells, I remember my grand-pappy telling me how some of my relatives way back in the late eighteen hundreds got into a feud. It seemed that folk were feuding at the drop of a hat. I forget how we were all related. I reckon they may have been grand uncles or something like that. Let's see. First there were Armadillo Moorhead and his cousin, Coon Massey. They were both tough customers. Now back in those days, Coon had an old dog, a mutt. Now that dog jes ran free and went wherever he wanted. Wal, that old dog took to chasin' Armadillo's hens and eating them. Now Armadillo got pretty mad and told Coon to mind his dog, but Coon paid no mind and his dog kept right on killin' Armadillo's chickens. Let me tell you, Armadillo got so fed up, so mad, that the next time Coon's dog came into his yard he killed it with his shotgun, skinned it, and cooked it, making it into a delectable stew. Armadillo then invited Coon to come over for lunch, and of course Coon hadn't a clue about what he was eating until the end of the meal when Armadillo told him, 'Coon, I'm glad you liked your lunch, 'cause you jes ate that miserable mutt of yours.' Wal, let me tell you, Coon got so mad he went plum berserk. He grabbed an axe that was lying on the ground and without blinking an eyelash he cut off Armadillo's head, took it with him, and put it on his fencepost as a warning: Don't mess with Coon."

"Remind me not to go to Texas any time soon," said Andy.

"Wal, it's not quite that way anymore. A lot of Texans, especially the ones in the big city, have acquired a thin veneer of East Coast civilization—you know, all the trappings of good manners—but underneath there still lurks the heart of a Texan. What's that old Irish saying? You can take the man out of the bog, but you can't take the bog out of the man."

"East Coast civilization is not all that civilized," said Martin. "We've got more crime here than anywhere, and don't forget all those big businesses that can be killing machines in their own right. Just pick your poison."

"Hey, I almost forgot; my story is not over," Jimmy broke in. "As I was saying, there was Armadillo's head adorning Coon's fencepost. Now Armadillo had a cousin, Wildman Woodman, who most folks were afeared of as he was prone to getting into terrible rages. When Wildman got word of what Coon did to Armadillo, he went berserk and said he would go gunnin' for Coon. Fortunately, the newly elected sheriff, the first in the area, intervened with his deputies and prevented further bloodshed. There was a heap of blood shed in them days."

≋ Chapter 41 ≋

Revels

People occasionally ask me about "Revels," and for lack of a succinct readymade answer (because there isn't one) I say, "You must go and see for yourself." That is not quite good enough, for such an admission—though well intended—leaves little to augment the imagination. At the other extreme, there is a temptation to tell them everything, which leaves them in a state of delicious confusion, but not better informed than if I had said nothing. I here opt for the latter, hoping to communicate the spirit in which Revels was conceived and continues to be performed and appreciated.

Revels is a celebration of the season in the form of music, put on at Sanders Theatre in Cambridge at Christmas and in Boston in the summer. Christmas Revels joyfully ushers in the New Year with song, dance, stories, and games, a seasonal rite of passage. The celebration of Christmas goes back to 320 A.D., when the Christian fathers in Rome decided to convert the birthday of the unconquered sun into a birthday more suited to their aims. The sun became the son.

Revels uses many traditional elements—a mummers' play, Morris dancing, folk tales, and carols, all artfully blended together by an interspersed broken narrative as well as by the structure of the performance. For its material, Revels draws on the traditions of Ireland, Scotland, Wales, England, Brittany, Cornwall, the Isle of Man, France, Russia, Armenia, Italy, Germany, the Balkans, Norway, and the United States.

Patrick "Paddy" Swanson, artistic director of Revels for many years, mentioned in the 2006 Christmas Revels brochure, which depicts a gaily festooned Santa Claus on the cover, "Christmas as we know it today is a mixture of three distinct elements, the Roman feast of Saturnalia, Christ's nativity, and the heathen Nordic German mid-winter festival of Yule. Saturnalia was a riotous time of fun, laughter, and gift giving which sets the tone of our modern Christmas; the nativity brings a sense of sacred mystery around Christ's birth and a rich legacy of sacred music and drama; but the underpinning of the ancient yuletide feast is the secular mystery of death and rebirth of nature, the great cycles of the seasons and the magical progress of life in all of its forms."

On the subject of rebirth, Easter, which celebrates the resurrection of Christ, coincides with the Jewish festival of Passover, the feast of the unleavened bread, an eight-day celebration of the Jews' escape from bondage in Egypt. Like Christmas, Easter is rooted in pagan celebration of seasonal renewal: "Out with the old, in with the new." Easter Sunday is welcomed with rejoicing, singing, parade processions, flowers in abundance, and the ringing of church bells. One of the pagan customs that is still observed is the lighting of fires at dawn for the renewal of life and the protection of crops. The association of the rabbit (the Easter bunny) and eggs with Easter suggests vestigial remnants of an ancient springtime fertility rite.

In his seminal though outdated work, *The Science of Folklore*, Alexander H. Krappe makes the point, which still stands, that festivals and their accompanying rites may be divided into three classes: (1) rites connected with certain days and seasons of the solar year; (2) rites observed on certain occasions, such as birth, marriage, and death; and (3) special rites of aversion and avoidance.

One year, Revels had a Southern Appalachian Christmas featuring Jean Ritchie, a singer from Kentucky. Another year, they celebrated Afro-Anglo (Gullah) traditions of the Georgia Sea Islands with Bessie Jones and her family. Those were unforgettable performances, transporting the audience's imagination into the very heart and marrow of those cultures.

The spring Revels celebrates our relationship with the sea in a robust, rollicking evening of stories about sailors, whalers, fishermen, and press gangs, an earthly flowing panorama of Jack Tars and their colorful lives and times.

I believe the success of Revels is due to the combined effort and expertise of many people. Jack Langstaff, a classically trained singer, was the founding father of Revels, which began in 1971. His passion was to restore the joyous celebration of the seasons. His vision succeeded in bringing together people of many backgrounds and talents, amateur as well as professional musicians. Instilling in them a belief in themselves, he became the invisible hand that leavens the individual and collective sensibilities of all. In Revels, the performers and the audience become as one, transfixed by their music circles, celebrating the mystery and meaning of life.

Jack's daughter, Carol, helped him get Revels off the ground in the early 1970s. With her musician husband, Jim Rooney, she established a companion organization, Revels North, and directed performances in Hanover, New Hampshire. Jim Rooney, performing with Bill Keith, one of the country's finest banjo players, contributed to the renaissance of old-time music in the 1960s. Though I never saw any of Carol's productions, I've heard that they were imaginative, consciousness-raising performances.

Others who have contributed to Revels include Susan Cooper, whose imaginative narration and poetry helped bind the many elements together like the sap that flows through limbs and branches. Raine Miller, who in the early days was "Jack's right-hand man," created the look of Revels through her imaginative costumes and beautifully textured props. Sue Ladr, the art director, created graphic designs that have given Revels its unusual identity. Besides having a strong creative staff in music, theatre, and art, Revels has dedicated and talented personnel who handle the practical side of things.

One evening during intermission of a concert featuring Jack Langstaff and Jerry Epstein, which I hosted at the Joy of Movement Center in Cambridge, Raine Miller told me a heartfelt story about

Revels putting on a Victorian Christmas at Sanders Theatre in the 1970s. In her words, "In the early days we didn't have much money and, like other fledgling groups, had to wing it creatively to make ends meet. It was opening night and we were lacking one indispensable prop; namely, a set of tails. There was very little time to get one. I did the only thing possible and that was to borrow one as quickly as possible. I realized that Brattle Street was out of the question as the houses were too far apart and I'd lose precious time going from one house to another, so I decided to go to Francis Avenue, and after knocking on several doors I finally got lucky. A woman answered. It was Mrs. Galbraith. She was very nice and invited me in. I then heard a familiar voice. It was my good friend Nancy Sweezy. Small world. Mrs. Galbraith then introduced me to her husband, John Kenneth Galbraith. I explained the situation to him and, being very sympathetic, he produced a set of tails on the spot. When I got back to Sanders I found an actor who was about the same height as Mr. Galbraith and gave him the tails, which, thank goodness, were a good fit. Thanks to Mr. Galbraith, Revels got off to a good start."

* * *

Having lunch at Not Your Average Joe's in Watertown, a watering hole popular with many of the Revels staff, I heard more about Revels from Paddy Swanson, its well-known and likeable artistic director. Reminiscing about his life in the theatre with a trace of an English accent, a remnant of his early years in London, Paddy said, "I got my education in England. It was basically the old-fashioned apprenticeship where I started off as an assistant stage manager at Arts Theatre in Leicester Square, which, by the way, is where they had the first production of *Waiting for Godot*. After that I moved up the ladder and became deputy stage manager. There I learned the nuts and bolts of the theatre, the basics, what makes it tick, how to make props, do sound and light, painting the stage, costumes, and doing publicity: the works. Having successfully auditioned, I became a spear carrier. After La MaMa, a well-known troupe that toured internationally, came to play at the theatre, I went to New

York in 1969 and studied world theatre at La MaMa. La MaMa had started in 1961 as a coffee house on Second Avenue with out-of-work actors. It was run by Ellen Stewart, who used to give people a place to sleep. She founded what's known as 'Off-Off Broadway.'"

"Off-Off Broadway?" I mused.

"Yes," said Paddy, "there's Broadway, Off Broadway, and finally Off-Off Broadway. Remember the musical *Hair*? Well, that came out of La MaMa. After that, I went back to England and studied at the London Academy of Music and Dramatic Arts. Eventually, in 1976, I returned to the States and ran an organic farm in Topsfield, here in Massachusetts, and that's where I met Jack Langstaff. At that time, he was teaching at a local school called New Audiences. Having joined Revels, I did some acting, played the part of Robin Hood, and directed a Mummers play."

"A Mummers play, what fun!" I said. "I remember sometime in the late '60s, I performed in a Mummers play at the Radcliffe Graduate Center. David Stacy, from Saffron on Walden in England, directed and acted in it. He was a fine traditional singer as well. That particular version of the play—I think it was a Wessex version—he got from Peter Kennedy at the Cecil Sharp House. It's fascinating that seasonal folk ceremonies have significance beyond mere recreation; they are survivals of ancient ceremonies intended to promote agricultural fertility. I remember St. George defeating his infidel antagonist, the Turkish witch, and the final resurrection. And the Mummers circling sun-wise, carrying wooden swords—I think we wore shredded newspaper coverings, which I gather were at one time animal skins similar to the shaggy world of carnival. As we know, the theatre has an ancient and glorious tradition that goes back to the Greeks: the pageantry, brilliant acting, clever lines, and the interaction with the audience are all part of the theatre. But don't forget all the little quirky things that can happen unexpectedly and how actors deal with it. Things like an actor falling asleep or fainting on stage, or someone's prop accidentally getting stuck on someone else's costume. I remember one play where a woman fell out of character and laughed so hard that she urinated down her leg.

"You mentioned that you played the part of Robin Hood," I continued. "Robin Hood stories are perennially attractive. He's a hero that has always been known and loved, if not in ballads and old legends as our ancestors did, then in the stories of Howard Pyle and the films of Douglas Fairbanks. We still agree with the ancient chronicler that Robin Hood is the most humane prince of robbers, a personification of generosity, sportsmanship, and resourcefulness. Scholars have long debated the origins of Robin Hood. Was he a real person and, if so, when did he live? Was he a mere yeoman who attained remarkable fame, or was he a disguised gentleman or member of the nobility in exile, or was he a creation of the gallant muse, as Professor Francis James Child put it? Perhaps he was a folk expression of inherited belief, a medieval modeling of some pagan woodland deity. If I remember correctly, the earliest allusion to Robin Hood is in William Langland's "Piers Plowman," written during the latter part of the fourteenth century. Paddy, what is it about Robin Hood that made you want to play him?"

"I think Robin Hood appeared to me on account of his association with the green man, a type of forest deity who has a human face, but with greenery growing out of his ears, mouth, and face. I remember once walking in the cloisters in Norwich Cathedral, where I encountered the green man in the form of a statue peeking out at me from behind the leaves. For some reason he reminded me of Robin Hood."

"Tell me, Paddy, in your experience as a director or actor, have you ever encountered anything that might threaten life or limb?"

"I once had a close call. In a production of *Dracula*, I played the part of Renfield, who was a mental patient of Dr. Van Helsing. The set design consisted of a series of mirrors created to put Renfield under the microscope, so to speak. There was a moment when a moth was flying around it and I, as Renfield, was mesmerized by the moth. My head was reflected in all of those mirrors. My hair, which at the time was quite long, suddenly burst into flame. At the time I was wearing a straightjacket. Quickly I rolled over on the floor and put it out. After the play was over, people came up to me and asked how on Earth I ever achieved that effect. Little did they know."

* * *

I also spoke with George Emlen, music director of Revels, who combined his talents and energies with Paddy's, shaping the musical material into a coherent whole and infusing it with beauty and light. At one time, George also sang in the chorus. In his words, "When you are on stage performing, surrounded by other people, it's difficult to hear the balance between voices and instruments. As a director, I have to know what's going on to get the whole picture. It's sort of a trade-off because when I was singing in the chorus, I'd energize it from within."

"George, what are some of your personal musical interests, and how do you implement them in a Revels performance?"

"Good question. One thing I like to do is to show the relationship between traditional folk songs and composed art songs. In our German Revels, the chorus sang 'Joseph Dearest, Joseph Mine,' an old German folk song, followed by a composed church piece with almost the same melody. Which came first is like the chicken and the egg."

* * *

I learned yet more about Revels at a symposium held on a cold November evening at Tommy Doyle's pub in Harvard Square, sponsored by the New England Folk Music Archives. The mission of the Archives, managed by Betsy Siggins, Millie Rahn, and Tim Mason, was to document the role of folk music in New England past and present. The featured speakers at the symposium were George Emlen; Paddy Swanson; and David Coffin, the master of ceremonies at Revels performances. David, the son of Rev. William Sloane Coffin and grandson of pianist Arthur Rubinstein, is also related to Tristram Coffin, a ballad scholar whose books I've read with interest and pleasure. The moderator of this special event was Scott Alarik, a connoisseur of folk music, writer for the *Boston Globe*, and a fine singer as well. Currently he puts on an informative program on

WUMB-FM called *Folk Tales*. Scott published an article in *Sing Out!* magazine on Jack Langstaff's life and mission with Revels.

While discussing Jack's role at Revels, David struck a resonant chord when he described the growing appeal of Revels, year after year in ten cities throughout the country, as people who come to a Revels performance feel included in what happens on stage. Performer and spectator come together in a collective celebration, making music and having a good time.

Chapter 42

Christmas in Newport

When I was growing up, Christmas holidays were a very special time for me. They brought a two-week reprieve from boarding school and a chance to renew old acquaintances and make new friends. There were plenty of parties at which I'd catch up on all the latest gossip that had accumulated during the school semester. "Is Mopsy Throckmorton still going out with Biddle Strawbridge?" or "Did you hear how Murray Forbes crashed Abigail Van Allen's coming-out party?" and other harmless but intriguing bits of news.

Christmas Eve was a family affair; my mother, my father, and I would spend a few hours finishing the decoration of our tall tree. I remember all the arrangements as beautiful works of art, made by the deft and loving hands of some European craftsperson. Later in the evening, the gardener and his family and the servants would be invited to the front part of the house, where my mother and father would wish them a Merry Christmas and give them their presents.

In retrospect, I felt like someone out of a Victorian novel, à la Thackeray, Dickens, or James, acting out the age-old, never-changing patterns of insular good breeding, whereby one's good manners, instinctive and/or socialized, lent substance and form to the rigidly choreographed charade. I suspect that the similarities between my mother and Lady Dedlock would far have outweighed the differences.

Christmas was a time to be enjoyed, relaxing with one's family. But I often felt strangely alone and would become anxious about seemingly inconsequential events. Like self-fulfilling prophecies, those little child's fears would actualize themselves as minor mishaps, mostly of the domestic variety, like spilling one's drink on the carpet or failing to say the right thing at the right time. Even on Christmas Day, the smallest transgressions would elicit a strong reprimand, and for the rest of the day I would bear the scar of that incident. I was very conscious of every move I made, feeling at times helpless, like a Dresden doll, ornamental and useless. As in a Japanese kabuki theatre piece, every move had to be performed in exactly the right way.

Such were Christmases for me then, full of a young child's fears, until, after my father died, I no longer went home for the holiday. At that point, I felt unable to submit to the kabuki-like rigors, and my mother became incommunicado toward me. I would have visited her had it been at all possible, but that opportunity never arose. I had been forbidden to take one step inside the house unless my mother invited me, and, of course, that invitation was not forthcoming. The only communication between my mother and me was an occasional card, inspired by my lingering sense of filial duty. Inspired, yes, but not inspiring. It was a dead feeling.

Fourteen years after my father's death, I plucked up my courage and decided to pay my mother a visit on Christmas Eve, despite not having been invited. Early in the evening I rang the doorbell at Ridgemere, bringing presents and not knowing what to expect. The maid who opened the door, failing to recognize me, did not ask me to come in. I waited until my mother suddenly materialized. She looked older than when I had last seen her. I politely wished her a Merry Christmas and gave her my presents, which consisted of several records I had produced on the Living Folk label, concert posters and reviews, and letters thanking me for performing at assisted-living centers and organizing musical events to benefit charitable organizations.

I waited. It was her move, after all those years. Looking at me almost curiously, she said, "It's nice to see you. I see that you have shed the mountain greenery."

I confess to having been a trifle perplexed by her mountain greenery image, which I surmised applied to the length of my hair, which was then and has always been cut short, and was usually neat. My mother, not wishing to prolong the impasse, concluded our brief encounter by telling me, "I'm terribly sorry that I can't invite you in. I'm having some friends over for cocktails, but do call again. Merry Christmas."

I politely bade her good night and went forth sadly, bound for places where I knew I belonged. Reconciliation was to come in the following decade, when I married and gave my mother a grandchild.

≷ Chapter 43 ≶

Teaching at the Museum of Fine Arts

In 1979, after having run concerts for nearly a decade, I received a note from a friend, Barbara Lambert, then Curator of the Department of Musical Instruments at the Museum of Fine Arts (MFA) in Boston. She asked whether I'd be interested in teaching a course in folk music at the MFA. I was delighted by her kind offer, but at first had reservations about accepting it, as I had no previous teaching experience. Following up by phone, she convinced me that I was up to the task. I spent the summer preparing for the course by listening to records and tapes of field recordings; reading or rereading books of ballads and ethnomusicology, as well as a few scholarly articles by folklorists; and talking with musicians.

Late that summer, I sent out a course description to everyone on my mailing list. The course was to include lectures, class discussions, field trips, recorded music, workshops with musicians who would play and discuss their material, and the opportunity to attend several concerts free of charge. It was to cover general characteristics of folk music; folk songs in their cultural context; the nature of folk tunes and their relationship to the text; the origins, structure, and themes of ballads; historical, romantic, and humorous ballads; supernatural ballads as archaic survivors of pagan cultures; and a comparison of folk songs to tribal music, classical music, and popular music. Andy Nagy, a friend who played the pennywhistle and hosted a radio show, *Black Jack Davey*, at Brandeis, was my assistant instructor.

Each week, I had twelve to fifteen students, some of whom had attended my concerts or knew of me through folk music channels. They all had at least rudimentary knowledge and appreciation of the music, which made my job easier and more enjoyable. Some were amateur musicians who played for their own enjoyment, others enjoyed the sociability of the music, and several expressed an interest in collecting folk songs in their natural habitat.

In one class, a student asked whether I had done any collecting myself. I explained that I had collected a few tunes, songs, and stories in Ireland and Cape Breton, but for the most part my collecting was highly specialized, as my informants had been my parents, repositories of the upper-class folklore of a bygone era.

A friend, Patsy Margolin, exclaimed, "I didn't realize that the upper class had folklore."

"Oh, yes," I said. "Folklore is not limited to any class; everyone has folklore. City people, country people, rich and poor, they all have folklore. It would be undemocratic to exclude them. Just ask my family."

At this mention of my family the class broke into subdued laughter. "Do we take him seriously or humorously?" Andy exclaimed.

More laughter.

After three or four classes, Kenny Goldstein, a professor of folklore at the University of Pennsylvania, who happened to be in town, came to discuss his experience in Scotland, where he had collected songs and stories from Jimmy MacBeath, Lucy Stewart, and Jeannie Robertson.

At one of our class meetings someone mentioned the great anthropologist Bronislaw Malinowski. I told how, after his death, Malinowski's wife discovered some of his letters and a diary that expressed his true sentiments—namely, that the Trobriand Islanders were smelly, loud, undisciplined, and treacherous people and that the only reason he devoted his life to studying them was to make his reputation in the field. Hearing that, several members of the class shook their heads and looked shocked. I cautioned that collectors must be careful about making such disclosures.

I then told the story of an acquaintance who received a handsome grant to make a documentary about an old fiddler who lived in the remote hills of West Virginia. On his arrival the scholar, who also played the fiddle, pulled out his instrument and played a few obligatory tunes to help set the stage. By winning trust and establishing a good rapport with your informant, I explained, you can fool him or her into thinking that you have something in common.

This fellow, having gained the confidence and the respect of the old man, set about accomplishing his tasks. Equipped with camera and recording equipment, he proceeded to film the old man at work. Later, he filmed the old-timer's house. Full of the noble conviction that poverty is honest and virtuous, he filmed the parts of the house that appeared rundown and dilapidated. He focused on such objects as broken furniture, paraffin lamps, walls where plaster was falling down or paint was peeling, and some rusty farm implements that had fallen into disrepair. He even went so far as to rearrange some of the furniture to make it conform to his notion of noble poverty. I needn't tell you that the collector's efforts paid off as the documentary was completed and made available to the public. The proud old gentleman, invited to see this masterpiece of deception, was naturally upset at being depicted this way.

Someone in the class volunteered, "The collector got paid for his efforts, didn't he?"

"Yes, of course, he did," I allowed. "Romanticizing poverty can be a way of keeping the poor impoverished, maintaining the status quo, guaranteeing a future fertile field for folklorists and anthropologists, and gratifying the middle-class desire to achieve a vicarious Rousseau-like innocence with little inconvenience. Remember that when Rousseau spoke about getting back to the origins of things, he strongly implied that because speech antedates the written word, it is closer to the Earth and morally superior to reading and writing. By keeping the noble, unlettered peasants in their place, preserving their incorruptible state of bucolic innocence, you will keep the middle classes happy, wallowing in sentiment. If the lower classes improved their lot in life, there wouldn't be anyone left to romanticize. Then where would we be?"

Robin Blecher, a friend I knew from my concerts, spoke up. "Peter, you're being very cynical. Most folklorists aren't like that. You don't want to misrepresent folk music and give it a bad name."

"No, I won't, but don't forget what the great English poet John Milton said—namely, that evil is more interesting and aesthetically appealing than good. The devil sells; God doesn't. Unless, of course, you're a priest who gets rich by selling indulgences. But then I suppose one could say that the priest was doing the devil's work. Robin, hear me out. By keeping the lower orders in their place, you are serving the will of God, which has it that society is divided into classes in accordance with the function each performs."

John Shaw, a graduate of Harvard's Celtic Department, volunteered, "Sometimes it works the other way, when the informant gets the better of the collector. Case in point is the account of Alan Lomax going into the Hebrides in Scotland to collect waulking songs—that's spelled w-a-u-l-k-i-n-g, but pronounced 'walking.' Waulking songs refer to the pre-Industrial practice of women sitting at a table and shrinking cloth by soaking it in urine and then pounding it with their hands, all the while singing to the rhythm of the work. While they were singing, Lomax was recording them. The women, knowing that he didn't understand Gaelic, made up funny verses about him, denigrating his manhood, like 'Maids, when you're young, never wed an old man. He went to bed and behaved like he was dead.' After a week of recording, Lomax took his tapes to England and had them played live on BBC radio! So, you can see that the first rule for a collector is that you should have at least a rudimentary knowledge of the people from whom you are collecting."

Rob Joel, a former president of the Folk Song Society of Greater Boston, opined, "Some of this stuff is way out. All of us collectors or performers have our little axes to grind. When I was at Fox Hollow, I heard the following story about a collector. There was a fiddler from the East Coast who had very stringent notions of authenticity. One time, he was learning a tune from an old guy down south who unfortunately, due to his arthritic arm, didn't have complete control of his instrument and consequently would make mistakes. The collector, listening to him play, learned the melody note for note, mistake for mistake. He duplicated those mistakes, all the wrong notes, the squeaks and the squawks, and incorporated them into his repertoire, all in the name of authenticity."

"It probably sounded awful," someone interjected.

"The irony is that the fiddler wasn't being traditional," Rob continued. "The folk process, that of learning a story, song, or tune, is not a slavish imitation of what one hears, but rather a re-creation of it in one's own personal and cultural terms. The essence of folk music is change, which is what gives a story, song, or tune its richness and life. Otherwise it's a dead thing. It's this process that accounts for the many versions of a song. As a song is passed on from singer to singer, it changes over time and from place to place. There are American songs and tunes, as you know, that are versions of Scottish, Irish, or English songs, and they are all different. Songs and tunes change as they adapt to new environments."

Jan Downey, a lovely singer who had performed at my concerts, said, "Most people who learn songs are not professionally trained musicians with perfect pitch. When they hear a song they might miss a few notes or words, and they might forget what they heard and make something up in its place. Or they might deliberately change what they heard to please a new group of listeners. It's almost Darwinian: songs adapt to survive. I'm from Arkansas, where one of my neighbors is Almeda Riddle, who is a wonderful singer. She sang at one of Peter's concerts not long ago. She never sings a song twice in the same way, and that's true of some of the other great women singers, like Jean Ritchie or Sara Cleveland from Scotland, Margaret Barry or Sarah Makem from Ireland, Shirley Collins and Frankie Armstrong from England; or the men singers, too, the really good ones like Norman Kennedy or Joe Heaney. Every time they sing the same song, it's a little different."

Another student jumped in, adding, "There's something magical and mysterious about how a song can be old and new at the same time. It's amazing how songs like 'Edward,' 'Lord Randall,' or 'Barbara Allen' that were sung hundreds of years ago and passed down through the generations, parents to children, are still alive today. Many of those singers couldn't read or write. It was all from memory. In the seventeenth, eighteenth, and nineteenth centuries, the Scots, Irish, Scots-Irish, English, and Blacks came to America for a variety of reasons, seeking freedom of religion or, in the case of the Blacks, were sold into slavery. People thought of America in different ways. These new inhabitants, with little in the way of material possessions, brought with them a wealth of folklore: songs, fiddle tunes, stories, legends, riddles, proverbs, folk recipes, and even instructions for building a house. Some of the songs took root, blossomed, and flourished, creating new American songs, while others, not so adaptable or fortunate, withered on the vine."

My good friend Freddy Lawrence, whose father and grandfather had been bishops, commented, "Good old America. What would we do without her? What was it that some seventeenth-century Puritan Divine called this country, with its wild animals, Indians, woods, and rocky shores—a 'howling wilderness.'"

"Well, that's an honest description," I said. "It's in keeping with the hellfire and brimstone mentality. I don't wish to appear cynical, but in all fairness, I should point out that back then investors, wishing to appeal to potential settlers, called America the new 'Garden of Eden.' That was good PR, pure and simple. Perry Miller, the dean of American letters, said that he who is without contradiction in his life, who sees everything black and white, is truly 'un-American.'"

On an amusing note, an elderly student, hearing someone mention a Child ballad, exclaimed, "Why is it a child ballad? There is no mention of children."

Freddy Lawrence then explained, "I don't blame you for being confused. When Peter mentioned 'Child,' he was referring to Professor Francis James Child, who taught at Harvard and wrote the definitive book on ballads."

In another class I started a new discussion: "Many people assume that the first great revival of folk music took place in the 1960s, a turbulent time not long ago when many people protested the war in Vietnam, pushed for civil rights, and looked for alternative lifestyles. There was a revival of sorts due in part to the collecting and writing of folklorists, with a boost from the radio and records. However, the first great revival of interest in folklore took place in Europe in the mid-nineteenth century, fueled by romanticism and nationalism, starting with the Grimm brothers going into the countryside. Other collectors followed suit, performing Grimm-like services for their countries. This led people to appreciate their own language, stories, and songs as having value in and of themselves and as a way of achieving political independence and establishing their national and cultural identity."

My friend Jack Whyte, a singing companion sitting in on the class, said, "I read somewhere about a festival in ancient Greece where the lower classes changed places with the upper classes and were allowed to rule for a week. This helped stabilize their society as it allowed the lower classes to let off steam, put people in touch with one another, and made everyone aware of the needs of others. At the end of the week people probably were glad to return to the status quo, as things must have been fairly chaotic. Paradoxically, what this accomplished was to reaffirm the existing social hierarchy."

Before the end of class I announced, "If you have any questions about the material, please feel free to call me at home. Several weeks from now, on Tuesday evening, I'm running a ceilidh at Passim. If any of you haven't performed at a Passim ceilidh, you are more than welcome to give us a song or play a tune. For those of you in the class, there will be no admission fee. I'll see you next week."

After the students had left, Andy confided, "I thought it went well today. People are enjoying it and contributing. I should tell you that one of the girls came up to me afterward and said, 'Andy, I really enjoy the course; everyone pitches in and I'm learning a lot, but it strikes me that Peter, well, not that he's negative, but he seems to take an ironic stance toward the material.' I told her that an unintended consequence of your approach is that you expose the foibles of human nature and the false romanticism that people associate with folklore. All in all, you're giving a balanced view, and a little humor won't hurt as it contains some truth. I told her that folklore, songs, and stories are never neutral and can be manipulated for psychological, economic, religious, or political purposes. That's what makes folklore so interesting. It's elusive and sometimes it's hard to get a handle on it."

"Yes," I agreed, "folklorists' attitudes may change. Nothing is written in stone. John Lomax believed one thing; his son, Alan, believed another. For a period of time, folklorists had a hard time defining their subject. Who are the folk? Are they just country people, or do they include city people? Is folklore just songs and stories, or does it include material culture as well as folk art? There is no agreement in the field, and that's one reason why it was difficult for folklorists to compete with anthropologists for government grants. Folklore is a two-edged sword. Some countries romanticized their folklore and saw value in its beauty and spiritual truths. It gave them an identity and, in some cases, political independence. Other countries, like Nazi Germany and Communist Russia, used folklore as a way of exploiting others.

"Next week we'll discuss the Child ballads. As you know, most of them are tragic. They deal with romantic and supernatural themes and historical events like border wars between England and Scotland, but a few are humorous. Often the latter get neglected, but we should at least look at one of those ballads. Bear in mind Thomas Hardy, who, in *The Return of the Native*, wrote about the tragic lives of, as he put it, the damned beautiful peasants, but somewhere along the line he mentioned that in the face of adversity they had a sense of humor. It's necessary for survival. It levels the playing field, gives a sense of perspective, an element of truth, and it's fun."

Chapter 44

Cousin Elsie, the Cambridge Buddhist

I f anyone was the intellectual in my family, it was my cousin Elsie Mitchell, Uncle Ted's daughter. I was very fond of her and always looked forward to visiting her house on Brattle Street in Cambridge, with its lovely garden tucked away in back.

On one visit, we reminisced about a conversation sometime in the late 1940s between Uncle Ted (Elsie's father) and my father (Elsie's uncle). I remembered Uncle Ted saying, "I'm concerned about young Elsie. As you may know, she's going to Miss Porter's in Farmington, Connecticut. She's very bright—precocious, really. She's made several good friends, is doing well academically, and appears to be well adjusted, but there's one thing that does concern me. She, God knows how, has gotten involved with Buddhists. I hope she hasn't gotten in over her head. I'm all for learning about different philosophies and religions, but that doesn't mean we have to embrace them to the exclusion of everything else. Perhaps rather than sending her away to boarding school, I should have let her continue as a day student at Milton Academy, my old school, which is close by and where I could keep an eye on her."

My father commiserated, "Ted, if I were you, I wouldn't give it a second thought; it might be a passing fancy. After all, the young are very impressionable. That sort of nonconformist behavior is very Boston."

Elsie laughed at my recollection. "I can just hear Uncle Pier saying that. Did you know that Great Aunt Amy took my father to China and Japan right after World War I, shortly after he came home from his stint in the British Navy? He and a friend visited many Japanese and Chinese temples together."

"Elsie," I continued, "here we are almost sixty years later, and here you are still rebelling. Not only are you a bona fide Buddhist, but a very good one. Over the years, you've made contributions to Buddhism and the Japanese intellectual community both at home and abroad. Just look at what you've done. You have tutored English at the Yenching at Harvard, published articles on different aspects of Buddhism, and written several books. You and John [Elsie's late husband] went to Japan, recorded traditional Buddhist rituals, and wrote an accompanying description of the ceremonies and chants, all of which were then made into a record for Moe Asch at Folkways.

"As a founder of the Cambridge Buddhist Association, you've hosted meditation retreats and made generous contributions to related organizations. Oh, I almost forgot: You are also a founder of the Ahimsa Foundation, which supports humane societies, wildlife sanctuaries, and some environmental groups. It's quite evident that you and Buddhism are inseparable and meant for each other—a felicitous fit.

"From what I can see, you are not just an armchair Buddhist, practicing dry principles learned from books; no, you've really lived it. I don't wish to sound overly dramatic, but it's in your bones and blood; it nourishes you and leavens your sensibilities. It's you! Over the years, you've learned Japanese language and customs; heard and appreciated the music; tasted the food; and marveled at the Japanese landscapes and paintings of mountains, waterfalls, and serene gardens. Elsie, I'm very proud of you."

"Oh, Peter," said Elsie. "You're a dear. I'm so glad you feel that way."

"You know, it's interesting," I continued, "how different members of the same family can go in very different directions. Case in point: your father took over a small mutual fund and made it very successful. Perhaps these contradictions are what some people loosely refer to as the New England mind—whereby, if you'll forgive the cliché, everyone does his or her own thing. It's been years since I've read it, but if I recall correctly, Van Wyck Brooks in his book *The Flowering of New England, 1815–1865* discusses how one generation rebels against the preceding one.

"Anyway, I am curious—how did you discover the Buddha? Was it an epiphany in which you were blinded by what Heidegger called 'the shining light of ontological truth,' or was it a kind of enlightenment that developed over time?"

Elsie replied, "Many years ago, when I was at Miss Porter's School in Connecticut in the 1940s, I read L. Adams Beck's introductory book on Buddhism. My grandfather's library was packed in a trunk in our attic, and it contained many books on Buddhist history and a few translations of Buddhist texts into German and French. Even before I graduated from Miss Porter's, I knew I didn't want to go to college. I wanted to travel and experience different cultures. I read the books that interested me. I didn't want a canned education shoved down my throat.

"Later, a month's stay with my husband in an old Japanese Zen Temple in a beautiful mountain setting, Eihei-ji, with its extraordinary big bells and gentle teaching that offers respect and compassion to all living beings, captured my heart and stimulated my mind. That's how I became a Buddhist."

"Elsie," I broke in, "your wish to travel after graduation reminds me a little of my mother. When she graduated from St. Tim's, she went to Europe with her chaperone, as well as to parties and balls. She saw the last of the Old World."

"Yes," said Elsie, "Aunt Lilias was very bright and curious about different ways of life. She spoke German, French, Italian, and even a little Hungarian. I enjoyed her company enormously, and I miss her. I recall how after your father died she became interested in Hinduism, not so much the metaphysical complexities, but the meditation practices."

"Elsie, I recollect that some years back some of your neighbors were up in arms against the Buddhist Association. What was that all about?"

"With my brother's generous help," she explained, "we bought a house on Sparks Street for the Association, and some of our neighbors objected to having a religious organization they knew nothing about so close to them. Actually, our members included psychologists and professors of Buddhism, Sanskrit, and comparative religion, not to mention Huston Smith, a theologian who wrote scholarly and popular books on comparative religion and whose lectures were shown on PBS. It took no more than a week for the Supreme Judicial Court of Massachusetts to decide in our favor."

"Well, I should hope so. After all, this is New England, rather individualist in its thinking—the home of Thoreau, Emerson, and transcendentalism. Tell me, Elsie, was your family religious at all?"

"No, they were agnostics," Elsie explained. "Usually they only went to church for weddings and funerals. I remember once going to church with my father in Milton. At the end of the service, I asked him what he thought of the sermon. He replied, matter-of-factly, 'I didn't hear it. I turned off both my hearing aids.'"

"Well, the same goes for my family," I added. "Once in a blue moon, maybe twice a year, Mummy and Daddy would go to Trinity Church in Newport and hear Reverend Scafe give his sermon. My mother said that the only reason she went to church was to see which of her friends were in town so she could have them over for drinks.

"Elsie, I hope I'm not coming across as a tiresome journalist with all my questions, but I really I know so little about you. Tell me, what writers were you drawn to when you were younger? Did they reflect Buddhism in any way?"

"That's a good question. When I was sixteen, I tried to read Montaigne in archaic French—rough going!—then in modern English. He was a Buddhist at heart, was very open-minded, and wrote a famous essay on toleration. He lived in a very intolerant time: Catholics in France were burning people alive. It was a ferocious period in the history of the Catholic church."

"Elsie, one more question. What is the relationship between Shinto and Buddhism? Are they in conflict?"

"Not really," she replied. "In Japan couples usually marry in a Shinto shrine, but their funerals usually are held in a Buddhist temple. The Indian king, Asoka, converted to Buddhism and forbade the consumption and slaughter of animals. He became a vegetarian and planted trees to improve the environment. He also built hospitals for animals as well as people. He ruled around 300 B.C., some years after Alexander the Great's departure from India. King Asoka had his Buddhist edicts carved into enormous stone pillars. These edicts, written in Sanskrit, proclaimed his Golden Rule of compassion for all living creatures, both animal and human. It was a central teaching that the Buddha Nature dwells in all living beings and can be activated to spread compassion for all beings in all spheres of life. Today our planet and all of its inhabitants cry out for this modus vivendi, this way of life. At the end of his life, Asoka became a monk."

"Refresh my mind on what you've written. There were two books, weren't there?"

"Actually, there were three," she explained. "First, there was *Sun Buddhas – Moon Buddhas*, which has to do with John's and my travels in Japan. It is a biography explaining why I became a Buddhist. The book is a sort of dialogue between East and West, between Buddhist and Christian values that I hope will broaden the perspectives of those on both sides of the cultural divide. Despite the many religious and cultural differences that separate people, I hope that in the search for one's own Buddha nature one may discover not only oneself, but all of humanity.

"The second book, *Our Own Day*, was based largely on a diary kept by my great-grandmother, Mary Josephine Faxon [b. 1834], and later edited by my Aunt Eunice Cabot for potential readers in the 1930s. It gives a picture of a Boston family, particularly the young people, living on Beacon Hill during the latter part of the nineteenth century. Finally, there was *The Lion Dog of Buddhist Asia*. The Lion Dog is a universal symbol of majesty. In the West, he adorns the coats of monarchs. In Asia, he became the benevolent guardian of the Buddha, who taught all activities that lead to good karma [peace and justice]. Though the Lion of Buddha originated in India, his attributes were most highly elaborated in China, Japan, and Tibet."

"Elsie, you traveled a long way, spiritually speaking, since our Puritan ancestors did a number on the Indians some four hundred years ago. If only they could see you now, they'd be spinning in their graves."

"With all due respect to those Puritan ancestors, I'm afraid I don't have much use for them. Cotton Mather, the Great Puritan Divine, once wrote a report on a ship bringing Quakers into Boston Harbor. He tried to prevent them from entering; in fact, he wanted to sell them all into slavery. I'm afraid Puritans are not my cup of tea."

"I don't blame you," I replied. "I feel we are closer to the Pilgrims' way of thinking than to the Puritans. The Pilgrims who came over on the Mayflower, including several of our ancestors, were separatists who broke away completely from the established church of England, whereas the Puritans simply wished to purify the church from within."

"It's my turn to ask you a question, Peter. What are your religious convictions or philosophic beliefs that have helped you through life?"

"Oh, God. That's a good question. I admire Socrates, who stood up for what he believed in, but I'm not so sure I'd be willing to die for my beliefs. I know it sounds jaded and cynical, but I think Hume had it right when he said, 'I'm a philosopher only when I'm at my desk.' Years ago, I identified in part with some of the pre-Socratics like the Sophists and the cynics, but I was being glib and sophomoric back then. Their thinking was shallow and had no substance. Medieval theologians believed that philosophy was the handmaiden of religion; they thought logic could go only so far and then faith would take you the rest of the way. I'm afraid I lack that faith.

"In prep school, where attendance at chapel was required, my various headmasters extolled the virtues of hard work and thrift and becoming captains of industry. They were spokesmen for the

Protestant ethic and materialism. They were good people, honest and sincere, but their sermons didn't reach me. We live in a secular age, where one doesn't hear the call like in the old days. I sincerely doubt that anyone I knew at school is now a minister.

"It's not in me to be blinded by some spiritual insight or meta-phorical truth. The shining light of ontological truth is not my beacon in the dark. Instead, some semblance of understanding of my limited universe comes to me in bits and pieces, which later I may discard in favor of something else. Empirical truths are so different from metaphysical ones. When Wittgenstein says that about those things of which we cannot speak, we must be silent, he is saying that metaphysical statements that have no empirical reference cannot be apprehended by the senses and cannot be discussed in any meaningful way. However, if we remain silent and don't find a way to speak about matters of ultimate concern, we may go mad and suffer spiritual death. We cannot remain silent.

"Look at ancient pagan, pre-Christian societies—the Greeks, the Romans, the Celts—or even contemporary tribal societies, the ones about which Frazer, Malinowski, Margaret Mead, and Ruth Benedict wrote. People in those societies are pre-scientific in their thinking and in their metaphysical anxieties. Their universe—animistic, alive with gods and supernatural beings—left them anything but silent as magic, manna, myth, and metaphor have explained their world to them and made that world richer than ours. I wonder—is something true because I believe it, or do I believe it because it is true? Perhaps, as the Buddhists say, 'all is illusion.'

"Elsie," I asked, "did you know Holmes Welch, who was a Buddhist?"

"Holmes and I were very good friends. Sadly, he is no longer with us. He was married to a nice Polish girl. When they were engaged, Bishop Fulton Sheen went so far as to try to dissuade the girl's family from letting her marry him. You see, she was a Cath-olic and he was a Protestant, a Unitarian, and a Buddhist. The girl's grandmother was quite rich, so naturally the Bishop took her into his confidence. He tried to prevent the marriage by telling the girl's family that Holmes was impotent. Can you even begin to imagine doing such a thing? That was a blatant lie.

"Well, I don't need to tell you that Holmes was livid. He was no Casper Milquetoast and wasn't going to take this lying down. Holmes rented a barge and married the girl in international waters, with a French priest officiating. Over the years Holmes sired a plethora of healthy children—I've lost count: four, five, six. At some point he got his revenge by introducing them all, one by one, to Bishop Sheen, which must have caused the bishop considerable embarrassment as he surely had lost face. Holmes was a dear. He also knew how to protect his family and just how to deal with mean-spirited prelates."

"Elsie, I think in some ways we are alike, simpatico. Both of us are more artistic than practical. There is not one mechanical bone in my body, and when it comes to finances, I'm helpless. God knows there are times when I wish I were otherwise."

"I dare say you're right. Finances and I were never made for each other. John took care of the money and mechanical things. It's been difficult with him gone."

Chapter 45

Brothers in Bipolarity

The film *Infinitely Polar Bear*, written and directed by Maya Forbes and starring Mark Ruffalo, premiered at the Sundance Film Festival in 2014 and was released commercially the following year. The film is a fictionalized dramatization of Maya and her sister China Forbes's experience growing up under the care of their father, Donald Cameron "Cam" Forbes, who suffered from bipolar disorder. The title comes from a phrase Cam once used to describe his condition.

When *Infinitely Polar Bear* came to one of my local theaters, I could hardly stay away—not only because I, too, am diagnosed with bipolar disorder, but also because Cam Forbes was one of my oldest friends. I met him in the early 1950s when we were campers at Camp Connery Cove in Little Deer Isle, Maine, run by Roger Eaton. Glad to get away from the stuffy, inhibiting social scene of Newport, I enjoyed the relaxed camp life as everything was run informally, with no schedules to be met or uniforms to be worn. Left to my own devices, I hiked in the woods; sailed with Mr. Garfield, a senior counselor, on his sloop *The Lively Lady*; played horseshoes in the garden and hide-and-go-seek; and shared stories and songs around the campfire in the evening. I recall an evening picnic on the beach during which counselors and campers discussed some of the games we played. Cam astutely observed, "Games have rules to be followed and strategies for winning that prepare us for later on in life."

After camp was over that summer, Cam and I lost track of each other until seven or eight years later, following my honorable discharge from the U.S. Navy. Then living in Harvard Square, I ran into Cam at the Hayes Bickford restaurant. Renewing our friendship, we would go to coffeehouses and sing folk songs at "hootenannies." Cam invited me to visit him at his home in Sudbury, where I met his parents, Faith and Donald Forbes; his younger brother, Ricky; and sisters, Dinny and Wendy. One evening, Faith and Donald were talking about folklore; they discussed how in some village communities riddles sharpened wits and proverbs gave sage advice and were used to settle disputes between families.

Cam, to his credit, was adept at fixing things. He once got my washing machine working and another time changed a tire on my Hillman Minx. But it wasn't until the 1960s that I realized that Cam and I were cut from the same spiritual cloth. At this time, Cam and a mutual friend, Freddy Lawrence, were strolling along the Charles River when he spotted some friends, Ricky Montagu and Chase Mellon, paddling a canoe. Cam called out to them and proceeded to take off his clothes—shorts and shirt. Naked as a jaybird, he jumped into the water and started swimming after them. Paddling fast to get away, his friends yelled, "Cam, go back!" Finally, Cam swam back to shore while Freddy exhorted him, "Cam, put your clothes on or you'll get arrested!"

My friend Cyril Phillips enjoyed spending time with Cam and me and hearing of our mischievous and eccentric adventures. He dedicated a short poem to us, which began with these lines:

> *In Cambridge I have two amazing friends*
> *Who tell me at times they're around the bend*
> *There's nothing these lads can't do*
> *They've got tricks and pranks to entertain you*

While working as a cameraman at WGBH-TV, Cam met an attractive young woman, Peggy Woodford. They married and had two lovely daughters, Maya and China. Then Cam was fired for getting into an altercation with his boss. Having little money to support a family, Peggy moved to New York to work at a brokerage firm. She became the breadwinner while Cam and the girls were still living in an apartment in Cambridge. Eventually Cam and Peggy divorced and Peggy remarried. Sadly, Cam died of cancer in 1998 at age 59.

Charmingly dramatized yet true to life, *Infinitely Polar Bear* captures the essence of Cam's story. Despite his impairment, Cam bit the bullet and did the best he could to bring up Maya and China—feeding and clothing them, playing with them, taking them to school, and helping with their homework. Those who see the film can empathize with and admire Cam, whose unconventional and unconditional love of his daughters enabled them to become distinguished creative artists—Maya as a filmmaker, screenwriter, and television producer; China as lead vocalist in the band Pink Martini. Cam's life has rightly been called "a great human victory" and Maya's movie "an artistic triumph."

I like the title *Infinitely Polar Bear*, which expresses an affinity between human beings and animals, what Thoreau called a "divine correspondence" among all living things. Old epics, myths, legends, folk tales, and songs tell how when the Earth was fresh and young, people and animals were the same in soul, spirit, and substance, communicating with and helping one another. Maya's name, too, evokes those ancient beliefs as it refers to the Native Americans of Central America and southern Mexico whose civilization reached its height around 1000 A.D., when the Mayan city-states were ruled by a king who was an intermediary between his people and the gods. Maya also is the name of the Hindu goddess of beauty and wisdom.

What is socially acceptable, or normative, in one culture may be considered deviant in another. Thus, in some tribal communities or in our own pagan, polytheistic, or pantheistic past, Cam's eccentric behavior might be understood and appreciated as making a connection with the supernatural, so that his bipolar energies could be harnessed and honed to benefit the community. As a shaman or medicine man, he would be an intermediary between the physical and spiritual worlds. With his esoteric knowledge, he would heal the sick, make the crops grow, and give advice.

In the same vein, my offbeat antics—painting the bulkheads of a naval vessel purple and pink rather than the traditional gray, dressing as the WBZ Turkey Man only to get fired for scaring an Irish farmer's bull, riding a motorbike into the Hayes Bickford restaurant—could be seen as socially beneficial. People who took vicarious pleasure in the heroic tales of my episodic life would be relieved of having to act out their fears, fantasies, or anger.

I hope *Infinitely Polar Bear* will help viewers better understand people who suffer from mental disorders. Recently I read an article in the *Boston Globe* about a chemistry professor at Boston College who took a leave of absence to get help for his bipolar disorder. Upon returning, he found that his colleagues were hostile toward him, and he was not rehired. He brought a lawsuit against the university and won. Boston College paid him one hundred and fifty thousand dollars and reinstated him. Good for him!

My friend and first editor, Don Kalick, a retired professor of psychology at the University of Massachusetts in Boston, agreed that mental-health professionals can do a lot to educate the public about bipolar and other mood disorders.

May Cam Forbes's rough-hewn and kindly spirit be with us and make us more accepting and understanding of ourselves and others. When I think of him—or of myself, for that matter—I recall this comment by John Stuart Mill: "The amount of eccentricity in a society has generally been proportional to the amount of genius, mental vigor, and moral courage it contained. That so few people now dare be eccentric marks the danger of our time."

⧽ Chapter 46 ⧼

Husband and Father

I met Lorna Palacios Porras in 1985 at a bus stop across from Symphony Hall in Boston. I sat next to her and we started chatting. She told me she was teaching English as a Second Language (ESL) at Harvard and French at Tufts University. As it turned out, we had mutual friends, Peggy and Daniel "Boone" Schirmer, as well as Anne Dow, head of ESL at Harvard.

Lorna was born in the city of Bacolod, land of "hacenderos," sugar barons, on the island of Negros Occidental, Philippines. Her father referred to Lorna and her siblings as "APPLES," an acronym of the initials of their first names: Arturo, Pepita, Phebe, Lorna, Edgar, and Solmar.

As Lorna told me, "In the midst of the Second World War, people were fleeing their towns. But my mother wanted to return and give birth in Bacolod. She said I was so tiny, like a Coca-Cola bottle. While in a water-filled air raid shelter, the midwife cautioned my mother, 'Keep the baby's chin up above the water.'" This was parallel to my experience during the 1938 hurricane when I was three years old.

Lorna's father called her a "war baby" because she was so tough. Due to the strain of war, her mother didn't have much milk. Thus, Lorna's aunt, Consolacion, became her wet nurse. Her mother would mash the "camote," sweet potato, with her teeth and feed it to Lorna. I told her that I, too, had a wet nurse, my nanny. But this

347

was under different circumstances. In the 1930s, most upper-class women had wet nurses for their babies.

Lorna recalled her mother's story that the only time she ever told a lie was when the Japanese soldiers asked her where her husband was. She told them that he was in the Japanese army fighting the Americans, when in fact he was in the U.S. Army fighting the Japanese. Trembling, her mother did her best to remain calm as she held Lorna, fearing the worst outcome for her baby. "We were all terrified of the Japanese soldiers then. There were stories about how they would throw babies in the air and then bayonet or shoot them. There was an incident when some Japanese soldiers saw my father and asked him what he was doing. Dad pretended that he was crazy. Getting down on his hands and knees, he told the soldiers that he was hunting for frogs. They decided he was harmless and left him alone."

After the war, Lorna's family moved to Jaro, Iloilo City. Jaro is also known as "Mestizo town" since many prominent Spanish-Filipinos live there. Lorna's mother was mestiza. Her maternal grandfather, Juan Palacios, was from Barcelona, Spain. Boone Schirmer used to say that the best part of Spanish colonialism was the "leche flan," the Filipino version of crème caramel.

Lorna continued, "My father was in the U.S. Army and was stationed in Okinawa. This was our family's first experience living abroad. After two years in Okinawa, my parents decided to move the family to the United States. The main reason our family came to this country was for the children to get a good education. During my junior year at the University of Washington, I went to Paris and studied French Language and Civilization at the Sorbonne. I hung out in cafés where I heard Edith Piaf and traditional French folk songs. Later, I made my way to Greece, Turkey, and Western Europe. From the word 'go' I wanted to travel, see the world, and experience a variety of cultures—how different people live and how they learn their songs, dances, and their cuisine.

"In 1971, I went to Senegal as a Peace Corps Volunteer, where I taught Senegalese students ESL at the *Lycee de Rufisque*. During the school break, I visited Mauritania, Mali, Morocco, Kenya, and Tanzania. By my mid-twenties, I had lived on four different continents: Africa, Europe, Asia, and North America.

"I returned to the United States in 1973. The following year, I pursued my Masters at the School for International Training (SIT) in Brattleboro, Vermont. My French internship was at the United Nations International School in New York, where I taught French to bilingual students."

"What a coincidence!" I said. "In my junior year at Salisbury High School, I went to France on a homestay and lived with a French family. This was with the Experiment in International Living."

"But here I am talking about myself," Lorna exclaimed. "How about you? Have you lived in Cambridge all these years?"

"Yes, I've been living in Cambridge for nearly thirty years. I came here after I was honorably discharged from the Navy in the 1950s. A friend of mine once commented that Cambridge was my mother, my womb. Even while I traveled to Ireland, Scotland, England, France, Wales, Brittany, and Cornwall to hear traditional music, I succumbed to the fatal charm of Cambridge."

I told Lorna about the bit of acting I had done and my concert organizing and record producing, which were starting to wind down. Perhaps it was too much of a good thing, not to mention all the work involved. Doing publicity, running around to radio stations, and contacting print media took a toll on me. At one point I was doing three concerts a month. It was too much. "Enough about me," I concluded. "Tell me more about your travels."

"Well, it sounds like you've been constructively occupied over the years," Lorna remarked. "Anyway, in 1978 I went to Carpentras in Vaucluse in Provence, where I lived with shepherds and observed how they herded sheep.

"In the early '80s I traveled to South America—Peru and Bolivia—upon invitation of Beatriz Fantini, a colleague at SIT. My host mother welcomed me with coca tea, which she said would help me acclimate to the extreme high altitude of La Paz. After drinking the tea, I fell asleep right away.

"After a few days, I decided to take the bus and venture to the rainforest Las Yungas on the eastern slopes of the Andean Mountains, the world's longest continental mountain range. The roads, known as the 'Highway of Death,' are considered to be among the most dangerous in the world. At dawn the next morning, I witnessed a breathtaking sunrise over the Andes. I was also in awe when I saw an Afro-Bolivian in her native costume.

"After a couple of days, I was trying to return to La Paz to meet my Bolivian students, but there were no buses running until the evening. So I decided to hitchhike. Several vehicles drove by, but to my surprise, no one stopped. Finally, I got a ride aboard a truck with men, women, and their babies all sitting on top of a shipment of oranges. So I climbed up and sat on the oranges with them. Passing under a waterfall, we would pull a tarp over our heads to keep from getting wet. At dusk, the truck stopped at the border and a young lady passenger talked to me in some Spanish mixed with Aymara, the indigenous language of the Andes and Altiplano region. She said we had to spend the night there. The next morning, upon reaching our destination, we were stopped by soldiers. They pierced through the oranges with pointed instruments like spears. They were looking for cocaine! Thank God there was none to be found.

"When I arrived in La Paz, I was covered with soot. My host mother gasped, 'Where have you been?' Exhausted, I replied, 'Let me go take a bath first and I'll tell you my story.'

"It was a good thing I returned to La Paz before midnight. My host mother had cautioned me that I had to be back at the house by twelve o'clock midnight, but I did not know why. It turns out the country was under martial law run by three presidents—a triumvirate.

"Goodness, there were so many adventures," Lorna continued. "Back in the late '60s, I stayed with my friends—Barbara from North Little Rock, Arkansas, and Pam from Salt Lake City, Utah—at a low-budget hotel in Istanbul. We decided to venture out to see the Black Sea. Barbara became suspicious and terrified of the driver. She thought he might have been running a slave trade and planning on enslaving us. So we went to the U.S. Embassy and a young marine escorted us to another hotel—the Istanbul Hilton.

"In the '70s, while in Rabat, Morocco, with my friends Marie-Claire from Toulouse, France, and Jane from Kansas, we booked a hotel near the train station. My friends decided to go out that night and I stayed alone in my room to rest. I asked the receptionist to wake us up in the morning so that we could catch our early train. A few minutes later, I heard a knock on the door. I said 'Oui?' and then I heard the receptionist say, 'Mademoiselle?' and he started propositioning me, speaking through the door. I was scared and angry. My door wouldn't lock. So I put my suitcase and some furniture against it and yelled and swore at him in French. I told him to leave and that if he did not, I'd keep screaming and he'd lose all his clients."

"My God, you sound like some heroine out of a picaresque novel!" I exclaimed. "One adventure after another."

Several weeks after we met, Lorna invited me to an ESL party with her students from Roxbury Community College at the Boston Business School. When I arrived, to my surprise and amusement, I saw Lorna dancing with one of her students, an elderly Russian gentleman who had a samovar perched precariously on his head. I held my breath in fascination, waiting for the inevitable, but for the duration of the dance, it remained there. He must have had it well trained.

In 1986, after Lorna and I had been seeing each other for several months, we decided to get married. The wedding was held at Peggy and Boone Schirmer's house in Cambridge. Lorna looked lovely in a simple white dress with muted lilac flowers and brocaded lace. Bishop Lawrence, the father of my good friend Freddy, married us. This seemed only fitting because Bishop Lawrence's father, who was also a bishop, had married my grandparents.

It was an idiosyncratic mix of people in attendance, including our host, Boone, a professor of history and an old-world Communist who had been blacklisted during the McCarthy era, and his colleague, the historian Howard Zinn. Also present, along with my fellow eccentric, Cam Forbes, were my Buddhist cousin Elsie Mitchell; her husband, John; and her brother, Ned Johnson, Uncle Ted's son and successor in business. Such incongruity is very Cambridge, known in some quarters as "the People's Republic of Cambridge," a city rich with history, ideas, and dissent that seems to have a mind of its own. My mother came from Newport, while a family friend, Caleb Loring, came from Prides Crossing. I was touched that Lorna's mother; sisters Pepita and Phebe; Pepita's husband, Joe; their son, Robbie; and a good friend, Gloria Ureta, drove three thousand miles from Seattle to the wedding.

Getting married in my mother's presence, I could not help but think back to some advice she had given me when I was young. "Peter," she had said, "when you consider getting married, what you do is go to the girl's house and thoroughly examine all the portraits of her ancestors to make sure they have good bones. In that way you can tell that there's no bad blood in the family. If the portraits pass inspection, then you can bring the girl home and your father and I will take a good look at her."

"Oh, what a good idea," I remember exclaiming enthusiastically in response, "but isn't it possible that the painter made the ancestors handsomer than they really were, just to be flattering?"

"Oh, sheer, absolute, and utter nonsense," my father had exploded. "It goes without saying that people of good family are always attractive. How could you improve on that?"

A year later, Lorna gave birth to our son, whom we nicknamed "PJ," a shortened and more manageable version of Pierrepont Edwards Johnson III. We moved to the Botanic Gardens, housing for Harvard University faculty. I knew that my life would never be the same again. Having a child presented me with a new set of responsibilities: changing diapers, sterilizing milk bottles, and singing lullabies—all the more so since Lorna was the primary breadwinner. Contrary to my upbringing, I gave our son all the attention in the world. I even refrained from giving him laughing lessons. Happily, PJ's arrival strengthened my reconciliation with my mother, who lived to enjoy her grandson's first thirteen years.

Several years after PJ was born, we moved to High Street in

Cambridge, on the third floor of a three-decker house owned and maintained by a kindly and wise Italian gentleman, Grandpa Lavignia. His family consisted of his three daughters, their husbands, and their children. The family frequently had parties, and the Italian influence was much in evidence: the food was delicious and plentiful, the beer and wine were continually replenished, and people never ran out of things to say.

While living there, Lorna, PJ, and I would walk around Fresh Pond and feed the ducks. I would also take PJ to Danehy Park, where we would kick a soccer ball or throw a baseball around or shoot baskets at the basketball court. On occasion, we would go canoeing on the Concord River. Not having a car, we would either walk to our appointed destination or take public transportation, usually a bus. PJ loved that neighborhood, where there were lots of kids to play with on the street.

In 1997, we moved to Belmont, where PJ attended Chenery Middle School. He then went to Beaver Country Day School in Chestnut Hill. Belmont Hill School would have been more convenient as it was nearer, but it was an all-boys' school, whereas Beaver was co-ed. I enthusiastically supported PJ's preference for a school where boys and girls could get to know each other in a natural way. When I was in boarding schools, I would see girls only at school dances or on vacations. I was terrified and tongue-tied, speaking in clichés and making every effort to avoid stepping on the girl's feet until our foxtrot or minuet mercifully ended. Students also had to wear coats and ties at Belmont Hill School, which seemed a throwback to the over-civilized boarding schools I had gone to, with all of their do's and don'ts, formal dress, and daily chapel attendance. I had had to put up with all that; half a century later, PJ did not.

At Beaver Country Day School, PJ left his mark by starting a jazz club, playing chess, being elected vice president of the senior class, and pitching as well as co-captaining the baseball team. On graduation, he received a commendation that characterized him as "a visible and joyous presence throughout the school. . . . Friendly, well rounded, and generous, you have a genuinely caring nature and a clear enjoyment of life that makes you a great friend to all your classmates."

PJ went on to Rollins College in Florida, where he majored in International Relations. During his junior year, he studied in Florence, Italy. Afterward, he led groups of students touring various European countries and cities. He returned to the U.S. and pursued his graduate studies at Fordham University, where he earned a dual master's degree in Economics and in International Political Economy and Development. He has led developmental efforts for non-profit organizations, mostly in New York: Children and Family Services, Harlem RBI, Sheltering Arms, Pablove Foundation, and the Bowery Mission. He disc jockeys on the side to fundraise for other philanthropic organizations. He knows, with varying degrees of fluency: French, Italian, Spanish, German, and Ilonggo, a Philippine language.

I am proud of PJ and likewise proud that in 1998 Lorna was given an award by the Cambridge Peace Commission for her work in defense of human rights in the Philippines, together with her support for tenants' rights in Cambridge. The award ceremony was held at the Harvard University Divinity School in the presence of former mayor and tenant advocate, Alfred Vellucci.

* * *

I did not give up music organizing entirely. After we moved to a Boston suburb, I resurrected Living Folk from its dormant state, trying my hand at running concerts, albeit less frequently than before as most of my time and energy was taken up with domestic responsibilities. Lacking a support system and being out of touch with the folk music world and the media, I was initially at a loss as to how to proceed. Fortunately, and none too soon, my friend and neighbor Gillian Charters, originally from England and a former president of The Scottish Royal Dance Society, came to my rescue. A whiz with the computer, Gill volunteered to design attractive posters to advertise our concerts. I didn't have much of a staff, but then I didn't need so much help as the concerts were fewer and farther between.

Lorna pitched in whenever she could, carrying recording equipment, taking pictures, and organizing the events.

I put on only four or five concerts, as opposed to the several hundred I had arranged back in the 1970s and early 1980s. The largest was a one-day folk concert at the Chenery Middle School while PJ was a student there, with the proceeds going to benefit the Belmont school system. Among the performers were Anne and Indigo Dow. We recorded the concert and made it into a CD. I also organized a benefit at Passim to raise money for Culture for Kids.

Later concerts were held at the First Parish Church of Watertown, where the Folk Song Society of Greater Boston staged their events. One of those concerts featured Bennett and Lorraine Hammond along with the Kossoy Sisters. Also on the program were a group from New York, Poor Old Horse, consisting of David Jones, Heather Wood, and Tom Gibney; and Little Blue Heron, consisting of Constance Cook and Adam Klein. Adam was a classically trained singer who also sang opera. There were also some local musicians—Joanie Bronfman, Neal MacMillan, and Ann Schneider. Appearing with them was Judy Cook, with her great repertoire of Civil War ballads.

Jean Morrell and her husband Peter Barnes, a fine instrumentalist, appeared at another concert. Jean sang in Irish and Scottish Gaelic as well as in English. Appearing on the program were the Gloucester Hornpipe and Clog Society, led by Nancy Koch and also featuring Diane Taraz, a lovely singer. They sang sea shanties and got everyone to join in. During intermission, George Emlen, music director of Revels, performed several songs and we all sang along.

The turnout for my few later concerts was disappointing, especially when compared to my concerts in the 1970s. There was less competition back then, as I was one of the few people doing it besides the Folk Song Society of Greater Boston, which still puts on top-quality concerts after all these years. In the heyday of the 1970s, there was—in my mind—a sense of adventure, of something always around the corner waiting to happen. Back then I was still young enough to be impressionable and receptive to whatever might come my way.

In 2010, for preservation and digitizing, I donated a collection of eighty-eight concert tapes and ten recordings of Cape Breton fiddle music to the Howard T. Glasser Archives of Folk Music and Letter Arts at the University of Massachusetts, Dartmouth. Howard, who had taught there for many years, participated in the ceremony. Five years later, I participated in a national conference of folk-music collectors in Connecticut to provide for the preservation of this priceless heritage. I have done my part. What happens from here on will depend on PJ's generation and those that follow.

Chapter 47

Passages

These days when I go to Harvard Square, I sometimes feel like Washington Irving's Rip Van Winkle, who, after falling asleep for twenty years, had a hard time getting his bearings when he awoke. I hardly recognize a soul, and the people I do know, the ones who have not died or moved away, look very different from when I first met them forty-to-sixty years ago. Most of the old coffeehouses, eating places, and bookstores that I frequented are gone. The old wooden buildings have given way to modern edifices, geometric in shape, most of them devoid of character or personality, looking as if they haven't a friend in the world. In cities like Cambridge, old New England charm seems just a memory. Thankfully, there are still a few familiar landmarks, like Passim coffeehouse, to ground me.

I have written this memoir as an ongoing exercise of memory and synthesis, of integrating the present with the past. I began this undertaking after Ezra Pound urged me to document the myths and rituals of the dying culture into which I was born, and later Robert Lowell advised me to write about the experiences and emotional conflicts that had brought me, like him, to McLean Hospital, the "giggle bin."

Encouraged as well by friends, I made this pilgrimage to the psychic underworld of my childhood—disinterring old family skeletons, making them dance to a lively tune, giving them their due but no more than that. Over the years, I continued to update the story while looking back on my past from the perspective afforded by my unfolding experience. I came to understand that my life was not a simple matter of one stage supplanting the previous one. Rather, each stage is inhabited by the ones that went before, each building on its predecessors like rings on a tree.

Through it all, in writing as in life, as my therapist, Dr. Harvey Mazer, put it, "Humor helped level the playing field, kept you in the ball game, and gave you some perspective. Laugh a little, cry a little, and learn a little. In some ways your life has been a tragic comedy, the bitter and the sweet, where one informs and gives meaning to the other."

"Perhaps this sounds sophomoric," I told Dr. Mazer, "but I feel that my life has taken the form of a Hegelian dialectic. Thesis was my early life as a passive recipient of what my family and surroundings dictated, when I didn't dare say 'Boo.' Then there was its antithesis, the wild and wacky self-destructive things I did in reaction. Finally came the synthesis of the two, as I became a productive person with my music. Wouldn't you say that my musical activities constituted a rite of passage, a successful synthesis of what had gone before?"

"Yes," he agreed, "but you've had several rites of passage. Certainly your music was one, as writing your memoir has been. Acting in the theatre, going to school, getting married, and having a child, as well as therapy, contributed to the synthesis. You passed through rebellion to a more stable, constructive, and mature middle ground, taking responsibility for yourself and your family. You've come a long way and I congratulate you."

"Thanks for your supportive words," I said. "Still, I hope I'm not too stable or mature, for then I might be just a little dull, and that's not me."